Multisensory Shakespeare and Specialized Communities

SHAKESPEARE AND SOCIAL JUSTICE

Shakespeare and Social Justice addresses the relevance and responsibility of Shakespeare work and production to the practices, processes and goals of social justice. It addresses the significant teaching and learning, performance and practice, theory and economies that not only expand the discussion of literature and theatre, but also refocus engagements dedicated to creating positive social change.

Series Editors

Matthieu Chapman, SUNY New Paltz, USA
David Ruiter, University of California, San Diego, USA

Advisory Board

Bernadette Andrea, UCSB, USA
Chris Anthony, DePaul and The Shakespeare Center of Los Angeles, USA
Lezlie Cross, University of Portland, USA
Ambereen Dadabhoy, Harvey Mudd College, USA
Nandini Das, Oxford University, UK
Carla Della Gatta, Florida State University, USA
Sarah Enloe, American Shakespeare Center, USA
Ewan Fernie, Shakespeare Institute, University of Birmingham, UK
Coen Heijes, University of Groningen, The Netherlands
Peter Holbrook, Australian Catholic University, Melbourne, Australia
Farah Karim-Cooper, Shakespeare's Globe, UK
Baron Kelly, University of Wisconsin, USA
Lee Chee Keng, Yale-NUS College, Singapore
Regan Linton, Phamaly Theatre, Denver, USA

Published Titles

Creating Space for Shakespeare
Rowan Mackenzie
978-1-3502-7265-1

Multisensory Shakespeare and Specialized Communities

Sheila T. Cavanagh

THE ARDEN SHAKESPEARE
LONDON • NEW YORK • OXFORD • NEW DELHI • SYDNEY

THE ARDEN SHAKESPEARE

Bloomsbury Publishing Plc, 50 Bedford Square, London, WC1B 3DP, UK
Bloomsbury Publishing Inc, 1359 Broadway, 12th Floor, New York, NY 10018, USA
Bloomsbury Publishing Ireland, 29 Earlsfort Terrace, Dublin 2, D02 AY28, Ireland

BLOOMSBURY, THE ARDEN SHAKESPEARE and the Arden Shakespeare logo are
trademarks of Bloomsbury Publishing Plc

First published in Great Britain 2024
This paperback edition published 2025

Copyright © Sheila T. Cavanagh, 2024

Sheila T. Cavanagh has asserted her right under the Copyright,
Designs and Patents Act, 1988, to be identified as author of this work.

For legal purposes the Acknowledgements on p. viii constitute an
extension of this copyright page.

Series Design: Tjasa Krivec
Photograph © Yevhenii Orlov / Getty and Joe Woods / Unsplash

All rights reserved. No part of this publication may be: i) reproduced or transmitted in
any form, electronic or mechanical, including photocopying, recording or by means of
any information storage or retrieval system without prior permission in writing from the
publishers; or ii) used or reproduced in any way for the training, development or operation
of artificial intelligence (AI) technologies, including generative AI technologies. The rights
holders expressly reserve this publication from the text and data mining exception as per
Article 4(3) of the Digital Single Market Directive (EU) 2019/790.

Bloomsbury Publishing Inc does not have any control over, or responsibility for,
any third-party websites referred to or in this book. All internet addresses given
in this book were correct at the time of going to press. The author and publisher
regret any inconvenience caused if addresses have changed or sites have
ceased to exist, but can accept no responsibility for any such changes.

A catalogue record for this book is available from the British Library.

Library of Congress Cataloging-in-Publication Data
Names: Cavanagh, Sheila T., author.
Title: Multisensory Shakespeare and specialized communities / by Sheila T. Cavanagh.
Description: London ; New York : The Arden Shakespeare 2024. | Series: Shakespeare
and social justice | Includes bibliographical references and index.
Identifiers: LCCN 2023032498 (print) | LCCN 2023032499 (ebook) |
ISBN 9781350296428 (hardback) | ISBN 9781350296466 (paperback) |
ISBN 9781350296442 (pdf) | ISBN 9781350296435 (ebook)
Subjects: LCSH: Shakespeare, William, 1564–1616–Dramatic production. |
Shakespeare, William, 1564-1616–Appreciation. | Acting–Study and teaching. |
Prison theater. | People with disabilities and the performing arts. |
Drama–Therapeutic use. | Social justice.
Classification: LCC PR3091 .C38 2024 (print) | LCC PR3091 (ebook) |
DDC 792.01/3–dc23/eng/20230912
LC record available at https://lccn.loc.gov/2023032498
LC ebook record available at https://lccn.loc.gov/2023032499

ISBN: HB: 978-1-3502-9642-8
PB: 978-1-3502-9646-6
ePDF: 978-1-3502-9644-2
eBook: 978-1-3502-9643-5

Series: Shakespeare and Social Justice

Typeset by Deanta Global Publishing Services, Chennai, India

For product safety related questions contact productsafety@bloomsbury.com.

To find out more about our authors and books visit www.bloomsbury.com
and sign up for our newsletters.

For:
Harry and Sue Rusche
Scott Jackson and Christy Burgess
John Watkins
Deborah Middleton, Barry Cassidy, and Katherine Cassidy
Curt L. Tofteland and the Shakespeare in Prisons Network

CONTENTS

Acknowledgements viii
List of Abbreviations xii

Introduction: 'The Five [or more] Best Senses' 1

1 'In Mine Own Throat': The power of breath and voice 29

2 Hearing the owl shriek: Shakespearean soundscapes 47

3 'Such Branches of Learning': Shakespeare and learning differences 65

4 'Touch of nature': Expanding Shakespearean sensory palates 85

5 'Weight of pain': Trauma-informed Shakespeare 107

6 'The rich advantage of good exercise': Physicality, art and mindfulness in prison Shakespeare 133

7 'The Open Ear of Youth': Shakespeare through physical and expressive arts 157

Notes 179
Bibliography 243
Index 263

ACKNOWLEDGEMENTS

I appreciate the support of Mark Dudgeon and Ella Wilson at The Arden Shakespeare; Series Editors Matthieu Chapman and David Ruiter and the Series Advisory Board.

At Emory, I thank and credit the University Research Committee, Emory College of Arts and Sciences, the English Department, the Stuart A. Rose Manuscripts, Archives and Rare Books Library, The Center for Faculty Development and Excellence, the PERS Fund, the Emory Center for Digital Scholarship, the Hightower Fund, the Michael C. Carlos Museum and the Halle Institute.

Among the many individuals I wish to thank at Emory are Rosemary Magee, former Presidents Jim Wagner and Claire Sterk, former Provost Earl Lewis, former Deans Michael Elliott and Robin Forman, Harry and Sue Rusche, Jennifer Gunter King, Gary Hauk, Dwight Andrews, Michelle Wright, Jim Grimsley, Ron and Keith Schuchard, Sally West, Jim and Lynn Morey, Joonna Trapp, Bobbi Patterson, Ron Calabrese, David Gowler, Eloise Carter, the late Gretchen Schulz, Sarah Higinbotham, Kelly Duquette, John Gulledge, Mary Taylor Mann, Nick Fesette, Buzz Morse, Steve Witte (and the entire classroom tech team) and our remarkable current and former library and museum staff (including their dedicated development team), especially Lisa Macklin, Erin Mooney, James Steffen, Kathy Dixson, John Klingler, Jason Lowery, Erin Glogowski, Erin Horeni-Ogle, Elizabeth Hornor, Leslie Wingate, Renée Stein, Julie Newton, Clint Fluker and the sorely missed Pellom McDaniels Jr., Chuck Spornick and CJ Jones.

Much of this work has been researched and written in the UK and I hold enormous gratitude for the many people who have made my time there so enriching and enjoyable (throughout these acknowledgements, people are not listed in order of precedence, even though the London livery companies like to organize things that way). The London Historians are a remarkable, welcoming group and I appreciate their hospitality, thanking in particular Tina Baxter, Mike Paterson, Dave Whittaker, Niki Gorick, Debbie Pearson, Diane Burstein Lynch, Peter Dodge, Margaret Willes, Colin Davies, Sue Sinton-Smith, Rob Smith, Joanna Moncrieff, Richard Watkins, Sarah McCabe and many others. In addition, among those I appreciate in London and beyond are Marion Wynne-Davies, Emma Smith, Michael Dobson, Tiffany Stern, Sonia Massai, Aideen O'Halloran, Jennie Hood, Tina Welch, Margaret and Nick Hodgson, Jasmine Seymour, Madeleine Neave, Ramona Wray and Mark Thornton Burnett, Celine Luppo McDaid, Sayuri Carbonnier, Colin and Annie Knowles. Rick Trainer and Marguerite Dupree, Richard Huzzey and Irene Middleton, Stephen Coates, Chris Ballinger and Ailsa McLean, the Worshipful Company of Educators and the Stationers Company. Many of these connections were made initially while I was on my Fulbright year in England and I am pleased to thank the Fulbright Commission for that opportunity.

From the world of arts and social justice, I am grateful to Scott Jackson, Christy Burgess, Curt L. Tofteland, Tina Packer, Kevin Coleman, Steve Unwin, Rowan Mackenzie, Harry Lennix, Sammie and Barbara Byron, Lue Douhit, the late Gail Deschamps, Esther Ruth Elliott, Robert Shaughnessy, Abigail Rokison-Woodall, Sergio Amigo, Maria Oshodi, Gregg Mozgala, Eric Mills, Laura Cole, Jeffrey Watkins and others from the Atlanta Shakespeare Company, the Shakespeare at Notre Dame team, Peter Holland, Jill Bradbury, Kate Powers, Kate Kenney, Frannie Shepherd-Bates, Matthew Van Meter, Allison Hobgood, Rob Pensalfini, Sheree Vickers, Alice Rayman and the Savvy Theatre team, Jonathan Shailor, Madeline Sayet, Bill Rauch, Jean Troustine, Jenna Dreier, Bill Taft, Caitlin Volz, Amy Cunningham, Christopher Davies and the Bamboozle team, Richard Conlon and the Blue Apple troupe, Darren Raymond, Carmen Mandley, Amanda Giguere, Amy Attaway, Lynn Baker-Nauman, Devon Glover, Debra Ann Byrd, Alejandra Luna, Leslie Currier, Alma Robinson, Jasper Norman, Yashaira Romilus, Ron Heneghan, Tom Magill, Kirsten Kearney, Arts Access Aotearoa, Stephan Wolfert, Dawn Stern, Nancy Smith-Watson, Bill Watson, Jim Tasse, Christopher Hunter, Keith McGill and Karen Saillant.

My numerous trips to India have enriched this book and my life greatly. For this, I thank Amitava Roy and the late Shreela Roy, Alokananda Roy, Indrani and Cchandam Deb, Aparajita Hazra, Tapu Biswas, Subir Dhar, Hulugappa Kattimani, the Kattamani/

Begre family and the many colleagues and students there I have been privileged to meet. Additional international thanks go to Katie Larson in Canada, Eve Nabulya in Uganda, Roderick and Gillean Deane in New Zealand, Lilith Acadia in Taiwan, Katherine Hennessey in China, Tom Bishop in New Zealand, Nicolette Bethel and The Shakespeare in Paradise team in the Bahamas, and the many international partners of The World Shakespeare Project.

The US contingent has also been consistently supportive and I thank many at the Folger Shakespeare Library, including the Reading Room staff: Rosalind Larry, LuEllen DeHaven, Camille Seerattan and the always appreciated late Betsy Walsh; Michael Witmore, Kathleen Lynch, Eric Johnson , Peggy O'Brien and Owen Williams. In addition, I am grateful to Joe Discher and Sean Hudock, Bruce Smith, John Watkins, Katherine Scheil, Katherine Eggert, Natasha Trethewey, James Siemon, Ann Ford, Lisa Gim and Kenny Fain, Valerie Friedline, Suzanne Holland, Terry Duggan-Jahns, Peter Henriot, Lena Cowen Orlin, Patricia O'Connor, Mitzi Loftus, Deborah Middleton and Barry Cassidy, Katherine Cassidy, May Lee Eckley, Mahin Nourraee, Sonya Freeman Loftis, Geraldo Souza, David Bergeron and the many members of the Shakespeare Association of America, the Shakespeare Theatre Association and the Shakespeare in Prisons Network who have supported this work. In particular, I thank Madeline Long for her expert editing assistance.

In true academic style, as I have been working on this book, I have been preparing for the next big project and want to thank those who have been supportive throughout my adventures in culinary history. Many thanks to Andy Hook, Giles Gaspar, Flo Swan, Toby Donegan-Cross, Anthony O'Shaughnessy and Nick Miles, from the outstanding Blackfriars/Durham University Eat Medieval collaboration; food historians Ivan Day and Paul Couchman and the participants of the Oxford Food Symposium, Ian Kelly, numerous teachers at London's Garden Museum and the Weald and Downland Living Museum, Gitanjali Shahani, Lauren Shook, John Tufts, Madeleine Neave, Tina Baxter, Peter Ross, Tamsin Lewis and the students who have enriched the food history courses I have taught thus far.

Those to whom this book is dedicated have heard far too much about my work. Harry and Sue Rusche have been wonderful friends and supporters from the time I interviewed at Emory; Scott Jackson and Christy Burgess have offered generous help, collaboration, feedback and adventures; John Watkins provided terrific textual guidance and is a great travel companion; Deborah Middleton, Barry Cassidy and Katherine Cassidy have kept tables filled with books and glasses filled with wine, while offering bountiful conversation. Working with Curt L. Tofteland and the Shakespeare in Prisons Network has been one of the greatest privileges of my lifetime.

My husband, Chris, and my son, Davis, have each had books dedicated to them before, but I once again offer my deep appreciation for their unstinting support of me and of my work. You will hopefully both understand why the people listed on the dedication page are there, but my love and gratitude for your presence in my life runs throughout this volume.

ABBREVIATIONS

ASC	Atlanta Shakespeare Company
ASL	American Sign Language
BSA	British Shakespeare Association
BSL	British Sign Language
CFTE	Center for Trauma & Embodiment
CSC	Chesapeake Shakespeare Company
ETC	expressive therapies continuum
FoC	Feast of Crispian
HHM	Hunter Heartbeat Method
HHSWT	Hip-Hop and Spoken Word Therapy
IOT	International Opera Theater
IYT	Intermission Youth Theatre
JRI	Justice Resource Institute
KATG	KNOCK AT THE GATE
NEA	National Endowment for the Arts
NT Home	National Theatre at Home
PP	Puck Project
PRUs	pupil referral units
PTALS	Pro-Tactile American Sign Language
PTS(D)	post-traumatic stress (disorder), also known as post-traumatic stress (PTS) and post-traumatic stress syndrome (PTSS); see note ## (Ch. 5)

PTT	ProTactile Theatre
RADA	Royal Academy of Dramatic Arts
RSC	Royal Shakespeare Company
RTA	Rehabilitation Through the Arts
RTP	Redeeming Time Project
SAA	Shakespeare Association of America
SBB	Shakespeare Behind Bars
SIP	Shakespeare in Prison
SiPN	Shakespeare in Prisons Network
SS	Signing Shakespeare
STA	Shakespeare Theatre Association
TALS	Tactile American Sign Language
TC	Tactile Communications LLC
TIIH	The Institute for Integrative Health, now Nova Institute for Health of People Places and Planet
ToM	theory of mind
VA	Department of Veterans Affairs

Introduction

'The Five [or more] Best Senses'

Detroit, Michigan

Frannie Shepherd-Bates, director of Detroit Public Theatre's signature community programme Shakespeare in Prison (SIP), is a warm-hearted, energetic and resourceful theatre practitioner who juggles innumerable figurative and actual balls as she helps craft Shakespearean experiences and interactions with a growing ensemble of incarcerated and released actors, musicians, as well as set and costume designers. Her talent and enthusiasm reap tangible results as evidenced by the delight and the detailed stories expressed by those now participating in SIP alumni events, such as those I attended with them in 2022. Their narratives about the Shakespearean exercises and performances they experienced while incarcerated provide insight into the reasons these gatherings remain important even after these actors have returned to society.

One year before the Covid-19 pandemic stopped in-person meetings, Erric, an SIP alumnus, started writing letters in character as he prepared for his portrayal of Gloucester in *King Lear*.[1]

Letter from Gloucester to Lear
January 17, 2019
Dear Lear (Beginning of Play)[2]
Words can't express my high regard and respect for your resilience in this turbulent times. Your heart beat inspires the kingdom in every possible way. I do have a confession that be twix my mind

& conscious my dear friend. How are you surviving and standing in the mist of an ugly kingdom. My eyes see thy strength and thy boldness you bestow upon thee. Even when your kingdom my lord has expanded beyond what your fathers can have ever live to see. Never in all my years have I seen the ocean so clear so beautiful so glorious. The enemies were no match for your strength. For your strength as I personally know is one of your crowns of jewels without your power.

He He oh Lear what fine days we have ahead of us, we known each other since we had been little kids. They used to call us Fear Lear and Goodie Gloster. Remember that time when we were playing in your mother's garden and you found that scarf and wrapped it around my head and promised me that your devotion to me as a friend shall never end. Well I still have that close by to remind me of your goodness.[3]

Soon, the other actors began writing similar letters from the perspective of their characters and a significant archive grew, chronicling the evolution of their understanding of the text and of the relationship between characters. Many of the letters were written in modern vernacular as these incarcerated Shakespeareans developed a deepening relationship with the figures and issues they encountered in the play. This detailed correspondence shows the considerable time and thought SIP's Shakespeareans devote to their theatrical endeavours. Erric learned what it could be like to live without sight, for instance, as all the cast members and crew delved into a world both far removed and very familiar.

Conversations with SIP alumni confirm that that their individual and communal work on Shakespeare provides multiple benefits. Sharie admits that she initially thought that acting was about lying and that since she is a 'good liar', this might be an appropriate activity for her.[4] Instead, she discovered that she learned an enormous amount about behaviour and emotions, not just about Shakespeare, that proved helpful in her personal life upon release. She learned perseverance, for example, and appreciated having a supportive group to talk with. In SIP, she did not encounter cliques or other warning signs signaling exclusion; instead, she found an entire ensemble ready to welcome her.

Kelly, moreover, found it helpful to be able to 'speak my own truth through words already written', just as Sharie found ideas from life that kept coming up in the plays, including love, betrayal, revenge and redemption. These actors work from the text as they prepare their performances, but memorization is not central. Several participants recalled Shepherd-Bates telling them that they mattered more than the lines: words that made an enormous difference for them. Shepherd-Bates draws heavily, but not exclusively, from acting techniques developed by Michael Chekhov, which she finds facilitate the kinds of changes these formerly incarcerated Shakespeareans report, '[Chekhov's] technique's emphasis on physicality and imagination allows participants to find new, safe ways of identifying and expressing emotions, and of reconnecting with their bodies.'[5] As participants in the groups discussed here often recognize, physical activities incorporating multiple sensorial experiences enhance the many intellectual aspects of Shakespearean drama and create theatrical activities that support positive physical, emotional and cognitive changes for these varied ensemble members.

Like the other ensembles featured in this volume, those formed in carceral spaces also create art that facilitates individual achievement in diffuse areas. None of these communities are monolithic, since their participants' circumstances range broadly; the characteristics shared between these dramatic communities have similarities but are never identical. Just as 'autism' and 'learning differences' are broad categories, individuals' experiences of physical differences or traumatic environments also encompass innumerable variations. Still, many of these individuals join together with others facing related challenges and create the artistic ensembles discussed here. Whether based in Baltimore, Buenos Aires, Detroit, India or elsewhere, many of these ventures are 'thriving', even though the Covid-19 pandemic ensured not all would survive.

South London, UK

Savvy Theatre in London's East Croyden area is unusual because its dramatic programmes reach many of the populations discussed throughout this study. Founded by Australian performer and director Sheree Vickers, Savvy offers a wide range of classes and performance opportunities to people with learning and physical disabilities, challenges with substance abuse and/or homelessness and those who have been incarcerated, as well as members of the community outside these groups. The various ensembles who include people of diverse ages, gender identifications, and ethnicities often perform together.

When I visited the Savvy studio, for example, they were rehearsing a joint production of *A Christmas Carol* that included ninety participants, as well as puppets, music, dance and innovative costumes and set designs. The company presents a range of devised and classic texts, including Shakespeare. A few years ago, for instance, after a workshop with the renowned Graeae Theatre Company, they cast Chloe, a blind actor, as Titania, a role she performed while riding a unicycle.[6]

In their 2022 Summer of Shakespeare, they presented several productions, including *The Taming of the Shrew Drag Show*, *Twelfth Night* (which they offered indoors in London, then at the RSC's outdoor Dell Stage in Stratford-upon-Avon), *Comedy of Errors* and *A Midsummer Night's Dream* (a play Vickers has directed several times). Vickers had an extensive previous career as a street performer and as a clown, which helped develop her strong commitment to collaboration and her ability to think quickly on her feet, thus supporting the diverse needs of Savvy's participants.

Savvy's *Taming of the Shrew Drag Show*, presented by their 'Crisis Averted' ensemble, whose members have experienced substance abuse and/or homelessness, illustrates the ways that such companies learn from long-time collaborations, while readily welcoming new members.[7] Most of this group have been together for about four years, including two during Covid-19. Having enjoyed the drag aspects of their production of *The Real Housewives of Grimm County*, it made sense to revisit this perspective in *Taming of the Shrew*, where problematic issues involving gender abound. While the facilitators were concerned that some participants might balk at Shakespeare, everyone jumped at the chance to create a music-infused production that addressed complicated issues. This approach seems to have made Shakespeare less intimidating.

The thirty-minute production included a number of energetic pop songs that kept things moving and the addition of a narrator enabled the company to address the issues in the play that give pause to modern audiences. Bianca's bevvy of suitors, for instance, is presented through a rendition of The Weather Girls' 'It's Raining Men.'[8] In Savvy's adaptation, Petruchio begins the play wearing male attire, but wears a dress in the wedding sequence. By the end of the show, Katherine and her husband have swapped clothing with each other, signaling a transformation both experienced over the course of the narrative. The production mixes modern lines with Shakespearean text and emphasizes considerable creativity in choreography and costuming.

Savvy's multisensory approach to performance exemplifies the kind of practices featured in this volume. They focus extensively on matching production expectations to the abilities and requirements of their actors. Thus, actors who need support with their lines receive a variety of verbal, silent, or musical cues, designed for their particular circumstances.[9] Since support workers' schedules do not always conform to rehearsal or performance times, Savvy helps ensure that their participants receive the assistance they require.

As later chapters will demonstrate, individuals do not respond identically to varied sensory experiences. Chloe, accordingly, gained significant information through touch, while some other performers avoid touch whenever possible. Savvy works hard to anticipate these varied needs, but the company's emphasis upon partnership also means that participants can freely indicate the brand of support necessary. During *A Christmas Carol*, seats were labeled with each actor's name so that no one would hesitate when they returned to their chairs during the performance. Similarly, actors who required someone to accompany them on stage and those with restricted mobility or lack of verbal speech were accommodated appropriately.

The company also endeavours to reflect their place within London. Their multicultural environment thus led to a production of *As You Like It* drawing from the plight of modern Syrian migrants. As the diversity of their Shakespearean productions suggests, Savvy's artistic range is noteworthy, just as the breadth of their participants' situations reflects a wide swath of individual circumstances. Savvy is geographically distanced from Detroit's SIP, but like many of the other groups highlighted in this study, both companies combine collaboration, respect, creativity and energy into their multisensory dramatic undertakings with specialized communities.

Members of the general public, however, often remain unaware of such socially conscious artistic programmes as the Shakespeare ensembles discussed in this volume,[10] unless they live in an area where a relevant group receives mention in the local press, have heard a pertinent presentation on radio or television,[11] or if they have encountered a documentary such as *Shakespeare Behind Bars*.[12] Although many of these initiatives rely on publicity for fundraising purposes, others remain under the radar. Nevertheless, the number of Shakespeare-related endeavors taking place with people in prisons; veterans; those with physical, intellectual or emotional disabilities; and other specialized communities are increasing, with many of them staying active despite all of the constraints introduced by the pandemic. A heightened awareness of broad-based social justice issues, desires for increased inclusivity and efforts to connect more effectively with diverse communities appear to be fueling the growing interest in such programmes.

Typically, the practitioners who instigate or engage with these proceedings are passionately committed to the programmes and their participants. The members of these groups often demonstrate considerable enthusiasm for such initiatives, sometimes remaining involved for considerable periods of time. While I have been working on this study over the past several years, I have visited numerous such groups, often in person, until the pandemic halted face-to-face encounters. Among the many initiatives included are Shakespearean programmess and performances for people currently or formerly in the criminal justice system; veterans; diverse, detained, homeless and at-risk youth; vision-impaired persons; d/Deaf and DeafBlind individuals; and those with varied learning needs.

The book is divided into sections discussing groups with physical or intellectual disabilities and those comprised of people deeply affected by traumatic or precarious circumstances. Unfortunately, most of the groups considered here are British or American, largely due to travel prohibitions during the pandemic, but there are also programmes included from India, Europe and Argentina.[13] Covid-19 inevitably restricted access to groups that I would have liked to include, such as initiatives connecting migrants with Shakespeare. Those interested in this topic can instead refer to pertinent essays included in 2021's *The Shakespeare International Yearbook*.[14] In addition, while there are an increasing number of actors in wheelchairs or with other physical differences performing in mainstream theatres and elsewhere, such practitioners are not included here in detail unless they belong to one of the communities discussed.[15] Regan Linton, however,[16] who performed as Don John in Oregon Shakespeare Festival's 2015 *Much Ado About Nothing* and as Titania/Hippolyta in Apothetae Theatre's *A Midsummer*

Night's Dream, offers an informative essay about actor training for wheelchair-using artists in Petronilla Whitfield's *Inclusivity and Equality in Performance Training*.[17]

As director of The World Shakespeare Project, I have participated with Shakespearean students in numerous countries, but, except in rare cases, classroom exercises do not correspond with the kinds of specialized communities presented here. I have, however, written about many of those engagements elsewhere.[18] While I regret the absence of some groups I aimed to include, I look forward to the research undertaken by others in related communities and in germane environments yet unknown. I also hope to have firsthand experience in the future with those the pandemic kept off-limits.

In general, the individuals and communities engaged in the wide range of endeavours included here have eclectic practices. Some focus on Shakespeare because of their previous professional experiences,[19] others for diverse reasons that will be discussed. Shakespeare appears not infrequently in work with specialized communities, but other artistic material is also used or created. This canonical author does not provide a magic bullet for all circumstances or communities, but many of the groups included here find his writing valuable in their environments. One size does not fit all, however, and these groups approach their work through a range of perspectives and practices.

Over the years, I have encountered many talented educators and enthusiastic participants in Shakespeare programmes aligned with specialized populations, similar to those reported by Ashley E. Lucas in *Prison Theatre and the Global Crisis of Incarceration*.[20] I have also met (and collaborated) with skeptics, including Sonya Freeman Loftis, who challenges Kelly Hunter's interactive performances for autistic children in her 2019 *Shakespeare Survey* article 'Autistic Culture, Shakespeare Therapy, and the Hunter Heartbeat Method'.[21] My work here identifies and integrates some of the theories, practices and questions informing these diverse Shakespearean initiatives. Some practitioners draw directly from studies on effective responses to the circumstances facing their participants; others craft their practices more instinctually or from their own practitioner training or experience. The most robust programmes create community, facilitate an expansive embodiment of human sensory experiences and establish safe spaces for reflection and experimentation, in accordance with the specific needs and challenges of individual groupings.

Diffuse facets of Shakespeare studies in general, of course, are receiving renewed scrutiny during our contemporary period of racial reckoning and reassessment and many of those included here are looking deeply at their practices and behaviours in light of such issues. 'Mohegan theatremaker' Madeline Sayet, for instance, who undertook doctoral studies at the University of Birmingham's Shakespeare Institute in Stratford-upon-Avon before serving as executive director of the Yale Indigenous Performing Arts Project and then joining the faculty at Arizona State University, cogently argues that Shakespeare's position in our educational and theatrical spaces contributes to a 'complex and oppressive role' for 'his work, legacy and positionality' in our society.[22] Jenna Dreier, who was recently appointed Minnesota Prison Education Program Coordinator, addresses these issues in prison Shakespeare programmes, arguing that

> Shakespeare's elite cultural status bolsters the sense of achievement and empowerment experienced by participants in prison performance programs; and yet, such engagements paradoxically risk further marginalizing participants by reinforcing a colonial mentality in which Shakespeare represents an offering from a morally superior white culture.[23]

Dreier's essay, which derives from her doctoral research, highlights the way that some programmes work to counteract the potential cultural problems associated with prison Shakespeare. Dreier also indicates, however, that all the prison practitioners she encountered intend their programming to be *'empowering* for those who participate'.[24]

Prior to the pandemic, Shakespeare programmes among what I am terming 'specialized communities' proliferated.[25] As the world constricted under lockdown and associated regulatory changes, however, these initiatives stopped face-to-face meetings. Some were able to continue virtually or through other communication modes, but others went on hiatus or switched their focus predominantly into planning or fundraising. This was a challenging time for those involved, but many made productive use of this unexpected cessation of ordinary activities.

The Shakespeare in Prisons Network or SiPN, for instance,[26] which includes participants from numerous countries, transformed its 2020 biennial live conference (SiPC 4), which was co-sponsored by the Folger Shakespeare Institute, into bountiful weekly gatherings that lasted for months. These sessions were recorded and made available on the web, creating a significant archive designed to support the work being done in carceral settings around the world.[27] Mary Irene Ryan Family Executive Director of Shakespeare at Notre Dame, Scott Jackson, and other members of the planning committee won the Shakespeare Association of America's 2022 Shakespeare Publics Award for this project.

Stephan Wolfert and Dawn Stern of the DE-CRUIT veterans programme also reconfigured many of their offerings into electronic events,[28] as did Flute Theatre,[29] by adapting their Shakespearean performance workshops for autistic children into international Zoom meetings, including sessions for Ukrainian children once the war there commenced. Rowan Mackenzie,[30] Artistic Director of England's Shakespeare UnBard, sent customized packets to her incarcerated participants so that they could continue to learn, communicate and stay connected during an intensive period of isolation and uncertainty. The Butler Trust, one of the many organizations honouring her work reports,[31]

> During the lockdown, which prevented her usual sessions from taking place, Rowan has produced weekly learning resources packs for three different abilities . . . we are amazed by the creativity and variety of the resources Rowan creates, and her commitment to producing them every week. They are interactive, thought provoking and engaging, and are a testament to Rowan's dedication and commitment to the people she works with.[32]

Shepherd-Bates and her team undertook a similar project with SIP, as their website shares,

> Though we cannot work with incarcerated ensemble members in person at this time, we have found a way to sustain our connection by sending ensemble members Shakespeare-based activity packets to help alleviate their isolation, boredom, and fear. Each activity pack consists of a piece of Shakespeare's text

and prompts for intellectual stimulation, creative expression, and self-reflection.[33]

The commitment and resourcefulness demonstrated during this challenging period corresponds with the creativity and dedication that are common among practitioners and participants in such initiatives. Some critics of these kinds of endeavours understandably fear what are sometimes labeled 'white savior' activities, such as programmes that do not reflect the needs and inputs of their targeted populations or offerings that displace texts more representative of their disparate communities.[34] Conversations with those involved as organizers and/or participants in the initiatives often highlight substantial thoughtfulness, care and intentionality in the creation and sustenance of these efforts.[35]

The primary reason that the 2020–21 SiPC 4 conference became so extensive,[36] for instance, was the conveners' shared determination to represent a wide range of voices,[37] including current participants and alumni of these programmes,[38] BIPOC perspectives, neuroscientists and trauma specialists, movement practitioners and contributors from those outside the United States. The core group participating in what eventually became known as 'the conference that never ends' consistently demonstrated efforts to engage with their colleagues and participants with integrity, while developing and following anti-racist practices and incorporating increasing knowledge of relevant modalities.[39] Since only a modest group of participants were able to meet consistently during this extended conference, the archive of these materials is particularly useful. Innumerable germane topics were considered that will be helpful in the future.

The 'specialized communities' considered in this study differ in terms of participants' personal circumstances, but, with few exceptions, they are all involved regularly in Shakespearean endeavours. Some of the individuals in these groups share related backgrounds such as veteran status, incarceration or age. Others possess shared or similar physical, mental or emotional circumstances. Sometimes groups like these are termed 'marginalized', but value judgments can easily be heightened by such terminology. 'Specialized' recognizes that these gatherings typically draw participants with identifiable common characteristics but avoids placing evaluative labels on them. It discourages any suggestion that these individuals diverge from 'normality'. 'Specialized' is here intended to signal inclusivity but remains a placeholder should a more appropriate term emerge.[40] The book is divided into two sections after this introduction and a chapter about breath, which is experienced by all those included here. The next section will look at Shakespeareans communities formed of those with congenital or acquired physical or cognitive differences, while the subsequent chapters focus on those coming to Shakespeare from trauma-informed and/or potentially unsettled circumstances.

As the title of my book suggests, the various human senses contribute significantly to the theory and practice underlying the work of the Shakespearean initiatives included here. Aristotle famously determined that humans possess five sense organs: smell, sight, touch, taste and hearing, which he describes in detail,

> The special is said to be that which it is impossible to perceive by any other sense than that appropriated to it and with respect to which that sense cannot be deceived. So it is that color stands to sight, sound to hearing, Flavor to taste: touch, however, it must be added, deals with a number of different qualities.

He goes on to distinguish these senses from what he terms 'common sensibles',

> The common sensibles are movement, rest, number, figure, magnitude; such properties being peculiar to no single sense but shared in common by them all. Movement for instance is perceived at once by touch and by sight.[41]

While Aristotle's named senses remain widely recognized and are regularly cited as common understandings of the senses, our current conceptualization of the human senses extends more broadly. There is often little consensus about the exact number and purpose of these additional senses, although they are typically seen to include aspects of human bodily experiences, such as movement and balance, and sometimes incorporate more amorphous elements like intuition. Waldorf School founder Rudolf Steiner identified a dozen 'senses', divided into the 'will senses', the 'feeling senses' and the 'cognitive senses'.[42]

Rob DeSalle talks about the many senses that do not appear in what he calls 'Aristotle's big five'.[43] His list is extensive, containing balance, pain and perceptions of hot and cold.[44] He also posits the potential inclusion of 'sensing time of day, magnetic and electric fields, changes in blood pressure, and hunger, among others'.[45] DeSalle suggests that many recognized senses are less monolithic than often believed, 'There are multiple brain regions where the pathways for each sense traverse. Vision, for example, processes all kinds of aspects of that sense, including color, shade, orientation, movement, and others.'[46] Especially pertinent for the topics discussed here, he further posits that 'the senses involved in language processing are primarily auditory and visual', but 'tactile senses are also used in braille and other means of communicating using touch'.[47]

DeSalle then suggests that 'it would not be surprising to me if a society for the creation of smell as a language crops up sooner or later. Certainly there are enough unique odorants that we humans have the potential to smell to provide us with a large enough vocabulary'.[48] The use of smell in drama appears later in this volume, in a discussion of ProTactile Theater for DeafBlind people, but there are other opportunities to incorporate smell in various realms where it currently does not figure prominently, whether or not that eventually includes language.

Individuals, of course, vary in their awareness and actualization of different senses.[49] As many of the groups included in this study illustrate, people's experiences of sight, sound, touch, taste and smell differ widely, as do their access to proprioception and various movement forms.[50] During the COVID-19 pandemic, moreover, those infected with this virus frequently reported loss of taste and smell as some of their earliest, most striking and longest lasting symptoms.

Notably, many of our senses are shared with animals, as Jackie Higgins demonstrates in her striking book *Sentient: What Animals Reveal about our Sense*.[51] Correlations between some human senses and those possessed by other species remain under investigation, but our senses clearly constitute only part of 'what makes us human'. Higgins' study, moreover, demonstrates that correspondences between human and animal sentience are more pronounced than many people realize.

The practices illuminated in this volume suggest that the varied benefits associated with the Shakespearean experiences undertaken as part of these programmes heighten participants' awareness and access to senses they may not otherwise engage with deliberately or productively. Some people, such as athletes and singers, for example, pay close attention to breath, movement and other sensory information, while others remain comparatively oblivious to these aspects of their bodies and consciousness. Increasing participants' cognizance and control over these bodily functions can lead to multiple benefits, however. Shakespeare enhances access to many of these advantages, although innumerable people obviously achieve heightened awareness of their sensorial capacities without recourse to this drama.

Shakespeare is clearly not a panacea for everything people contend with in their lives, but many of the acting practices aligned with the performance of his plays offer physical and emotional benefits in accordance with the results reported by those involved with these initiatives. Those programmes include set, costume and musical design and offer further sensory benefits.

Surprisingly, despite its frequent dominance in discussions of the senses, the role of sight is not often emphasized in these groups, so will not be examined in depth here, even though Erric mentions sight several times in the passage earlier. Sight is central in many theatrical presentations, but, as Susan Hrach observes in her volume investigating 'how physical space, sensation, and movement affect learning', this sense does not necessarily offer the objective information many expect:

> In the case of sight, we have an opportunity to help students interrogate vision as a source of unfiltered reality, or the belief that our senses provide us with reliable, objective perceptions. The brain interprets signals sent by our eyes, but exactly what we perceive can be complex.[52]

DeSalle, moreover, reminds us that if we 'go to the theater or a concert, and you will most likely see a wide range of people with differing levels of visual acuity'.[53] He then details the extensive 'variation in seeing that you wouldn't outwardly recognize at this performance'.[54] Many of the groups included here may well discuss such issues, but I have not witnessed these conversations, except in groups, such as Extant Theatre, specifically focusing on the vision of their performers and audience. The subject offers intriguing possibilities for future research, as Shari Tishman indicates in her description of 'slow looking',

> Slow looking is an important and unique way of gaining knowledge about the world. It is important because it helps us to uncover complexities that can't be grasped in a quick glance. It is unique because it involves patterns of thinking that have a different center of gravity than those involved in critical thinking, and different as well than those involved in creativity, though it shares many cognitive capacities with both these areas.[55]

Visual aspects of production are undeniably important in many performance events and deserve further attention in the current context. In addition to the need to focus more on uses of vision in these theatrical ventures, there are a number of philosophical limitations evident across the theoretical underpinnings of these endeavours that will hopefully expand over the next few years. While some programmes incorporate diverse traditions, written and practical sources often rely heavily upon Western modalities, although more inclusive work is gradually becoming available. The initiatives under discussion here draw from numerous modern theories about acting, trauma, movement, vocalization and so on, but Western perspectives often predominate.

Some non-Western practices include yoga and Buddhist methodologies, but they do not yet typically incorporate significant research addressing cultural and ethnic contributions to sensory studies, such as those referenced in Mark M. Smith's *A Sensory History Manifesto*. Smith lists many researchers who are investigating perspectives that integrate geographic, ethnic and other influences on the ways that the senses are experienced and analyzed.[56] As Smith notes, 'Structural shifts in sensory environments, changes in sensory perceptions and habits, shifts in the ways the senses were (and are) produced and consumed were (and are) not merely incidental to key historical developments but constitutive of them.'[57]

Given the predominantly Western background and training of many of the practitioners considered here, only a portion of these global conceptualizations of the senses will be addressed, leaving many interesting perspectives available for future investigation, particularly among communities whose traditions and belief systems may not figure prominently in current Shakespearean work.[58]

Shifts in such directions are already appearing. One group in New Zealand, for example, that developed a Shakespeare Behind Bars programme when Curt L.Tofteland completed a residency there a few years ago, subsequently shifted its focus from Shakespeare to local Maori materials, according to Arts Access Aotearoa, an organization devoted to 'increasing access to the arts'.[59]

Additional complex issues surround some of these initiatives, as many contemporary disabilities activists maintain a vocal insistence upon 'nothing about us without us', a phrase drawn from James I. Charlton's 1998 book of that name.[60] This slogan, which demands the involvement of individuals with disabilities in the planning, implementation and assessment of programmes, services and other entities designed for them, sometimes comes into play with regards to the programmes considered here. Flute Theatre, for example, has been criticized for being developed initially by persons not identifying as autistic and for situating itself within the 'medical model' of autism. These concerns will be considered.

Like numerous of the practitioners involved in these initiatives, I do not share many of the circumstances affecting participants in these performative ventures, and I am careful not to make assumptions about what is 'best' for individual groups of people. Currently, there is widespread focus on positionality, with the ethical aspects of a researcher's shifting status as an 'insider' or 'outsider' raising questions.[61] Anna CohenMiller and Nettie Boivin discuss contemporary research into this fluid and shifting binary but highlight the ways such distinctions may becoming obsolete.[62]

For my part, I remain aware (and wary) of the many times that researchers have unconsciously or deliberately misrepresented or misunderstood the circumstances or perspectives of those who figure in their research. Accordingly, I have spent significant time with many of those featured in this volume and endeavour always to respect their agency, privacy and trust that they will be represented appropriately. I acknowledge the danger of inadvertent errors and apologize for any mistakes made in these pages, many of which are written on complex and contentious topics.

Thus, while I have spoken to numerous group participants whose personal circumstances align with the organizing principles of these communities and I share some of these conversations, I make no attempt to speak in their stead. This volume's focus on multisensory Shakespeare emphasizes the human conditions highlighted in these programmes that broad swaths of people engage with. Nothing proscriptive is implied or endorsed here. The vast majority of the groups discussed in this study aim for inclusivity.

Mackenzie, for instance, shares governance with the incarcerated members of the theatre groups she works with. All decisions are made communally by the ensembles. SIP works similarly, although staff operate as 'facilitators' within this framework.[63] Some of these specialized communities rely more heavily upon sensory experiences than others. Collectively, they illustrate the many benefits for those who emphasize sensory awareness in their theatrical activities, although individuals invariably encounter diverse experiences.

Occasionally, the practitioners in these realms hold therapeutic credentials, but most of those working in these areas emphasize that they are not offering treatment.[64] They also make it clear that these initiatives neither imply that the participants need to be 'fixed' nor that Shakespeare specifically (or theatre more generally) can or should be seen as an avenue towards remediation. While these engagements aim to create positive outcomes, practitioners typically are careful to not to make claims outside of their training or licensure. In addition, as Clark Baim's recent writing on safe and ethical practices demonstrates, increasing attention is being paid to the foregrounding of ethical perspectives within such work.[65]

Many of these programmes emphasize integrated physical, emotional and intellectual engagement. Exploration into interactions between mind and body, which are key to these practices, emerge in a number of disparate fields, including what is termed 'embodied cognition', as explained by developmental psychologist Esther Thelen,

> To say that cognition is embodied means that it arises from bodily interactions with the world. From this point of view, cognition depends on the kinds of experiences that come from having a body with particular perceptual and motor capabilities that are inseparably linked and that together form the matrix within which reasoning, memory, emotion, language and all other aspects of mental life are meshed.[66]

Embodied cognition, whose rise in public and scholarly visibility is often attributed to collaborative work by cognitive scientist Francisco J. Verala, philosopher Evan Thompson and psychologist Eleanor

Rosch, has gained significant attention in performance studies. One key text was written by actor/director/scholar Rick Kemp and another edited by a team of theatre and cognition specialists, including Experience Bryon, J. Mark Bishop, Deirdre McLaughlin, and Jess Kaufman.[67] Kemp, for example, describes the way that many traditional dramatic training programmes separate mind from body:

> While many training programs include movement classes, or activities such as Alexander technique, yoga, or dance, these are generally separate from the 'acting' classes, and offer the student little information on how to synthesize the two. On the other hand, physically-based approaches tend to neglect textual analysis, again leaving the student without linking information.[68]

By adding elements of cognitive research into this equation, Kemp supports an alteration in theatrical training, 'A shift to a holistic concept of the bodymind will support practices that embrace the reflexive and integrated relationship between physicality, thought, emotion, and expression.'[69]

In his study, Kemp discusses a number of prominent theatre theorists and details the ways that different acting styles resist or facilitate 'embodied acting', endeavouring to bridge 'the gap between the categories of theory and practice by applying some of the most significant discoveries of cognitive science directly to the work of key practitioners of the twentieth century to create a praxis-based understanding of acting'.[70] The work of many of the practitioners considered in this study similarly interrogates and often includes embodied practices.[71]

Cheryl Pallant, for instance, speaks about the importance of movement, even while deeply acknowledging the power of stillness,

> As sacred as stillness can be, movement is a game changer. Movement alters the environment within our body. Movement stimulates the heart, breath, blood, brain, gut, energy, our proprioception on continual alert, situating and resituating the body on the move.[72]

Movement obviously confers many physical and psychological benefits that regularly manifest themselves in these Shakespearean initiatives.

McLaughlin also conceptualizes embodiment through a relevant lens, in a piece she labels as a 'provocation.' Here, she offers her understanding of the intersection between cognition and performance:

> The fact that embodiment has emerged as a primary issue for consideration in both cognitive science and actor training (and actor-based performance training) as just two examples of a wider range of disciplines and research programmes grappling with the concept reflects a concrete change in thinking about the nature of the mind and cognitive processing which extends beyond individual disciplinary projects. In many ways, the concept of embodiment has served as a pivotal catalyst or fulcrum between various disciplines within the sciences, arts, and humanities.[73]

McLaughlin's view that embodiment brings together a number of different disciplinary perspectives concurs with the work being drawn upon by many Shakespearean endeavours with specialized communities.

Despite Kemp's belief that mind and body are largely kept separate in actor training, some of those writing in the field of 'embodied acting' find that major figures in these realms frequently offer practices that are congruent with understandings of embodiment. Ysabel Clare asserts that prominent theatrical figure Konstantin Stanislavski's training practice demonstrates embodiment,

> it evokes the embodied mind and demonstrates its circularity by extracting conceptual principles shaped by physical experience before converting them back into physical experience for the purpose of acting; it addresses processes of which we are usually unaware; and the metaphorical concepts that originate in perceptual experience of the material world are situated in relation to the body in space and time in three dimensions.[74]

Kemp does not specifically address Clare's assessment of Stanislavski, but indicates that this arts practitioner supported a division between mind and body that correlated with 'the rudimentary knowledge of the mind at that time'.[75] He also suggests, however, that the common Anglo-American conflation of Lee Strasberg's work with Stanislavski's led to an unfortunate misunderstanding, whereby 'for a large part of the twentieth century, many directors and actors considered [Stanislavski's] work as a purely 'psychological' approach'.[76]

Nevertheless, much of the work done by groups included here incorporates exercises from Stanislavski, Michael Chekhov and others, that emphasize integration of physical and psychological perspectives. In contrast with what is often considered the more cerebral training presented by Sanford Meisner and others or the more specifically body-focused work of Rudolf Laban, these Russian-developed practices encourage integrated approaches, although Soviet political pressures helped suppress acknowledgement of such aspects of this work for many years.

Recent research by Sergei Tcherkasski traces influences on Stanislavski's practice from the hatha yoga principles presented by Yogi Ramacharaka and describes the active censorship that elided these influences from view,[77]

> In the late 1920's, all or almost all, mention of philosophy and the practice of Yoga disappeared from Stanislavsky's manuscripts and published works. According to Stalin's ideologues, the great man of socialist realism in the theatre could not derive inspiration from the mystical teaching of Indian hermits. Thus began the silencing of one of the most important sources of the System.[78]

Tcherkasski reintroduces the yogic background of Stanislavski's work and draws attention to similar integrative influences upon the practice of Stanislavski's notable student Michael Chekhov, who incorporated yoga and the sensory perspectives of Rudolf Steiner[79] into his own actor education practice,[80] although Charles Marowitz reports that some of Chekhov's students were 'frightened off by his immersion in yoga and reincarnation'.[81] Chekhov famously spent most of his career working outside of Russia, due to political concerns about the direction of his work. As Marowitz explains, after Chekhov and his wife left Russia,

> there would be several attempts to negotiate a return to his homeland, but they would all be broken off. Chekhov would journey from Berlin to Paris, from Latvia to Lithuania, from Devonshire to California, but never again step foot on Russian soil.[82]

At least some of the objections generated from Chekhov's work came from what Marowitz describes as 'Chekhov's admiration for the teachings of Rudolf Steiner' whose 'anthroposophical ideas were spiritual tendencies smacking of religion which had become anathema to mainstream Communist ideologues'.[83] Despite this initial political resistance from Russia, however, Chekhov's work remains important to many of the practitioners included here.[84]

In my 2021 *Shakespeare Survey* article discussing prison programmes in India, I detail the close correlations found between the practices of prison arts practitioners Hulugappa Kattamani in Mysore and Alokananda Roy in Kolkata and those recommended by many expressive arts practitioners, movement instructors and others encouraging the integration of mind, body and spirit.[85] Common acting exercises often incorporate many of the elements highlighted in such modalities, as do other movement regimens such as yoga. Those who engage in studio arts, either as part of their group work or in preparation for performances, also engage with a range of sensory experiences. Heightened sensory and physical involvement are key to these practices.

Central to the theoretical and practical materials contributing to these programmes are the well-known works of Paolo Freire and Augusto Boal, who wrote highly influential texts that resonate through many social-justice environments. In his preface to the fiftieth anniversary edition of Freire's iconic *Pedagogy of the Oppressed,* Donald Macedo suggests that Freire's goal in writing this book was

> to launch the development of an emancipatory pedagogical process that invites and challenges students, through critical literacies, to learn how to negotiate the world in which they find themselves, in a thoughtful and critically reflective manner, so as to expose and engage the tensions and contradictions inherent in the ongoing relations of oppressor and oppressed.[86]

Freire's work has been revered in many circles, influencing much additional work, including that of the Brazilian director and theorist Augusto Boal, who published *Theatre of the Oppressed* and *Games for Actors and Non-Actors*, among other texts that expand Freire's philosophies into theatrical realms.[87] Adrian Jackson, translator of *Games for Actors and Non-Actors*, lists some of the places incorporating Boal's practices.[88] These locations resemble the Shakespearean environments discussed in this book:

Schools, factories, day centers, community centres, with tenants' groups, homeless people, disabled people, people in ethnic minorities, etc. – anywhere where there is community which shares an oppression. Its aim again is to stimulate debate (in the form of action, not just words), to show alternatives, to enable people 'to become the protagonists of their own lives.'[89]

Not surprisingly, Boal's methods correspond with many of the practices detailed in this volume.

I use the word 'exercise' to designate all physical, muscular movement (respiratory, motor, vocal) which helps the doer to a better knowledge or recognition of his or her body, its muscles, its nerves, its relationship to other bodies, to gravity, to objects, space, dimensions, volumes, distances, weights, speed, the interrelationship of these different forces and so on. The goal of the exercises is a better awareness of the body and its mechanisms, its atrophies, and hypertrophies, its capacities for recuperation, restructuring, reharmonisation.[90]

For Boal, as for many others included in this book, theatrical endeavors designed for personal or social change involve extensive multisensory engagements.

While not directly connected with Boal, another Brazilian theatrical event illustrates the multifaceted nature of the Shakespearean performances undertaken by communities not commonly associated with such drama. Dani Snyder-Young recounts a story along these lines told by Paul Heritage, who

> stag[ed] a reading of *Romeo and Juliet* in a Brazilian prison for an audience of inmates, guards, dignitaries and journalists. A string of 12 incarcerated teenage boys played Romeo in this reading. Some boys handled the complex language with fluency and passion, while others slowly sounded the text out word by word. Heritage describes initially feeling as though these rough performances represented failure on his part-until he realized that 'the audience was seeing something different. They were watching them read.' Incarcerated boys in the audience were able to 'see them as extensions of what they might be capable of doing.'[91]

As Heritage and Snyder suggest, professional performances are not always an appropriate goal in such settings, although many of the ensembles considered here set that standard for their participants. Snyder also reminds us, citing Tim Prentki and Sheila Preston, that applied theatre initiatives range widely and that one should not make too many assumptions about their deliberate or unconscious methodological or ideological precepts without investigation.

> It might be tempting to assume that applied theatre is, per se, a left-wing or socialist methodology. This would be a false assumption: applied theatre is no more or less at the service of a particular ideology than any other kind of theatre. Its processes are as available to fascist regimes seeking to inculcate messages of obedience as they are to democratic regimes seeking to mobilize active citizens.[92]

Personally, I have never recognized anything resembling a 'fascist regime' among the practitioners included in this volume,[93] but it remains important to remember that good intentions cannot be taken for granted and that many of these environments are vulnerable to exploitation both by professional staff and volunteers. Nevertheless, I continue to question how prevalent what Todd Landon Barnes calls 'the perils of redemptive performance' are in these realms.[94] It is also pertinent to note that the benefits available through these ventures, such as reading aloud in public, may not correspond with the standards associated with professional theatre. Many of the groups included here tend to be more intent upon 'process' than 'product;' others need to work within external power structures that are outside their control. They operate within complicated circumstances that the practitioners typically approach with care.

While I have great respect for many of those involved in the specialized communities discussed later, I feel compelled to be forthright about some of the challenges attendant within the communities included in this study. The first may seem slight, but it is, in fact, often significant. The academic world and the realm of arts practitioners remain significantly distinctive, in many cases.[95] Widely divergent perspectives often frame these varied realms of inquiry and presentation. These groups regularly approach their work from disparate perspectives.

Scholars and those teaching at tertiary institutions tend to meet regularly at national academic gatherings such as the Shakespeare Association of America (SAA), the British Shakespeare Association (BSA), the Shakespeare Society of India, the Australian and New Zealand Shakespeare Association, the Armenian Shakespeare Association, the European Shakespeare Research Association and various regional groups. Theatre professionals are sometimes welcomed and occasionally made to feel out of place at these events.

The Shakespeare Theatre Association, on the other hand, and other gatherings of theatrical personnel predominantly feature arts practitioners: actors, artistic directors, education specialists, designers and others who are closely associated with the presentation of Shakespearean drama. There is often little overlap between those who attend these conferences and related activities, although some gatherings, such as the American Shakespeare Center's Blackfriars Conference, Southern Utah University and Utah Shakespeare's Wooden O conference and the University of Waterloo/Stratford Festival Shakespearean Theatre Conference in Stratford, Ontario include representatives from both academic and artistic realms.[96]

I feel fortunate to be able to work closely with both theatrical professionals and academicians but acknowledge that there are times where this study predictably and/or unexpectedly sheds light on the distinctive cultures, norms and expectations of these disparate communities. My training as a scholar inevitably informs how I perceive and describe these Shakespearean activities; I greatly appreciate the guidance of the many theatrical practitioners who have offered their time and expertise to help ensure that I am presenting things accurately and respectfully about theatrical practices, expectations and assessment.[97] Any errors are, of course, my own.

In this study, the questions emerging from the scholar/practitioner divide, as well as the scientist/literary scholar/theatrical practitioner spectrum, are sometimes mundane and comparatively benign: should typographical errors in course materials or student writing be noted, for example, or should distinctive vocabulary choices made by practitioners, scholars or participants be pointed out? Such choices can lead to embarrassing decisions, but typically do not trigger momentous outcomes.

The potential stakes become higher in some of the contexts emerging in this study, however. The fields of trauma studies, yoga and those associated with autism, for example, contain points of contention. At least two prominent yoga figures, Yogi Bhajan and Amrit Dessai, for instance, have been identified as sexual offenders.[98] Trauma specialist Bessel van der Kolk, whose book is a long-term *New York Times* bestseller and whose work appears regularly in the realms included here, was accused of bullying. He then lost his trauma center position and instigated legal action as a result.[99] In addition, the scientific conclusions of both van der Kolk and trauma specialist Stephen Porges have been questioned, even though both remain prominent presences in trauma studies.[100]

van der Kolk earned his MD at the University of Chicago and completed his psychiatric residency at Harvard. Porges' educational background is less clear, but he appears to have studied at Michigan State University.[101] He is a professor of psychiatry at the University of North Carolina at Chapel Hill and director of the Kinsey Institute Traumatic Stress Research Consortium at Indiana University. Both have published widely. From an academic perspective, therefore, their credentials seem solid, if not unassailable.[102]

The same cannot be said of some of the other figures whose works loom large in these fields. Cathy A. Malchiodi, an arts therapist who often appears on panels with van der Kolk and Porges, has significant professional experience and has published extensively. Her 2009 PhD, however, seems to have been granted by Northcentral University, an online, for-profit institution, which carries limited cachet in academic environments.[103] The source of her PhD is not indicated on her website or in the biographies included in the books under her authorship that I have seen.[104] Similarly, Jamie Marich, a counselor, writer and practitioner in expressive arts and trauma, received her 2009 PhD (in human services) from Capella University, another online, for-profit institution and she does not provide this information on her website.[105]

Such educational backgrounds do not necessarily erode these practitioners' contributions to expressive arts initiatives, but they make it more difficult to assess them academically. At the same time, academic credentials often do not figure centrally in practical theatrical enterprises. I am including these contributions in my study, therefore, while recognizing potential questions, such as those raised by somatic practitioner Cheryl Pallant who describes 'a somatic perspective' in the context of scientific skepticism:

> A somatic perspective recognizes the body as the site where personal and collective experiences meet . . . The scientific perspective tends to ridicule and suspect many of the findings of the subjective somatic perspective which science considers unreliable and unreproducible. Many times, such findings are unreliable and unreproducible, but that is precisely their strength. Personal experience provides a potent, at times unique insight into ourselves and seeds a broad understanding that is constantly undergoing revision and development.[106]

Pallant's observation underscores a key dichotomy that deeply affects the practices incorporated into Shakespeare for specialized communities.

Funding sources and other bodies offering 'stamps of approval' frequently demand scientific evidence and results. At the same time, many of the somatic, expressive arts and movement modalities often relied upon sometimes correspond with scientific findings and sometimes operate according to alternative measures of success and efficacy. Since financial and other resources remain limited, these diverse interpretations can generate significant controversies.

Not surprisingly, hesitation or resistance has already emerged surrounding the work of some of those working and writing in areas relevant to Shakespeare in specialized communities. David Fontana, for instance, who died in 2010, was a professor in transpersonal psychology at Liverpool John Moores University and a Distinguished Visiting Fellow at the University of Cardiff when his helpful *Meditators' Handbook* appeared in print. He published numerous books that have been widely translated and his volumes contain substantial information about germane topics. At the same time, he delved deeply into paranormal studies, which situates him outside many conventional academic and scientific parameters. His interest in poltergeists and related phenomena do not figure into discussions here, but in the relevant chapter I place his work in a footnote rather than the main text due to the skepticism his paranormal research could generate.

Such less conventional perspectives often acquire derogatory labels, such as 'woo-woo', but the dominance of Western scientific thought warrants examination in the context of alternative perspectives, particularly if we are going to make room to explore explorations of mind and body from diverse cultures. Some ideas may not bear close scrutiny, but others could contribute fruitfully to our understanding of a wider range of valuable embodied practices.[107]

Throughout this project, I endeavour to be scrupulous about respecting issues surrounding respect and consent. Despite living in a social media saturated world, I am not including photographs in this volume. Several years ago, I was challenged for not showing images of 'red Indians' when I was giving a talk about work with a group of North American tribal colleges. This demand deeply influenced my decision not to include photos. Many of the groups discussed here use photos in their own outreach or publicity materials, but I do not wish to supply any room for the people included to be 'exoticized' or exploited in any way. In keeping with these principles, I am not correcting writing errors of group participants unless necessary for clarity. Many of those involved in these Shakespeare groups do not write with standard spelling, phrasing, or punctuation, often for reasons associated with their current or former circumstances. Highlighting deviations from academic prose in the writing created by those within these specialized communities is contradictory to the tenets of respectful inclusivity that undergirds this study.

Similarly, since some of those discussed here cannot legally and/or ethically give consent for their names, images or words to be presented, I am careful to quote only those individuals whose words appear in print elsewhere or those who can unequivocally agree to be identified. Incarcerated Shakespeareans are not, therefore, cited directly, except as they present themselves in theatre programmes or other public materials, such as those involved in Emergency Shakespeare,[108] who provide pseudonyms in performance documents. Those who have returned to society, on the other hand, including the SIP alumni, are mentioned when they have given consent.

I am also not emphasizing race, sexual orientation or gender identities of the participants. As mentioned, many of these programmes are pursuing expanded training and revised practices in diversity, equity and inclusion, which I applaud. The groups included are diverse in many ways, some of which are visible and predictable, others which are not. The incarcerated Shakespeareans

I met in India, for example, appear to be predominantly, if not exclusively, from the areas around the correctional facilities where they live. Shakespearean-involved prison environments in some other regions and countries often house people of multiple nationalities. The United States notably incarcerates disproportionate numbers of BIPOC citizens. That practice is reflected in many of the American prison populations included here, except in some of the institutions located in less diverse communities. Sexual orientation and gender identity sometimes come up in discussions taking place among the groups participating in these Shakespearean activities, but those narratives are not mine to tell.

While much sensory information comes from Westernized perspectives, this study is still focused on the broader human characteristics shared by members of these groups, rather than gender identity, race, or ethnicity, even though these would be informative topics to investigate. I look forward to appropriately crafted studies conducted in these areas. The incorporation of more non-Western perspectives on the human senses and on performance will undoubtedly alter many approaches in initiatives for specialized communities, as these influences spreads.[109] These programmes will inevitably evolve, as knowledge and experience shift what are perceived as best practices. In addition, some of these initiatives rest heavily upon the engagement of dedicated individuals whose departure would be challenging for their groups; others have well-defined succession plans in place. The paths they will follow are likely to be as diverse as the members of these communities.

Perspectives about Shakespeare remain in continual flux and are likely always to be fluid. Some of these programmes focus nearly exclusively on this canon, while others incorporate a range of other writers and artistic creations in their endeavours. Some facilitators and participants in these groups believe strongly in the particular applicability of Shakespeare to such undertakings; others welcome and encourage a broader perspective. Conversations about multiple aspects of these endeavours will undoubtedly continue. I remain grateful to the many people who welcomed me into these diverse creative environments and look forward to experiencing what pathways these gatherings follow in the future.

1

'In Mine Own Throat'

The power of breath and voice

In September 2021, Detroit's Shakespeare in Prison (SIP) programme posted a Facebook message quoting one of their participants:

> When I came into Shakespeare, it was just like a BREATH. A stress reliever. Somewhere I could spend my energy in a positive way while having a good time and not getting in trouble. That's what I wanted to get out of it and, by god, I did.[1]

This remark emphasizes one of central concerns of this chapter, namely, the importance of oral speech, breathing and breath training in much of the Shakespearean work included in this study.[2] The related sense of smell will be considered in a later chapter, but breath and speech can claim identification as embodied experiences, even if Aristotle excludes them from his taxonomy of senses.[3] Other understandings of the senses offer far more capacious understandings that incorporate corporeal functions such as breath. In addition, along with movement, breath constitutes one of the few bodily experiences currently engaged with by all the groups discussed in this volume.

'The voice is by no means necessary for language', as John Colapinto rightly reminds us,[4] but many of these specialized communities use spoken language nonetheless.[5] For such speaking individuals, voice work offers participants opportunities to become more consciously attuned with the numerous parts of their body involved in vocalization and to experiment with a more extensive range of speech patterns than twenty-first-century people typically experience. Many of the exercises described in these works also help ameliorate the physical and psychological effects of traumatic life experiences. Thus, those who participate in these activities can gain physical and emotional benefits, including results that many vocal trainers attribute specifically to Shakespeare.

Those who do not use spoken language can potentially access the power of breath training and learn from other avenues about the characteristics of Shakespearean text that distinguish his works from modern writing and speaking.[6] Famed Shakespearean vocal teacher Kristin Linklater,[7] for example, maintains that 'we do not express our passions regularly and the twentieth-century voice goes pretty much unexercised in the language of extreme expression'.[8] Patsy Rodenburg, another vocal coach with extensive experience with Shakespeare at the Royal Shakespeare Company (RSC) and elsewhere, supports Linkater's assessment in her critiques of modern communication styles.

> Many of our habits today are about non-communication. Perhaps we don't trust what we say or believe that others are listening. We're often frightened of committing to any powerful idea or passionate feeling. Our communication grows indirect, surrounded by an aura of studied casualness; we hesitate and mumble; we rely more and more on glibness, cynicism or denial.[9]

Like several of the other vocal and trauma specialists included here, she also maintains that people today often restrict their vocal and experiential range.

> Our modern voices tend to be held and tight–tight jaws, riddled with urban stress. We either fight the world vocally, pushing aggressively at it, or avoid committing ourselves to speech, underusing our voices. Both options reduce the range and enjoyment of the voice. Tension locks sound and words into the speaker. We have to unlock sound in order to release every quality embedded in Shakespeare's language.[10]

These and other Shakespearean vocal masters are widely influential, so it is not surprising that their exercises and beliefs often appear in practices undertaken by Shakespeareans in specialized communities. They also offer significant potential answers to the 'why Shakespeare?' question that regularly emerges in conjunction with the initiatives.

Similar to other famed Shakespearean vocal coaches such as Linklater and Cicely Berry, Rodenburg frequently differentiates Shakespearean language patterns from modern speech practices.

> The world Shakespeare creates is full of inquisitive speakers and attentive listeners. His characters use their language to connect to the world, not to hide from it. They use it to survive, to probe to explore, to quest. They are not afraid of profound expression. If they mock, it is direct and to the point, not under their breath.[11]

Linklater further elaborates upon Shakespeare's embodied speech, which demonstrates how and why delving deeply into the language of this playwright can be particularly beneficial for a wide range of people.

> When words are mainly experienced in the head and the mouth they convey cerebral meaning. In order to transfer Shakespeare's full emotional, intellectual and philosophical intent from the page to the stage, words must connect with the full human range of intellect and emotion, body and voice. They must be allowed to rediscover old neuro-physiological routes of appetite to bring back taste and texture to speaking and to spark the animal response mechanisms which fire creative processes long buried under layers of 'civilized' and 'rational' behaviour. Only the fullest access to the humanity of the speaker allows one to speak Shakespeare fully.[12]

These insights correlate with the differences between cognitive and affective learning, which feature in Bloom's taxonomy, the psychological model for the hierarchy of learning and which emphasize how people learn from a range of different perspectives, including physical, emotional and experiential situations.[13] Like the relationship between mind and body often referenced by theorists and practitioners in this study, both cognitive and affective learning play central roles in these acting and breathing exercises.[14] Linklater also describes the problems she finds in the speech patterns prevalent in our current environment, noting, 'Today's adult voice is deprived of the nourishment of emotion and free breathing. Society has taught us that it is wrong to express ourselves freely'[15] and, 'The adult voice is, in most instances, conditioned to talk *about* feelings rather than to *reveal* them.'[16] In addition, she suggests that Shakespeare's language provides access to more 'truth' than modern speech facilitates.

> Shakespeare's 'truth', therefore, is different from our daily experience of 'truth'. The scale is larger than our domestic reality. But he does not express his truth in a different language, he expresses it in a different experience of language. When today's actor starts to *experience* Shakespeare's language as a whole-body process, s/he is led to a larger and deeper experience of thought and emotion, and from there to a more fundamental, more individual an enlarged experience of 'truth'.[17]

According to such perspectives, therefore, voice and breath training, particularly when focused on Shakespeare, can help participants access both physical and emotional benefits that are not associated with ordinary modern speech.

Fay Simpson makes a similar point in *The Lucid Body*, a book containing considerable Shakespearean material, which additionally links these perspectives with aspects of the yogic practices associated with numerous Shakespearean initiatives.[18]

> Positioned between the heart and the mind, the throat [fifth] chakra transforms our feeling and ideas into speech.
>
> The fifth chakra is the spokesperson of our physical systems with the ability to communicate our deepest truth. Revealing yourself honestly through the voice is not easy and takes years of training. Most of us hide behind made-up voices, devised to give a specific impression, like an outfit. When the naked truth does emerge, however, it rings out like a bell. You can recognize it in the tone, or timber, of the voice.[19]

In contrast to the restricted speech models described by these vocal coaches, learning to speak with what Linklater terms one's 'natural voice' enables vocal participants to gain more intimate understandings of their physical speaking apparatuses as well as a broader familiarity with innumerable forms of expression. As Linklater remarks,

> The basis for all my work is the belief that voice and language belong to the whole body rather than the head alone and that the function of the voice is to reveal the self. This book, in consequence ... aims to recondition both mind and body so that the voice can express the visceral and spiritual urgency that was its subject matter in Shakespeare's day.[20]

The work of Linklater and other influential Shakespearean voice teachers helps illustrate why their breath-training exercises remain prominent in the settings discussed here. Integrating breath work and physical awareness into the study of the emotional breadth associated with drama, leads to many positive outcomes, as Michael Lugering, founding director of the Expressive Actor, a nonprofit associated with integrated methods of actor training explains,[21]

> The purpose of breath training is to develop flexibility, dexterity, strength, control, and freedom in the muscles that make breathing possible. A telltale sign of faulty breath management is excessive muscular tension. When this occurs, the muscles of the throat, tongue, jaw, neck, shoulders, and rib cage desperately attempt to supply, bolster, and stabilize an unsteady and weak breath stream. The body fights the breath, and the breath fights the body. Inhalation is forced, audible, and overtly muscular. Exhalation is strained, pressed, and congested.[22]

The introduction of breath work to these specialized communities, therefore, can facilitate the release of significant muscular tension, which is often associated with stress and trauma, as van der Kolk details,

> One of the ways the memory of helplessness is stored is as muscle tension or feelings of disintegration in the affected body areas ... The lives of many trauma survivors come to revolve around bracing against and neutralizing unwanted sensory experiences and most people I see in my practice have become experts in such self-numbing.[23]

van der Kolk also includes yoga exercises in his work, a practice he adopted after extensive studies into the ways that yogic breathing counteracts the numbing described earlier, allowing people, in his terms, to 'inhabit their bodies'.[24] It seems fitting, therefore, that yoga appears in many of the programmes included here. As indicated in the introduction, van der Kolk often collaborates with Stephen W. Porges, Director of the Trauma Research Center at Indiana University's Kinsey Institute, who also stresses the importance of such physical models of intervention for trauma survivors, stating,

> One area (i.e., nucleus ambiguus) is linked with the regulation of all the facial muscles – muscles of ingestion, muscles of listening, and muscles of engaging others. Our social nervous system is intimately related with the newer vagus – and so is our breath.[25]

Porges further remarks upon the ways that the tensions these practices endeavour to lessen may have begun as defensive mechanisms that served useful purposes.

> I try to explain to trauma survivors what their body has done. There seems to be a prevalent implicit feeling for many survivors of trauma that their body has done something wrong, something very bad. They need to be informed that their bodily response strategies may have been protective and saved their lives. Their bodily responses may have enabled them by immobilizing and dissociating to minimize physical injury and painful suffering by not fighting back. The immobilization may be very adaptive, since it may not trigger additional aggression.[26]

Given the backgrounds of many of the individuals in these specialized communities, it is predictable that these groups include populations contending with significant, ongoing stress and trauma in their lives. Shakespeare in Prisons Network (SiPN) members, for example, engage in Shakespearean activities in a large number of international carceral institutions and also work with those who have been released from custody. SiPN practices vary, but each group engages individuals possessing complex, frequently traumatic, life histories and many SiPN practitioners work closely with trauma specialists.[27]

Similarly, programmes connecting veterans with Shakespeare, such as DE-CRUIT, Feast of Crispian and Chesapeake Shakespeare Company, as well as those performing Shakespeare with those experiencing homelessness or at-risk youth, involve people facing long-term challenging circumstances with practices designed, in part, to help ameliorate the effects of their trauma. While not all of the featured Shakespeare initiatives work explicitly with survivors of trauma, breath and movement modalities enhance diverse participants' ability to develop more productive physical habits that contribute to their personal growth.

Those who are not typically involved in yoga, acting, singing, athletics or congruent activities requiring pulmonary awareness, however, may not pay close attention to their breath, their voice or the other physical processes linked with these practices.[28] For many people, especially those without respiratory concerns, breath is something they take for granted, not a sense or experience they actively attend to or cultivate. Although life requires breath, it rarely captures attention unless impaired or emphasized through particular activities. When people are new to various movement and therapeutic settings, they regularly need to be reminded to breathe. While breath is normal and necessary, many individuals also often 'get it wrong'. As pulmonologist Michael J. Stephen notes, 'Only someone who is short of breath gives the lungs a second thought.'[29] In response to this common disregard for the ongoing importance of respiration, Stephen underscores the significance of breathing, arguing that alertness to this process can promote healing in numerous parts of the body:

> Science is beginning to investigate in a serious manner something humanity has known for centuries – that the breath can be used to heal the body. Every year more papers are being published on the healing power of breath ... The scientific evidence has started to go even deeper, to the level of our blood, and even our genes. In those who practice breathing exercises, levels of inflammatory proteins in the blood are significantly lower, especially under certain types of stress. Mobilizing the power of the breath has also been shown to turn on anti-inflammatory genes and turn off pro-inflammatory ones, including genes that regulate energy metabolism, insulin secretion, and even the part of our DNA that controls longevity.[30]

Numerous trauma specialists make similar points about the healing properties of breath. van der Kolk, for instance, describes his first encounter with a new patient and his immediate focus upon her breathing,

> Annie shuffled into my office . . . barely breathing, looking like a frozen bird. I knew we couldn't do anything until I could help her quiet down. . . I breathed with her and asked her to follow my example. . . She stealthily followed my movements, her eyes still fixed on the floor. We spent about half an hour this way. From time to time I quietly asked her to notice how her feet felt against the floor and how her chest expanded and contracted with each breath. Her breath gradually became slower and deeper, her face softened, her spine straightened a bit, and her eyes lifted.[31]

As van der Kolk indicates here, since breathing and emotion are closely related, attention to breath can facilitate therapeutic results. Calapinto also notes, moreover, in alignment with Linklater's assertions about the constraints of modern speech, that many individuals today often restrict the range of their vocal expression.

> One way that our massive cortex affects our emotional vocalizations is by editing, or censoring, them –modulating the spontaneous noises that might otherwise burst from us. So, in a hostile encounter with a boss, a teacher . . . we might experience a flare of activity in our amygdala, which ordinarily would trigger a loud, angry growl and hostile snarl. But to blare forth with such a noise would usually come at too high a social cost, so we control the vocal noises we make, keeping the overt hostility out of our tone, and preserving relations with our family, friends, and the line cutter [in traffic].[32]

For many people dealing with trauma, numbness can often coexist with aggressive outbursts, so a more healthful model for 'controlling' breath and vocalization could lead to more productive habits.

James Nestor offers a complementary perspective in his best-selling *Breath: The New Science of a Lost Art* that expands the physical purview of breath. His book incorporates wide-ranging research done on breathing, some of which suggests that 'many modern maladies – asthma, anxiety, attention deficit hyperactivity disorder, psoriasis and more – could be reduced or reversed simply by changing the way we inhale and exhale'.[33] While to my knowledge, none of the Shakespeare programmes discussed are seeking directly to cure illnesses, they are helping participants access practices that can provide relief for a number of physical and psychological constraints. Nestor and others suggest that the potential healing available through breath has yet to be understood fully.

In accordance with such possibilities, therefore, many acting regimens and trauma therapies, as well as martial arts and mindfulness practices, teach individuals how to access the physiological and emotional benefits, as well as the performative strengths, of breathwork. By emphasizing breathwork during actor training, yoga and other movement regimens, the practitioners working with these specialized populations offer their actors the opportunity to enhance their emotional and physical well-being, as the work of Sankalpa in India, Shakespeare & Co., the International Opera Theater, among many others, demonstrate. Breathwork can benefit participants from many backgrounds, whether or not they communicate vocally. Furthermore, integrating breathwork with Shakespearean dialogue can help offset common habits of restricting deep breathing and the full range of emotional resonances available through spoken language.

As Colapinto notes, moreover, human recognition of the correlation between breath and health has a lengthy history.

> The healing power of breath was recognized as far back as 7000 BCE, in the Zoroastrian religion of Persia, now Iran, where breathing exercises were routinely practiced. This tradition was carried to the West, where both the ancient Greeks and Romans regularly engaged in breathing exercises and reflection. Meditation and chanting have remained an integral part of Judaism, Christianity and Islam. But while Western religions talk and write about the breath – the Holy Spirit, and *ruach* – Eastern religions have made a strict focus on the breath being a part of spiritual enlightenment.[34]

Nestor makes a similar observation about the extensive, multi-cultural history of studies into what he calls 'the basics of restorative breathing': 'These slow and long techniques are open to everyone – old and young, sick and healthy, rich and poor. They've been practised in Hinduism, Buddhism, Christianity, and other religions for thousands of years, but only recently have we learned how they can reduce blood pressure, boost athletic performance, and balance the nervous system.'[35]

Similar to some of the other practices adopted by those seeking beneficial results for their particular groups of Shakespeareans, however, the research on breath studies that Nestor references does not always emanate from mainstream scientific realms. Thus, he acknowledges,

> Many early pioneers in this discipline weren't scientists. They were tinkerers, a kind of rogue group I call 'pulmonauts,' who stumbled on the powers of breathing because nothing else could help them. They were Civil War surgeons, French hairdressers, anarchist opera singers, Indian mystics, irritable swim coaches, stern-faced Ukrainian cardiologists, Czechoslovakian Olympians, and North Carolina choral conductors.[36]

However, he remarks that 'over the past several years their techniques were being rediscovered and scientifically proven'.[37] One of the challenges facing us as we endeavour to expand our cultural knowledges, will be determining how to assess practices that may not immediately align with standard Western beliefs. Nestor, therefore, is one of the many writers currently addressing this dilemma – or opportunity.

Clearly, however, there are a number of prominent long-term vocal coaches still influencing Shakespearean practices, who focus intently on the relationship between mind and body. Linklater, for example, co-founded Shakespeare & Co. with Tina Packer in 1978 and taught there until the mid-1990s. Her vocal practices are still a key part of the curriculum there, and many of the practitioners with specialized communities draw from her books and exercises. Her work, like that of long-term RSC voice coaches Rodenburg and Berry, extensively highlights the importance of breathing and other modes of physicalization both through acting preparation and in the delivery of Shakespeare's lines in ways that resonate significantly with the communities included in this volume. Packer and Bella Merlin regularly refer to Linklater's ongoing influence on the popular and respected 'month-long intensive' at Shakespeare & Co. that reaches innumerable practitioners working with Shakespeare in many environments relevant to this discussion. They suggest that a key aspect of the intensive 'is to own Shakespeare's language to the extent that you barely know where *you* stop and the character begins'.[38] Packer and Merlin offer detailed information about the content of the intensive, including the 'ground rules', the first being,

> *This is embodied training* (as athletic as sport). You're invited to take Shakespeare's narratives into your body and not just your head, to understand why physically, politically, psychologically, dramaturgically he has written a particular moment.[39]

Whether or not everyone would agree, these practitioners find resonance in Shakespeare that other texts do not replicate and believe that actors take full advantage of this when they

> listen more and more intently and open [themselves] to the psychic charge that the language transmits…Innate in the process are two important points of attention . . . First your *breathing* is constantly noted (the *Training* always begins with breath).[40]

Breathing is clearly key here. Undertaking the exercises imbedded in the intensive then leads the participating actors into Shakespeare, through Linklater's work, in conjunction with text work developed by Packer and famed Shakespearean director John Barton that asserts,

> As your voice becomes physically freer, your *imagination* opens up. And your opened imagination builds your capacity for Shakespeare's powerful thoughts – as well as your ability to express his big *emotions*. Your new ability to express big thoughts and powerful emotions demands more *breath* of you, so your lung capacity increases. And then, in a kind of metaphorical infinity sign, your increased capacity for breath expands your receptivity to Shakespeare's language! So now, you don't just take a breath because you're supposed to speak your lines: you allow a breath into your body and – *because of that breath* – a new insight suddenly dawns on you.[41]

Because so many practitioners included in this study have participated in trainings at Shakespeare & Co. and/or learned from their facilitators at other venues, these approaches have had widespread influence in these environments.

Berry's publications provide detailed instructions for her equally prominent vocal work, with both illustrations and directions indicating how to proceed through the exercises. Although neither Berry or Linklater are still with us, their books and students continue their influence. Like the other voice specialists, Berry comments on the ways that people's voices reflect their circumstances.

> The voice is incredibly sensitive to any feelings of unease. In everyday life, if you are slightly nervous or not on top of the situation, this condition reacts on the voice. The basic feeling of fear puts all the defence mechanisms into action, and the result is tension, particularly in the upper part of the body, the neck and shoulders.[42]

While these kinds of insights eventually become commonplace for those deeply engaged in actor training, the people involved with Shakespeare in specialized communities frequently begin this work without the understanding of breath and self-awareness that grows through practice. For those lacking prior education in breath and voicework, these texts can be especially revelatory about the ways that mind, body and voice intersect and influence each other. As Berry remarks,

> What you are doing is reaching down to your center for the sound. The breath goes in and the sound comes out – you are touching down to your centre, you are finding the 'I' of your voice. When you find this it is as though you belong, you are present in what you are saying. You will then find the breath touching off a sound like a drum. You will find that you will not have to use a great deal of breath, because the breath will be made into sound. It is economy of effort. When you find this absolutely right use of breath the voice will be effortless. It will impel itself. This is where your true energy is. This is what I mean by rooting the voice.[43]

Giles Block, another prominent Shakespearean voice trainer, has worked on voice techniques with actors at Shakespeare's Globe in London since Mark Rylance was artistic director. He does not interact with specialized communities to my knowledge, but *Speaking the Speech: An Actor's Guide to Shakespeare* helps illuminate the ways that this dramatist's work facilitates effects sought by voice coaches and many facilitators of Shakespeare with specialized communities.[44] Block asserts that the aim of this book is to answer two simple questions – 'Why does Shakespeare write in the way he does, and secondly, how can actors get the most out of these incomparable plays?'[45] He then offers one answer to the 'Why Shakespeare' question: 'If you were to ask me "What makes Shakespeare so great?", high on my list would be his extraordinary ability to bring his characters to life by a simple turn of phrase, by a breath they take, by a pause they mark.'[46]

Block writes at length about the power of Shakespearean rhyme structures, with a particular emphasis upon the meaning conveyed through the stresses in the lines.[47] Like the other voice coaches, he puts a lot of emphasis upon the importance of breath training and explains why the length of breath associated with speech in Shakespeare makes such a significant difference in the emotional meaning conveyed by the lines. Drawing from a speech of Isabella's in *Measure for Measure*, act 2, scene 4, for example, he notes the importance of the length of her exclamation 'or with an outstretch'd throat I'll tell the world aloud'.

> The middle line is long. It has twelve syllables in it and you can feel the effort behind Isabella's utterance of it. If you took out the word 'aloud' at the end of the line, it would be a line of normal length, but Isabella doesn't only want to let the whole world know of Angelo's depravity, she wants to shout it from the rooftops. And so the line seems to call for an 'outstretch'd throat' in order to say it all, and it needs a deeper than normal breath in order to achieve this.[48]

He follows this observation with an important point, based on the aspects of Shakespeare's writing that facilitate these effects.

> So Shakespeare's verse is based on two things: a line length that corresponds with our breathing, and an underlying rhythm that corresponds with our heartbeat. So although the idea of a play in verse might at first have seemed somewhat intimidating, it is simply a mimicking of those two vital forces that are keeping us alive – our pulse and our breath.[49]

Block offers innumerable additional examples of the intersection between breathing patterns and the emotion emanating from the way this influences lines spoken by both central and more peripheral Shakespearean characters.[50] Noting that we typically don't notice breathing patterns in speech or on stage because we are focusing on meaning, he draws attention to a speech by Lucilius in *Julius Caesar*, 'The gods defend him from so great a shame' and examines how the line is enriched by considering its association with breathing,

> We can all say that easily on one breath, and once any one of us had said it we would all do the same thing: we would all take another breath in order to go on speaking some more. If, however, you tried to do the next *two* lines on one breath,
>
>> When you do find him, or alive, or dead,
>> He will be found like Brutus, like himself.
>
> – well, it would be possible, but you would probably feel that you were getting a little short of breath by the end of the second line in a way that doesn't really happen to you in everyday life. But more importantly, it would have sounded as if you were a little less emotionally involved. The lines and the thoughts within them would have sounded less caring.[51]

Block's further analysis indicates the kind of insights available to those who learn the intricacies of breath and line delivery. Suggesting that a speaker 'top up' their breath before the line, 'He will be found', Block emphasizes the crucial role such a breath can play, even if the audience is unaware of it,

> Now this breath is in no way special. It's not something you do because you're on stage and no one, not the audience or your fellow actors, should even notice what you've done. In the end you shouldn't even be aware of it yourself. But you do it so that, when you come to say that second line, the words in it sound as if you are creating them, choosing them, *as* you are speaking. These words are expressing Lucilius's love for Brutus, and to convey that love we need to give colour and emotional strength to his key words. And this needs the right amount of breath. But we need no more breath than that which is natural to the situation. We breathe in order to speak, and we breathe again in order to go on speaking, and Shakespeare's lines tell us where to do that.[52]

While only some of the specialized communities examined in this volume raise professional-level expectations for those involved in their initiatives, these examples from Block and from the other vocal coaches demonstrate the kinds of lessons all participants can gain from modules addressed to breathing and speech in Shakespeare. Such undertakings bring participants' attention to the power of their own breath from multiple perspectives, while also providing important opportunities to recognize the way that breath is often linked to physical, psychological, emotional, intellectual and spiritual aspects of human life. In Rodenburg's terms, the Shakespearean actor needs to attend to the following aspects of physiology and the text:

> Oxygen and breath power the voice, feed the brain and fuel the heart. You are about to embark on some of the most passionately felt plays ever written, full of long and often complex thoughts. You will need oxygen to explore them. Your voice will need breath to be free, to have full range and to be propelled forward on the wave of the iambic, the line, the thought, the scene. You will need breath to explore the many specific emotions in a part, the reflections in a character's soul, the transformations they undergo. You will need to alter the rhythm of your breath. Every human being breathes differently and Shakespeare writes each character with a different rhythm of breath that changes as they change.[53]

For many of those engaged in Shakespeare through various specialized communities, these perspectives also help them recognize aspects of their own and others' humanity that they may not have understood previously.

As Rodenburg observes, all humans breathe differently and those involved in Shakespeare with specialized communities differ similarly. Sammie Byron, a founding member of Shakespeare Behind Bars (SBB), has continued his Shakespearean endeavours with Tofteland and others since then.[54] He credits significant changes in his life to his SBB breathwork. Since he left prison, he has remarried the same woman he divorced prior to his lengthy incarceration. Both Byron and his wife Barbara report that his voice has changed substantially since their first marriage, a transformation that he attributes to SBB. Before SBB, he spoke softly and was afraid to raise his voice, due to the dire consequences of yelling. Recalling his abusive childhood, he remarks upon being a 'broken child', who wanted to be heard, but was afraid to speak out. In addition to his acting involvement, Byron is a champion powerlifter, so he is deeply engaged with both artistic and athletic activities requiring considerable attention to breath.

Joining SBB introduced him to life as an actor, where it is important to be heard and to connect with the other performers and the audience. He participated in the array of theatre games shown in the SBB documentary,[55] and while these activities are playful, they helped him learn how to speak from the gut and open up his vocal canal.[56] After a lifetime of living in his head, he learned to take in more oxygen and to project. In his early days in SBB, he often injured his throat when he would shout, but he now knows how to breath appropriately enough to avoid the throat trauma he once suffered during rehearsal or other SBB sessions. By stepping outside of his vocal comfort zone, Byron grew in confidence and now projects strongly whether on stage, in a classroom, or in a social situation. He attributes these changes in part to SBB's 'Circles of Truth',[57] because he finds that a consistent commitment to the truth leads to a more powerful vernacular and a deeper resonance that he previously experienced. As the Shakespearean voice coaches maintain, Byron believes that Shakespearean language requires him to enunciate and hear everything, and that if the iambic rhythms are off, the emotional content of the speeches are also off. He insists that focusing on telling the truth leads to a more open and authentic presentation, something that he finds serves him well on stage and in life.[58]

The specific directions conveyed in Berry's writing (and others) provides insight into how the physical attention to breath described by Byron can lead to the transformation he relates. While *Voice and the Actor* gives the misleading appearance of being a slight volume, Berry devotes considerable attention towards the goal of being as explicit on the page as one can be in an in-person setting. Here, for example, she offers a breathing exercise using detailed information about how to enact the actions required:

> Breath in slowly and easily, hold a moment, make sure the shoulders and neck are free, then breathe out slowly to ten counts (by that I mean counting in your head, not aloud). It is

vital to feel the muscles between the ribs controlling the outgoing air – this is the main point of the exercise. Breathing out should be quite noiseless as the throat should be open. If there is noise in the throat, however, it means you are controlling the breath there by a certain constriction, which means there is a concentration of energy there, and when you come to vocalize there will be tension. Always wait before you breathe in again so that you feel the muscles between the ribs needing to move.[59]

Tara McAllister-Viel cogently challenges the work of Berry, Linklater and Rodenburg, along with Linklater's conceptualization of the 'embodied voice', for their seeming disregard of the full range of bodily circumstances that exist. The current practices such as those presented by Berry, however, benefit many of those participating in the specialized communities featured here. Nevertheless, McAllister-Viel's call for a 'change in voice training expectations, practices and normative values' provides a thoughtful analysis of the ableism and narrow cultural perspectives that these now conventional approaches can inadvertently inculcate, especially since actors with 'differently abled bodies' may not fit into practices created for what McAllister-Viel labels as what is too commonly perceived as '*the* body'.[60] As McAllister-Viel notes, 'An actor's body/voice carry with them particular socio-cultural and historical contexts and in this way can be understood as embodiments and reenactments of cultural values and ideas of what voice can/should be and what voice can/should do.'[61] She indicates profitable directions this field can follow as it evolves and expands its understanding and implementation of inclusivity.[62] While McAllister-Viel's objections to these traditional breathwork practices do not reduce their value in multiple environments, the points raised in her work offer ways to amend them fruitfully for a more broadly inclusive perspective on voice training.

   The focus on breath correlates with other expansive practices found in the communities under consideration. Many of these voice teachers make emphatic cases that Shakespearean drama is the best route for the kinds of outcomes they seek. At the same time, they point to specific physiological activities that work in concert with Shakespeare's writing in order to facilitate numerous emotional and physical enhancements for those who engage in such endeavours. The power of breath joins with other mindfulness, movement and creative undertakings to enrich the experiences of many of those included herein. As one of the 'five [or more] best senses' recognized in *Timon of Athens* and referenced in the title of my introduction, breath – and voice – enable diverse (but not all) Shakespeareans to access diffuse aspects of their humanity, often to their benefit.[63]

2

Hearing the owl shriek

Shakespearean soundscapes

Sound provides enhanced access to Shakespearean drama, whether within the theatre or through noises cited in the text. The members of the communities discussed here, which include actors, students and audience members, lack the visual acuity required by many conventional theatrical performances and rely heavily upon sound during performances. Some are legally blind; others possess limited vision.[1] One of the groups was disbanded recently due to the controversial, abrupt sale of their building.[2] The other, Extant Theatre, is ongoing, despite the pandemic, producing Christopher Hunter's *States of Mind* (a modernized *Venus and Adonis*) during the 2021 Bloomsbury Festival.[3] *Theatre London* describes,

> Extant's cast of visually impaired actors take the words of the world's most visual dramatist and demonstrate how a vivid physical and emotional landscape can be created through the power of language. By delivering integrated audio description through the theatricality of a medical observation room, this feature of the production – though primarily for a visually impaired audience – is designed to include sighted members to enhance their own enjoyment of the piece.[4]

States of Mind (which was also streamed during the 2021 Bloomsbury Festival) has evolved from Hunter's one-person show into a piece with two actors on stage, plus an unseen 'clinical' narrator. It does not yet benefit as powerfully from Shakespeare's visually evocative text as performances drawn from his writings often do (or as the solo version Hunter performs himself does), but it demonstrates how Shakespeare's writing can be presented successfully by and for those without the kind of vision demanded by conventional dramatic presentations.[5] In this instance, the audio narration alerts audience members to what is happening on stage.[6] Since this text is integrated into the play, the audience does not face the aural conflict that often occurs when stage dialogue and audio description through headphones or other devices occur simultaneously. In addition, as Maria Oshodi, Extant's Artistic Director, notes, 'It is tiring to wear equipment to access what's on stage. It's better to be unencumbered.'[7] In Hunter's piece, the actors, set and actions performed, as well as the colours used and lighting design, are described at length. The narrator also serves as a character in the drama, offering interpretive comments about the individuals and interactions being presented. Gillian Dean, who appeared in *States of Mind*, states a clear preference for the way audio description was handled for the production, contrasting this process with what often appears, in an interview with disability and theatre blogger Shona Louise.

> I personally don't have a problem with audio description being something that you choose to watch [*sic*], but I do have a problem with it being tacked on in such a way that nobody on stage is leaving any space for it to happen, they're not even aware of what audio description is. I do think it has to be considered right from the beginning of the process so that everybody on stage and in the audience knows its happening and gives it the space and respect is deserves.[8]

Extant works continuously to ensure that their audio description practices work well for everyone in their audience. This Bloomsbury Festival performance at RADA Studio did not appear, however, to make any accommodations for patrons with other access needs.[9] Typically for London, toilet facilities are down a long, dark corridor and a flight of stairs. The audience, many of whom appeared to know each other, seemed to be in good spirits, despite the constraints often associated with buildings designed and constructed before such issues were addressed extensively or successfully. These kinds of physical and electronic access anomalies are unfortunately frequent in venues hosting purportedly accessible performances, something Shona Louise addresses in her October 2021 'open letter to the commercial theatre about accessibility and disability representation',[10] which was signed by a wide range of theatrical practitioners. Changes in this realm will be expensive, but in order to promote equal access, they need to be enacted.

States of Mind creator and director Hunter has enjoyed a lengthy career as an actor, director and drama teacher, including a period with the Royal Shakespeare Company. He has also worked regularly with Extant, which was established in 1997. According to the company website, 'Extant is the opposite of extinct', and describes itself as a 'group of professional visually impaired artists', working to 'redress our invisibility as artists and explore new creative spaces'.[11] Oshodi further indicates that Extant provides 'a safe place for learning', both for those, like Hunter, who succeeded professionally after what she terms 'mainstream training', but later experienced vision loss, as well as for those with vision impairments who 'fall by the wayside' after completing conventional training programmes.[12]

Hunter's initial 2017 production of *Venus and Adonis*, moreover, was developed after close consultation with Katherine Cox, a staff member at Survivors UK, a service for men and boys who have experienced sexual assault.[13] In 2021, Hunter adapted *Venus and Adonis* from a one-person presentation into a two-hander with Extant specifically in mind. *States of Mind* retains this earlier contextualization. Hunter's personal and professional dealings with vision impairment and his detailed research on the kind of intimate abuse resonating through *Venus and Adonis* reflects the care, sensitivity and desire to respond appropriately to specialized communities that many of the arts practitioners included in these chapters demonstrate.[14] In this instance, Hunter engaged an intimacy director for *States of Mind*, due to the content and interactions involved. Intimacy directors are fairly recent additions to acting environments, helping ensure that physical touch, emotionally charged dialogue and behaviors and issues of consent are being addressed effectively.[15] *States of Mind*, therefore, was created within a framework of respect for actors and audience members of diverse circumstances.

Hunter's approach to his adaptation of *Venus and Adonis* also draws from his long-term engagement with Shakespeare, which aligns closely with Extant's aural emphasis. Hunter maintains that Shakespeare's 'words explode in one's head and make you think', and thus, Shakespearean actors need to 'inhabit words', while modern playwrights prompt actors to 'inhabit characters.'[16] Throughout our lengthy conversation about *States of Mind* and its earlier Edinburgh Fringe Festival incarnation as *Venus and Adonis*, Hunter regularly illustrated his points by returning to this poem's resonant and linguistically rich phrase, 'melodious discord'.[17]

He also talked about Cicely Berry's deep influence upon his work emanating from vocal workshops at the Royal Shakespeare Company (RSC) where actors sat in a circle working through the text in small increments.[18] Recalling Berry's reminder that speeches are comparatively rare in daily life, except when given by politicians or during wedding receptions, Hunter also emphasized the importance of focusing on particularly powerful words, such as 'melodious discord', during rehearsal and performance to allow the actors learn to embody rather than recite Shakespeare's vocabulary. From Hunter's perspective, Shakespearean acting is a 'muscular activity'. He states that Shakespeare is 'vocally incredibly physical' in contrast to cinematic acting where movement, even in actors' faces, is reduced. Shakespearean language 'demands' embodiment and that this process can lead to physical pain for speakers without regular practice in this realm.[19]

Fellow vision-impaired actor and director Esther Ruth Elliott also speaks about the physicality of speaking for in-person aural-based performances, noting the contrast with radio where 'you have to make your breath invisible. If you can hear it [in radio], you're doing something wrong'.[20] To be effective in the environments described by Hunter and Elliott, however, the sounds of breath and other physical aspects of vocalization remain paramount.

As many will acknowledge, Shakespeare's language can also be painful for everyone when it is performed poorly. The *Times*' review of Hunter's *Venus and Adonis*, for instance, notes that 'Sitting through more than a thousand lines of poetry in the middle of the afternoon may be demanding'. However, it continues, 'Hunter's performance, the way he inhabits the work's shifting ambience and characters, more than repays the commitment.' Further remarking that 'the performance requires us to listen', the review points out that

Hunter 'takes palpable delight in the sensuous language, at times appearing literally to chew on the words'. For a performer such as Hunter, who loves Shakespeare's language intensely and whose own vision has diminished, creating this dramatic rendering of *Venus and Adonis* facilitates the presentation of Shakespeare's powerful language in an environment especially conducive to aurality.

When Shona Louise interviewed Gillean Dean and Robin Paley Yorke, the stars of *States of Mind*, they both expressed appreciation for the fact that their visual impairments were not included in the script.

> They both also shared with me how refreshing it was that the fact that they are visually impaired has no bearing on their characters. So often in this industry when we cast disabled performers we often cast them in roles that are disability specific, believing that if we cast a disabled performer then their characters story must completely revolve around their disability. Gillian told me: 'I think that's what is really refreshing because as a visually impaired actor I have it listed on all my profiles and it's always lovely when you get approached for a role where you're like, okay, where is the blindness? And they respond, "Oh, nowhere really!" That's always lovely.'[21]

While they experienced frustration regarding many aspects of typical conditions for disabled actors, they also enjoyed working with others facing vision issues.

> We finished off by discussing what it's like for them both to work alongside another visually impaired performer. 'It is lovely. I certainly feel it's really nice not to be the blindest person in the room, especially as Chris, the director and creator, is also visually impaired. So, there's 3 people in the room, and not one of has got the same access needs or level of useful sight', Gillian shared.[22]

The interview does not address the actors' response to working with Shakespeare, but Oshodi indicates that Extant performers have taken on projects of many kinds and that Shakespeare fits well within their remit.

Elliott also worked with the RSC but stepped away from her professional acting career when her sight limitations became increasingly intrusive.[23] In 2018, she undertook a research and development project with Extant entitled *The Man Who Saw Backwards*, which combines facets of *King Lear* with the experiences of modern Londoners receiving treatment at Moorfields Eye Hospital. She discusses this residency in Extant's podcast series in 2018,[24] in *Shakespeare Studies* (2019)[25] and in a private interview in 2021. In this dramatic piece, which has not yet been fully staged, she draws from the many references to sight and blindness included in *King Lear* and presents both sighted and blind characters as well as actors with diverse visual abilities.

She is alert to the many issues that arise in these environments. Her article highlights the logistical challenges encountered when working with students or actors with diverse visual needs and abilities, such as the difficulty many vision-impaired actors have with reading scripts and learning dialogue and the need for everyone to refrain from changing the physical spaces used for rehearsals or performance. Actor Karina Jones, who has participated in Extant's Pathways Training Programme,[26] similarly discusses the specialized requirements necessary for practitioners with visual impairments. In 2019, she became the first blind performer onstage with the RSC. She and now-retired artistic director Gregory Doran note the benefits and challenges associated with such casting decisions on BBC Sounds's show *In Touch*.[27] Jones's vision, for instance, often keeps her highly alert to light, which prompted several adjustments to the RSC stage and lighting design for *Measure for Measure* and *As You Like It*.

Since individual actors present a range of visual circumstances, however, such particularized alterations are unlikely to transfer directly to other productions. Consultation with those involved remains critical. Notably, Jones is a vocal coach as well as an actor, so she brings her aurally astute practice to the RSC and elsewhere in a variety of forms. Such involvement is key, as many practitioners have emphasized, including Dean, who mentions this issue in her interview with Shona Louise.

> Both of them [Dean and Paley York] talked about how often conversations about accessibility are being had by people who don't have the right knowledge to guide others. Gillian said, 'the more people representing all aspects of the industry, the better the access is going to be, because you've got people

talking about what they know, rather than assuming what is required'.[28]

Accordingly, one of the goals of Extant's Pathways programme is to train professionals to fill advisory positions dedicated to such issues, and Shona Louise's 'open letter' addresses the urgent need for similar changes across theatrical culture,

> Statistics on just how many disabled people work in the theatre industry are almost impossible to find. We are completely missing from conversations about diversity and inclusion. We must work harder to train and hire disabled people. The fact that accessibility has barely improved in the industry in recent years is partly down to the fact that we don't have a seat at the table. This means that it's down to audience members to pick up accessibility issues, when it's often too late to change anything. Increased visibility of disabled people will lead to more awareness, and more conversations that will give us the space we deserve.[29]

As these examples indicate, many of those addressing these issues serve both as practitioners and as activists intent upon changing the environment in the arts for performers and audience members with diverse needs and abilities.

The Man Who Sees Backwards included support workers in their incorporation of 'line-feeding' into the rehearsal process, a practice that the veterans' programme Feast of Crispian also includes in their Shakespearean work with veterans (more on the Feast of Crispian in Chapter 5). Other companies use similar techniques, as will be discussed here. This production also benefitted from the contributions of BBC foley artist Alison Craig, allowing Elliott to further her aural experimentation in the piece.[30] Elliott often incorporates music in her work and presented each actor in this piece in association with a particular musical instrument in order to help the audience recognize and differentiate between them. At the same time, however, she is sensitive to the resonance of silence and descries productions that rely too heavily on music instead of silence, since music can 'kill the story.' She observes, moreover, 'When you drop a sound into space you have to think about where you're going to place it and also whether that sound exists in the dark or whether it happens in the light. That also has a big effect. Silence is a sound.'[31]

This observation accords with other prominent performative interactions with 'silence', including the American-based (with roots from the Republic of Georgia) Synetic Theater's acclaimed 'wordless' Shakespeare series.[32] They were initially deemed incorrectly as 'silent', since they lack spoken dialogue; however, they include considerable sound and music. Susan Bennett discusses composer John Cage's iconic *4'33"* from a similar perspective, noting that the original 1952 audience 'demanded to know what was the intention behind Cage's silent piano'.[33] As Bennett describes, however, this piece is far from silent,

> Of course, while there was no audible rendition of music from [pianist David] Tudor on stage, the performance in its fullest sense was not silent. Sounds from the pianist's and the audience's movements and expression, as well as those from the contextual environment, filled the sonic gaps '4'33' appeared to create in the auditorium . . . His composition was designed to retrieve the usually inaudible as both the subject and object of the audience's experience.[34]

As these examples of both Shakespearean and non-Shakespearean productions indicate, the work of artists focusing on aurality instead of, or in addition to, visual aspects of Shakespearean production offer opportunities for audiences of diverse visual abilities to experience many facets of the drama with a heightened awareness of the breadth of sonic expression. Extant caters primarily to a cast and audience with visual limitations, although their performances generally welcome everyone.

Elliott also participated in Shakespearean activities with a group of older women living at London's Mary Feilding Guild. According to an article about this establishment,

> The Mary Feilding Guild was set up in 1857. Lady Mary Feilding became aware of the difficulties facing well-educated, unmarried women who were effectively abandoned by society when they retired from professions like nursing and teaching. Lady Mary acquired a block of 50 flats in Kensington to provide accommodation for them, enabling them to live with

care, companionship and dignity. The women paid their rent by producing and selling crafts.[35]

The group from this setting all had fascinating and accomplished life stories and many of them continued to remain involved in important activities as much as possible.[36] One retired professor, for example, got up early every morning in order to work on translations from Russian literature. Elliott worked with an eager group of Shakespeareans there until the property in Highgate was abruptly and controversially sold.[37] The women met weekly to read and perform Shakespeare – and apparently paid little heed to Elliott's background with the RSC. Since many of them had the declining vision often associated with advanced age, the aurality of the sessions was key. Elliott, therefore, emphasized the sounds associated with these texts, often bringing recordings from significant productions. Many of these arts-oriented women had seen the original stage versions of the performances Elliott shared with them. The closure of the Mary Feilding Guild was a blow to many, including Elliott and her Shakespearean performers.

As part of her work with actors and students who are visually impaired, Elliott explores Shakespearean 'soundscapes',[38] a topic that features prominently in the realms presented in this chapter. Investigating such soundscapes illuminates the avenues into Shakespeare followed by these specialized communities, but also demonstrates the ways that aural Shakespeare can deepen many actors', students' and audience members' understanding and appreciation of this dramatists' craft. Audio renditions of Shakespeare, which have been popular for many years, also include some of the features bringing attention to Shakespearean soundscapes.[39] Whether or not it is true, as some argue, that early modern audiences would go to 'hear' rather than to 'see' a play,[40] the sounds embedded within these texts and those added during production reveal important answers to the 'why Shakespeare?' question and how his works can be relevant, enjoyable and informative for these particular specialized communities.

'Sound Studies' is a burgeoning academic field,[41] with many implications for early modern scholars, arts practitioners, and students,[42] not just those with vision impairments. Corresponding to the voice training discussed earlier, these aural-based investigations emphasize how Shakespeare incorporates significant aspects of sound into his plays. Some of them also remain alert to the sounds that early modern audiences would have experienced in their daily lives. Accordingly, these perspectives bring our attention to the association of sonic events with many people's experiences of the world. Michael Bull, editor of the *Routledge Companion to Sound Studies*, rightly notes that the 'disciplinary coming together through the study of the sonic provides an enormous range and diversity of intellectual enquiry and subject matter'.[43] This abundance is clear in the work of the Shakespearean groups featured here, which draw from a multitude of sound-based performance elements.

The rise of sounds studies in conjunction with Shakespeare seems appropriate, given Jonathan Sterne's account of historical sound.

> Plato purged flautists and flute-makers from his ideal state; 17th-century Londoners complained of the new noises filling their city – 'he that loves noise must buy a pig' – and people in positions of power all over 19th-century Europe were so worked up about the different standards for orchestral tuning that many countries passed laws to resolve the problem.[44]

Sterne also points out that sound studies 'is a global phenomenon as well. Work that self-consciously defines itself as sound studies has now appeared in English, German, Dutch, French, Italian, Portuguese, Japanese, Korean, Hebrew and Spanish, among other languages'.[45] Shakespearean sound studies fit well within the parameters of this expanding global and historical field of enquiry.

Bennett provides a valuable overview to the state of the field. Much of her scholarly work has focused on Shakespeare, so it is no surprise that her volume draws heavily from examples in this canon. In her introduction, she remarks on one of the key aspects of theatrical history that underlies this chapter's emphasis on sound,

> Scholarship in theatre and performance studies for a very long time emphasized, sometimes almost exclusively, matters of visuality and embodiment, even as it was recognized that sound in its various forms is an intrinsic part of any performance experience.[46]

As Bennett and Bull indicate, the field of sound studies is extending its academic reach, making the significance of these aural Shakespeare interactions even more pertinent for audiences of all visual abilities. Bennett also remarks on the centrality of sound for performances in Shakespeare's time, 'Whether open air or indoors, the theatres of early modern London were also acoustically sophisticated spaces that the early modern playwrights and the newly formed theatre companies sought to exploit.'[47] Clearly, sound has been key to the performance of Shakespearean drama ever since it was first composed and put on stage.

A number of scholars and practitioners describe how Shakespearean soundscapes operate. Elliott, for example, notes that 'Poor Tom's line to Lear, for instance – "Let not the creaking of shoes, nor the rustling of silks, betray thy poor heart to women" (3.4.94–95) has a full soundscape in it.'[48] At the same time, she points out that 'such specific sound descriptions speak volumes for sight-impaired audiences. Focusing on these instances of highly descriptive text enables sight-impaired audiences to experience an expanded 'hearing journey'.[49] Not every reader or audience member will focus deliberately on the sounds imbedded in these lines or even consciously recognize their aural significance. Nevertheless, these moments illustrate Shakespeare's skill at creating evocative auditory images that communicate, subtly or overtly, a talent Hunter notes often. Referencing creaking shoes and rustling material conveys vivid images to audiences and performers, even when they do not live in a time when the 'rustling of silks' is a common sound.

For those either accustomed to listening rather than viewing or for those who are guided in this direction, attending to these moments in Shakespeare helps us better comprehend the world he fashions. As Wes Folkerth indicates, 'Listening closely to Shakespeare himself listening to the world around him, we gain a much better understanding of why his works continue to reverberate so strongly amongst us today.'[50] While people have long complained about the purported difficulty of Shakespeare's language, his soundscapes, like the one noted earlier, help alleviate the gaps some find between his environment and our own. Creaking shoes and rustling garments have not vanished over the intervening centuries.

Bruce R. Smith's important scholarship on sound in Shakespeare further links the voice work presented by the vocal practitioners earlier in this study and the experiences of many scholars, actors and students as they delve into the world of Shakespearean sound.[51] Smith begins his study on what he terms the 'O-factor' by encouraging his readers to experience the physicality of sound through 'feeling' the sound *oh*, 'Instead of *seeing* the sound, however, try to *feel* the sound. Put a thumb and a finger on each side of your larynx or Adam's apple and make the sound [O] again.'[52] Smith goes on to describe the physiology associated with the creation of sound, recalling the early authors, including Galen and Helkiah Crooke, who wrote about these processes.[53] Although he acknowledges that 'the fact that our only access to the oral cultures of early modern England comes via written texts points up the political differences that separate one speech community to another',[54] he insists that 'if it is Presence that this book is after, it is not the Presence of the Word, but of *sound*', and the goal is to encounter 'people whose voice-based cultures are available to us only if we come at them through indirection'.[55]

Shakespearean scholarship does not often encourage readers to engage physically with their bodies in the way that vocal coaches and others involved with the practice of theatre frequently do. This engagement with the physical, however, helps explain how Shakespeare performances designed for audiences and actors with limited or no vision encourage the benefits associated with embodied texts, while forging links between current experiences of spoken language and those emanating from the early modern period through Shakespeare's texts. Soundscapes can emanate from a wide range of texts, but as Elliott, Folkerth, Bennett, Hunter and Smith indicate, Shakespearean drama seems particularly well-suited for this kind of historical and physiological intercommunication.

Scholarship focused on the importance of sound in Shakespearean performance is raising a number of issues that are pertinent for this chapter. While only a few of these specialized communities appear to be moving deliberately in this direction at this point, for instance, Sonia Massai's insightful book, *Shakespeare's Accents*, outlines ways that closer attention to sound studies and aurality can widen other kinds of access in Shakespearean performance.[56] In her introduction, she details the important scope of her monograph and analyses how individual accents influence numerous aspects of Shakespearean performance, both now and in the past,

> accents are now increasingly being used, along with other crucial markers of social identity, like race and gender, in order to activate a different interpretation of the fictive worlds of the plays and to

challenge a traditional alignment of Shakespeare with cultural elitism. However, while a considerable amount of attention has been paid to the benefits and challenges of unconventional race and gender casting, there has been no sustained attempt to gauge the impact of marked voices on the production and reception of Shakespeare in performance. The topic is therefore ripe for further exploration.[57]

Massai's illuminating study demonstrates, once again, that the Shakespearean practices undertaken by these specialized communities offer the potential for wide-ranging benefits beyond the specific groups they aim to serve. While not everyone accesses Shakespeare through sound, innumerable performers, students and audience members do. As Massai indicates, accents have long played a central role in determining who appears on Shakespearean stages and who hears – or doesn't hear – familiar intonations when they congregate in diverse dramatic spaces. As she demonstrates, however, the ability for actors to use their regional accents onstage for professional Shakespearean drama has only emerged fairly recently. These accents have long been suppressed, in large part, due to widespread prejudices about perceived correlations between accent, social status and the high-culture status accorded to Shakespeare, as Massai explains,

> Even in the 1960s, when new voices were starting to emerge in the writing of post-war playwrights, most actors were still well-versed in what Carol Rutter calls 'verbal camouflage': Albert Finney, Tom Courtenay, Peter O'Toole, Anthony Hopkins and Alan Bates were effectively 'bi-lingual,' because they were trained not to use their regionally inflected accent on stage. When exceptionally used on the Shakespearean stage, regional accents caused outrage. Most memorably, Nicol Williamson, who was born in Scotland and raised in the Midlands, used his natural accent to play Hamlet in Tony Richardson's production at the Roundhouse in 1968.[58]

The wave of social changes that was putting many societal practices under scrutiny helped create a space for Williamson to present his accent without camouflage, but not everyone was prepared to approve of this decision.

> Reviewer John Simon found Williamson's accent objectionable and utterly inappropriate for the role. In his review, 'My Throat

is in the Midlands,' Simon first remarks on the acoustic quality of Williamson's voice: 'Williamson has a tendency to sound like an electric guitar . . . [and his] lips seem to part only for visual effect.' Simon then turns to Williamson's accent: It has been called Midlands, North Country, and Cockney with a loose overlay of culture. Only Henry Higgins could correctly place it South of the Beatles and North of the Stones and identify the veneer as grammar- or council-school. But even Colonel Pickering could tell that it isn't Hamlet.[59]

The insensitivity expressed here correlates with attitudes often expressed about actors outside conventional expectations. As these accounts suggest, therefore, multiple benefits emerge when additional attention is paid to aurality in performance. The work of companies such as Extant can help inform the broadening range of options being implemented in more traditional theatres. Linguistic diversity adds to the range of more widely inclusive practices being highlighted here. While Massai is not focused on specialized communities in her study, her rich analysis points to key aspects of an increased focus on the aural in Shakespeare.

Notably, the Covid-19 pandemic also helped expand the development of Shakespearean productions designed for hearing rather than seeing.[60] During this period, KNOCK AT THE GATE (KATG) productions produced *Julius Caesar* and *Macbeth*, the latter in conjunction with Theater Emory.[61] They are currently developing a new production called *The Tempest: A Surround Sound Odyssey*.[62] This company combines the talent sets of theatre and film practitioners in order to create high-quality audio Shakespearean productions.

> KNOCK AT THE GATE builds high-fidelity immersive audio experiences for adventurous listeners around the world. Born over a bonfire during the pandemic and fueled by the works of Shakespeare, this collaboration between theatre and filmmakers in isolation tests the boundaries of immersion and resonance through a series of feature length surround sound experiences designed for in-home listening on a pair of headphones in the dark.[63]

The productions are both consistently engaging, using high-quality audio techniques to craft engrossing presentations of classic drama.

Incorporating striking sound effects and strong verbal renditions of the dialogue, KATG's Shakespearean tragedies bring elements to the forefront that are often lost in traditional stagings.

It is not always easy, for example, for audiences to differentiate between the assassins in *Julius Caesar*, particularly when the roles are filled by men of similar ages and ethnicities. In KATG's version, it is difficult at the start to identify all of the characters, but as the play progresses, the actors' varying vocal styles successfully create distinctive characters. Both productions also take full advantage of the key storms and fights in these plays and *Macbeth* highlights the role of travelling by horseback in the text. These sounds are expected and would likely be included in any radio rendition of the dramas, but modern audio facilitates a richer soundscape than was available for earlier audio presentations.

Immersive theatre has become increasingly popular in recent years, at least prior to the pandemic when live theatre was possible. KATG demonstrates that Shakespeare can be conveyed successfully through sound alone to audiences with the necessary aural acuity. These performances do not now engage those who are d/Deaf, but as Sonya Freeman Loftis, among others, reminds us, even the best-designed 'universal design' projects cannot attend to all access needs simultaneously: 'universal design is desirable in theory, but an unattainable goal in reality: it is impossible to design an environment that will equally accommodate everyone's needs simultaneously.'[64] Just as a production emphasizing visual aspects of the plays may not provide optimal access to Shakespeare for those with vision impairments, Shakespeare that is primarily or exclusively vocal needs appropriate adjustments for d/Deaf audiences and KATG probably cannot currently accommodate their needs. They are, however, raising money intended to expand 'inclusion initiatives, and provide subsidized access for visually impaired listeners, students, veterans, low income and historically marginalized audiences'.[65]

Fittingly, Joe Discher and Sean Hudock crafted their idea for KATG next to a campfire during the pandemic summer of 2020.[66] They were not interested in creating a 'typical' Zoom production, nor were they intending to recreate a radio production.[67] As Hudock explains, these three-dimensional sound productions are best appreciated 'in the dark with a pair of headphones'. One inspiration came from Hudock's fascination with NASA's

Sonification Project, 'which allows audiences – including visually-impaired communities – to experience space through data.'[68] As the project website explains,

> NASA's distant telescopes in space collect inherently digital data, in the form of ones and zeroes, before converting them into images.
>
> The images are essentially visual representations of light and radiation of different wavelengths in space, that can't be seen by the human eye.
>
> The Chandra project has created a celestial concert of sorts by translating the same data into sound. Pitch and volume are used to denote the brightness and position of a celestial object or phenomenon.[69]

On their website, KATG describes *Julius Caesar* accordingly,

> The second full length immersive listening experience from Knock at the Gate, created in isolation and designed for a pair of headphones and lunar light. Inspired by the cosmic images and caveats in Shakespeare's *Julius Caesar* and the work of NASA's data sonification project. The project was streamed to listeners around the world May 25–29, timed to air with the 'Super Blood Moon' and the first full lunar eclipse since 2019.[70]

Working with a team of sound engineers, sound designers and editors, in addition to a number of actors participating through Zoom from multiple locations, the team began to create a soundscape that entices audiences to respond as though they were actually present within the action of the play. Discher and Hudock note that 'Shakespeare's language is imbued with imagery, storytelling and emotion', while Hudock remarks that as an actor in this context, 'I have to use my voice, I cannot use my body.'[71] One of the main obstacles faced by the actors, it seems, was accepting the directors' instructions to whisper when the conspirators were meeting. Given the kind of technology in use, an actual whisper was required, but many actors are far more familiar with the use of 'stage whispers'.

KATG largely avoids adaptations of Shakespeare, although they do not hesitate to cut lines or combine characters if that makes the storyline clearer.⁷² Still, they maintain that 99 percent of the lines they include come directly from Shakespeare's texts. They focus on storytelling with close attention to the sensory experiences present in the plays as their description of their process and audience reactions indicate.

> People have been saying I feel like I'm in the middle of this action. So then do that with a storm and a shipwreck [in *The Tempest*], and it makes it seem like you were hearing people who are drowning and are under the water, with the sound of thunder above the water in the sky. Yeah, there are also interesting questions about how to keep these things kind of natural or all the sounds feeling organic. In some ways it's like, what Shakespeare would have heard, or what would he have imagined in all these sounds sort of coming together.⁷³

While KATG aims for a wide audience, rather than restricting themselves to a specific specialized community, their work offers insight into the kinds of emergent modalities made possible by technology that should make these plays accessible to a broader range of people.

Like many of the practices undertaken by the specialized communities discussed throughout this volume, the attention paid to aural aspects of Shakespeare's texts offers significant benefits to a wider group of people than the initial goals these developments may target. While many contemporary soundscapes are not accessible to d/Deaf performers and audience members in the forms currently devised, such performances can bring attention to aural aspects of the plays that could potentially be emphasized for d/Deaf communities. The NASA Sonification Project demonstrates ways that new forms of communication for many people are being developed.

The role of sound in Shakespearean performance is a growing interest both for specialized and general audiences. The increasing attention being paid to sound suggests that both access and interpretation gains will grow. For performers and audiences with vision impairments, the importance of sound in Shakespearean performances is central. Shakespearean sound studies continually bring fresh insights into the importance of aural interpretation. Megan Lloyd and Elizabeth Brown, for example, in their intriguing

'Staging "Skimble-skamble Stuff"': *1 Henry IV* and the Welsh voice', raise important questions about the various directorial decisions made following Lady Percy's admonishment to Hotspur: 'Lie still, ye thief, and hear the lady sing in Welsh.'[74] The Welsh song is not included in the ensuing text, however, and Hotspur rudely responds that 'I had rather hear Lady, my brach, howl in Irish.'[75]

Lloyd and Brown's discussion about Shakespeare's possible reasons for not putting the text of the song in his script as well as the dramatic implications of directors choosing to include or omit a Welsh song in their productions draw renewed attention to significant interpretive ramifications of sonic Shakespearean decisions. Michael P. Jensen announces that he 'want[s] to advance the cause of audio in [Shakespearean] scholarship'. The productions highlighted in this chapter suggest that the time is ripe for Jensen's self-proclaimed 'manifesto' to be heard.[76] Hearing actors and viewers have much to gain from further attention to aural Shakespeare.

3

'Such Branches of Learning'

Shakespeare and learning differences[1]

The historic Normansfield Hospital and Theatre in South London situated itself at the intersection of neurodivergence and the arts with its Victorian arts facility within the hospital complex, which doubled as a site for religious activity.[2] Founded by John Langdon-Down (for whom Down Syndrome is named) in 1868,[3] the facility was designed for people with Down Syndrome, the chromosomal configuration trisomy-21, although in keeping with norms from the era, it was unfortunately described as housing and treating 'imbeciles, idiots, and the feeble'.[4]

While the significant problems often associated with similar kinds of residential facilities are becoming increasingly clear,[5] Normansfield's apparently caring treatment of the children and its commitment to theatre bears noting in this chapter.[6] Although the regular entertainments at this hospital location tended to emphasize Gilbert and Sullivan and farces rather than Shakespeare,[7] part of the Victorian decor includes a portrait of Shakespeare.[8] One of the prologues delivered at a concert there in 1887 contained words thought to have been written by a member of the orchestra, 'For soothing care that all misfortunes bring, We feel with Hamlet that 'the play's the thing'.[9] Andy Merriman, a historian who documented Normansfield's development, reports that residents and employees performed together often and that staff members with theatrical abilities in addition to their other skills were regularly recruited in order to use drama therapeutically,

> In order to use the drama and music as a form of treatment it was vital that the staff who were to be employed at Normansfield were not only skilled attendants, but also possessed theatrical talent . . . Attendants, recruited through employment agencies, thus had to have some performing talents and it was Mary Langdon Down who pursued suitable candidates to ensure that all the staff were appropriately qualified in this respect.[10]

Merriman further cites *Dr. Langdon Down and the Normansfield Theatre*, a 2004 thesis written by Francesca Byrne, that suggests these productions were respectful of everyone involved.

> The Langdon Downs fostered an inclusive environment where both patients, staff [sic] cooperated in their theatrical endeavours . . . The idea of voyeurism was still at work in asylums such as Bethelem during the nineteenth century, but at Normansfield the asylum inmates were no longer viewed as objects of curiosity and fear; they were both performers and audience mixing with the local community and all experiencing the same excitement provided for their amusement and education.[11]

Similar to many more recent theatrical programmes for specialized communities, Langdon-Down's events actively encouraged sensory education for the intellectual betterment of Normansfield tenants, 'They should be taught the qualities, form, and relation of objects by their sense of touch; to appreciate colour, size, shape, and relation by sight; to understand the varieties of sound when addressed to the ear.'[12] Merriman also notes fairly recent unsuccessful efforts to revive theatre at the venue.[13] Future plans for this historic site remain uncertain but it is in little danger of falling into disrepair. The theatre is Grade II listed and the property now holds offices of the Down Syndrome Association and occasionally hosts entertainments, including a performance of *Lucia di Lammermoor* that I attended in 2022.[14] The theatre is beautiful, with numerous original details intact. It was clearly designed and built with care; Normansfield's theatricals were taken extremely seriously, even though many of their philosophies were sadly representative of that era. While the provenance of Down's apparent belief that the population at his facility possessed theatrical talents and interests as part of their chromosomal make-up remains unclear and readily prompts skepticism,[15] there are a number of current programmes providing acting training or dramatic exercises to people with specialized learning profiles. Some of these aim towards expanding professional opportunities for their participants, some offer theatrical experiences for targeted communities, and others endeavour to serve both the professional and personal goals of those engaged in their activities.[16] These groups rarely explicitly link theatrical ability to the intellectual or emotional constitution of their populations, however. Notably, the late twentieth-century opportunities pursued for the Normansfield Theatre also reflect some of these disparate possibilities. According to Merriman,

> In 1987, an application was made to turn the theatre and other facilities into a National Arts Centre for Disabled People ... There was, however, opposition to this ambitious plan on a number of fronts. Arts bodies were not keen, some local residents were concerned about the creation of a 'ghetto' for the handicapped and many disabled people themselves understandably preferred to be integrated into mainstream arts schemes'.[17]

A few years earlier, there was a plan for the Strathcona Theatre Company to establish residence at Normansfield, though this endeavour stopped when Strathcona dissolved due to economic challenges. In Merriman's account, this company apparently 'employed a number of actors with disabilities . . . unlike other 'inclusive' theatre groups, Strathcona was never tokenistic and the disabled actors and actresses played a full part in productions'.[18] At the moment, the theatre hosts visiting companies that do not have any apparent connection to the location's initial intention.

Over the past several years, however, a number of theatre companies have been dedicated to expanding access for ensemble members of varying abilities, often partnering with some of the groups considered here. While not every initiative bringing theatrical endeavours to those with learning differences focuses on creating professional opportunities for their participants, some organizations, such as Ramps on the Moon UK, build partnerships between training schemes and theatre companies seeking to expand inclusivity.[19] Dark Horse Theatre in Huddersfield, Yorkshire, was thus able to place one of their members, Rebekah Hill, in the Leeds Playhouse Production of *Oliver Twist*. Covid-19 truncated the run of this impressive show, but it was made available throughout 2022 on National Theatre at Home (NT Home).[20] Apothetae Theatre in New York similarly casts performers across a range of abilities, demonstrating that this model of inclusivity is gaining traction internationally.[21]

Dark Horse Theatre has offered an artistic training programme for those with learning disabilities for many years.[22] The ensemble typically receives less immersion in Shakespeare than the other groups considered here, but they emphasize what they term 'the silent approach' in their rehearsal room activities. They find this broadens accessibility by increasing physicality, reducing extraneous distractions and limiting the need for words.[23] They include significant movement training, such as study of Laban techniques[24] and provide theoretical background through connected learning, images and kinetic experiences rather than lectures.[25] Music, for example, is used extensively in their training as a way to convey meaning. Vanessa Brooks, former artistic director of Dark Horse Theatre describes the silent approach as

> a way to remove the biggest barrier to equality in a rehearsal room-language. It's a technique based on Stanislavski precepts of action, objective, given circumstances and character. It's a dynamic way to direct general audiences to standard timescales with casts with all kinds of neurodivergencies. It's also a great way to work creatively with lots of different kinds of people. The silent approach is for everyone.[26]

Brooks has experimented with the silent approach in several venues, including a three-day exploration at London's Royal Academy of Dramatic Arts (RADA) in 2017. Several members of the Dark Horse Theatre ensemble participated there in scenes from Shakespeare, including excerpts from *A Midsummer Night's Dream*; *Henry VI, Part Two*; and *The Tempest*.[27] There is a short Vimeo clip presenting part of the RADA workshop available online.

The Dark Horse core group includes eight to ten members who remain with the company as long as they choose to. While not all of them enter the theatre professionally, Dark Horse sets a drama school standard for these participants, many of whom are represented by agents. The company also designs their shows so that the performers will not need assistance on the set.[28] In addition to their acting training and various youth programmes, Dark Horse advises police officers and nurses on how to provide assistance for vulnerable populations effectively and appropriately. During the pandemic, they moved many of their operations to Zoom, while the ensemble also turned their attention towards creating short films and other digital materials. At the time of this writing, Ramps on the Moon, a theatre company that focuses on inclusion for d/Deaf and disabled people, is partnering with Sheffield Theatres on a touring production of *Much Ado About Nothing*, but it is unclear whether any Dark Horse Theatre ensemble members are involved, although some of them auditioned.[29]

Blue Apple Theatre (Artists in Residence at the University of Winchester, UK)[30] also has a lengthy history of facilitating actor, dance and musical training for those with learning differences.[31] Statements on their website indicate their goals for these endeavours,

> Through producing high quality theatre, dance and film we aim to challenge prejudice and transform the lives of people with a learning disability . . .
>
> Blue Apple is committed to the development of integrated and progressive opportunities within the arts for people with learning disabilities to raise the ceiling of expectation and advocate for the development of a more inclusive and equal society. The increase in confidence gained through stage performances has helped Blue Apple participants to enhance their social, personal and artistic skills and achieve public recognition for their talents.[32]

The company performs regularly, has toured internationally and has also placed ensemble members in professional roles. Tommy Jessup, for instance, who has played a number of key Shakespearean parts for Blue Apple, received great acclaim for his performance as Terry Boyle in Jed Mercurio's popular police drama *Line of Duty*[33] and has been given numerous awards and accolades, including an honorary doctorate from the University of Winchester and full membership in BAFTA.[34] Blue Apple offers a wide programme of classes and performs classic texts, devised pieces and adaptations of familiar tales. Their 2022 production of *The Wizard of Oz*, for example, added a frame story with new material as well as segments drawn from L. Frank Baum's original text and from the iconic film. Before the pandemic, they presented *Winchester, the First 100,000 Years*, derived from the lengthy history of their home base in southern England. Over the years, they have offered Shakespeare regularly. In my numerous visits with the company, several of them have spoken at length about their fascination with Shakespearean plays and films. Blue Apple productions have included *Macbeth*, *The Tempest*, *Much Ado About Nothing*, *Hamlet* and *A Midsummer Night's Dream*. Like Dark Horse Theatre, Blue Apple sets professional standards for their core acting ensemble members, even though many of them have no vocational acting aspirations.

Unlike some groups, they do not involve their participants in set design, costuming and such, since most professional theatre companies have staff dedicated to such roles. Their artistic director oversees the choice of plays and similar details. The cast freely offers their opinions during the development and rehearsal of these productions and help create additions to original scripts, but the collective management model sought by many prison or veterans' ensembles is not a goal here. Artistic Director Richard Conlon is a warm, talented and energetic leader who ably shares his expertise and guides this ensemble towards offering performances that receive considerable attention. Blue Apple has also gathered a dedicated group of staff members and volunteers who assist with those needing specific support during rehearsals and performances.

The schedule of Blue Apple's 2022 *Macbeth* was severely altered due to the pandemic, but Conlon notes the timeliness of the ways they shifted the drama in response,

> 'Macbeth' has been told and retold since 1606, but we're confident that you'll not have seen a version like this. We like to take liberties and this year, as our winter show crashed into Easter, limiting our preparation time – we took more liberties than usual. This is the real Macbeth (albeit tightened up from the longer original) with all the hits but with an added surreal

or absurd flavour. The extra song and dream sequences here have been created by the cast with the volunteers who tirelessly help get our pieces on stage. They take us to new places which Shakespeare never thought of, but they bring us back to what is at the heart of the play – toxic ambition.[35]

Their production incorporates segments from Shakespeare's *Macbeth* intertwined with a modern narrative about an ambitious Shakespearean academic, Stratford Williams, who spends most of the play in the hospital after being hit by a bus while en route to a conference presentation. The script includes substantial text taken directly from 'the Scottish play', but it also includes puppetry, music and dream sequences where Williams appears to 'enter' the play and encounter the witches while in his own identity, who then try to tempt him towards malevolent action by a tarot card reading that places his academic rival in a position of triumph over him. The performance is less conventionally Shakespearean than many of their previous productions from this canon, but the Covid-19 pandemic influenced their re-imagining of the text.

The period since spring of 2020 has been a bumpy ride for all of us with many of our cast being more vulnerable than most. They have struggled on valiantly to keep doing what they do; taking their place in the community of national storytellers, sharing their take on the world and making us see through a new lens. Our 'Macbeth' has elements of the surreal and the absurd shot through it, but perhaps we have spent the last year or two learning that both the surreal and the absurd are closer than we used to think was possible? Thanks for joining us for this show – without you we would be like the sound of one hand clapping![36]

The Blue Apple Company offers a dizzying array of programmes for their participants, and this production of *Macbeth* demonstrates their continuing experimentation with both modern and more traditional perspectives in their work.[37] Their use of writing, music and broadly based creativity, along with their bountiful regimen of physical and vocal acting exercises and their staunch support in their community, has led to impressive experiences and credentials.

Blue Apple also recognizes that shared discussions are valuable for those engaged in such work. In November, 2022, therefore, they hosted a Be IN! (clusive) Festival under the theme of 'Surviving or Thriving?' in order to share and discuss the artistic achievements and practical difficulties associated with each company. Among those represented were Poland's Teatr-21; Divadlo Aldente from Brno, Czech Republic; Open Theatre, Birmingham, UK; Savvy Theatre, Croyden, UK; Magpie Dance, Bromley, UK; and Blue Apple. Teatr-21, Divadlo Aldente and Blue Apple are in the second year of a collaborative project, partially funded by the European Commission's Erasmus+ program, which has supported theatrical and research events in all three countries and enabled joint artistic and programmatic partnerships.[38] The 'Surviving or Thriving Symposium' that concluded the festival provided an opportunity to view some of these companies' artistry, and to hear their shared concerns and aspirations. Among the sentiments expressed was the hope that 'inclusivity' will no longer need to be a necessary word, that these groups can remain the most 'civil' of civil rights groups and the most 'social' of social justice endeavours that artistic performances can shift towards being 'actor-specific' rather than focusing on 'abilities' versus 'disabilities' and that the participants in these ventures could be paid without threatening any funding they receive as citizens with learning differences. Not all of these groups present Shakespeare as part of their repertoire, but they are all committed to furthering dialogue among everyone involved.[39]

Savvy Theatre, which was discussed in the introduction, has formed several ensembles at their home in South London. Participants sharing circumstances similar to many of the other initiatives perform Shakespeare as part of their extensive repertoire. They shorten the plays and emphasize music, movement and creative interpretation. They also match the productions to the needs and interests of their various constituencies. In a performance of *Macbeth* cast with youth offenders, for instance, they included guns and knives into the drama and brought in a fight director to train the actors in stage combat. Given their legal status, it would be a crime for these performers to take the weapons outside the rehearsal space. Since they were committed to doing the show, they all took this responsibility carefully and treated the rules and their fellow ensemble members with respect. Some Savvy groups need extensive social time built into their rehearsal schedules, while others thrive with an expanded role in crafting the drama. Numerous participants require a range of physical and/or emotional support. Many of these actors, for example, have lengthy histories of trauma. Like many of the other practitioners included in this volume, Savvy founder Sheree Vickers has studied with Shakespeare & Co and incorporates many techniques featured there, including a strong emphasis upon Kristin Linklater's approach to breath work. Vickers also trained with Linklater during drama school. Close attention to breathing is a key element within Savvy's practice, particularly since many of their actors use little or no vocal speech. Those actors who do speak, moreover, often do not live in environments conducive to learning lines, so the work done in the studio, including breath work, is particularly critical.

The facilitators also emphasize the rhythm of the texts, which frequently helps their participants in diverse ways. The woman playing Hermia, for instance, in one of their productions of *A Midsummer Night's Dream*, often became anxious and struggled to speak, but the iambic rhythms of the play enabled her to perform her role and present her lines comfortably. Music and movement strengthen these ensembles' ability to offer these plays well. Like the *Christmas Carol* described in the introduction, these different groups rehearse individually, then come together for the public performance. Thus, since Savvy provides three daytime groups for people with learning differences, *A Midsummer Night's Dream* was divided into a trio of casts, comprising the faeries, the court and the players who rehearsed independently.

Vickers and her talented team of facilitators believe strongly in co-creation with their participants and remain ready to adapt, change and cut the plays as needed.[40] Both Vickers and the Leicester-based Bamboozle Theatre's co-founder, Christopher Davies, draw heavily from the dramatic pedagogical practices of Dorothy Heathcote. As Brian Edmiston and Iona Towler-Evans remark, 'Heathcote's humanizing pedagogy is rooted in a commitment to equity, diversity, inclusion, and social justice.'[41] Not surprisingly, her influence is strong in these companies' practices.

Bamboozle Theatre also designs programmes and offers classes and tutorials for those displaying a range of educational needs. It does not structure its activities towards professional opportunities for its youthful participants, but presents itself as 'creating possibilities for disabled children'.[42] Bamboozle performs regularly, works with a number of schools in England and abroad and circulates two weekly e-newsletters for subscribers: 'multisensory bites' and 'behavioural bites' which offer suggestions from Bamboozle's toolkit for home and school use. Co-Founder and Artistic Director Christopher Davies has published two books drawn from the ensemble's artistic practices.[43] The company offers both devised and classic dramatic exercises and performances, including a version of *The Tempest* (*Storm*) that has been presented in numerous venues, as distant as Sweden and China.[44] This production is crafted specifically for students identified as autistic, although many of Bamboozle's offerings can be adapted for varied audiences. Bamboozle indicates that their work demonstrates 'How exploratory play builds trust, reduces anxiety and provides child-centred opportunities for expression and learning.' They also discuss

- how child-initiated engagement and interaction can be developed – key behavioural and linguistic strategies;
- adapting free exploration into more structured learning.[45]

In addition, the company provides innumerable practical suggestions for creating and using multisensory environments as they

- show ways to use cheap [or free] materials/props/objects to create stimulating environments with learning potential;
- demonstrate how to build an environment in minutes that can be used in a variety of ways – drama, problem solving, playing, storytelling;
- show how to create environments where exciting discoveries can be made;
- explain ways of structuring the space to accommodate a range of abilities;
- give lots of simple ideas to take into school/home/specialist settings to use immediately;
- look at ways to use the Multi-sensory Environments when they are in place;
- reach the end of the day inspired to make use of simple materials with your children and young people.[46]

Having had considerable success with their practices, Bamboozle offers adjustable suggestions for presenting material through a range of 'different sensory channels' such as 'Visual, auditory, kinaesthetic and olifactory/gustatory' that may engage disparate audiences.[47]

While Davies acknowledges that taste and smell are less prominent in their presentations than desirable, the inclusion of broad multisensory opportunities for their young audiences is paramount.[48] This model of engagement was highly visible in the production of *Rain Rain* I attended in 2022. Children were actively engaged with instruments, props, sets and a variety of implements throughout the performance, which offered diverse, attractive possibilities for involvement that children could choose or ignore.

The children were regularly addressed by name and sat or interacted as they pleased, in an environment clearly designed for flexibility.[49] Davies emphasizes that the ensemble draws both from scientifically based research and intuitive practices. Their dance practitioner, for example, works through intuitive movement with their non-verbal participants, while the company also collaborates regularly with academic institutions and hopes to receive funding to have a PhD student on site with them.

On their website, Bamboozle provides a *Storm* 'companion pack for teachers & support staff' as well as a 'visual story' that describes the performers, the story and what audience members can expect. In the companion pack, they detail 'the Bamboozle Approach' that is used in the production,

> *Storm*, as with all Bamboozle productions, has been designed to put the audience at ease from the moment they enter the performance space. The team of highly skilled performers will guide the students and staff through the production and ensure that they feel safe and comfortable. There is no right or wrong way to experience the show and, at various points during the piece, the performers will invite the audience to explore and interact. The performers will be sensitive to the students' reactions and will build on what they see; they are not looking for any particular response or specific result.[50]

Bamboozle resembles many of the other programmes included in this study through its emphasis upon 'invitation' rather than 'requests' for those involved with their performances. Those in the audience are presented with opportunities to interact with actors, props and so on but no one is physically or verbally directed in a particular manner. The team designs their interactions for the children in their audiences with the clear goals of creating multisensory environments. When they are planning productions, for instance, they discuss whether the story can be communicated through a disparate set of sensory avenues so that children can experience the drama without being dependent on specific or limited modes of communication. Davies insists, moreover, that the most important aspect of the 'Bamboozle Approach' is giving children time and space.[51]

In *Storm*, the company explains that they are drawing some characters and situations from *The Tempest*, but that they are not attempting to present the play in its entirety. 'Instead, elements of the story have been selected for their contribution to a simple narrative and for their theatrical potential . . . [and] allows us to take advantage of the highly theatrical potential of the storm and magic.'[52] In a subsequent description of their creative process, they indicate various ways this technique operates with their production of *Macbeth*, 'You could create the blasted heath from the beginning of *Macbeth* with witches who want to mix a spell in their cauldron – the students could venture out to find or create the different ingredients and then bring them back to the cauldron and cast the spell.'[53] They also note, however, that 'we once spent a week exploring *Macbeth* with a group of students who gave it a happy ending where everyone said sorry and made friends'.[54]

Bamboozle's Shakespeare productions are pared down considerably, although they acknowledge that 'most of the words you hear spoken in *Storm* are lifted directly from the script of *The Tempest*'. They suggest, however, that 'it is possible to strip the text down to its essential elements or create atmosphere and mood with the original language'. In *Storm*, Prospero and Ariel shout out many of the lines assigned to the sailors in the opening of *The Tempest*, but that the words' 'meaning is less important than the mood of fear and confusion that they communicate'.[55]

The Hunter Heartbeat Method (HHM), which works with a similar population, by offering 'drama games for children with autism', seems to be the most divisive, at least in certain academic realms, among the programmes discussed in this chapter.[56] HHM, presented by Flute Theatre Company, was developed by British actor and director Kelly Hunter, who was inducted into the Order of the British Empire in part for this work.[57] In its 2022 rendition of *Pericles*, the actors enact snippets from the play, then engage the participants in movement and musical exercises, adjusted individually for each person's circumstances by the actor who accompanies every participant on stage. The sensory aspects of these games, and those in HHM's prior productions of *The Tempest* and *A Midsummer Night's Dream*, are prominent. The company performs in person and on Zoom for autistic children and their caregivers in many different countries. Individual performances vary significantly, whether face-to-face or electronically, because the participating actors remain closely alert to the responses of children in the performative circle. Children engage with the activities much as they please, so long as they do not harm themselves or others and they always have at least one Flute ensemble member directly 'playing' with them individually.[58]

Hunter is not a scientist, but HHM began as a joint endeavour of the Royal Shakespeare Company (RSC) and The Nisonger Center for Excellence in Developmental Disabilities at the Ohio State University (OSU).[59] Flute is presently working with scientists at Goldsmiths University and University of London 'to understand how new technologies – like wearable sensors – might be used to uncover, and help us understand, social behaviours in autism'.[60] When HHM shares Shakespearean drama games with autistic children, they are billed as theatrical endeavours, not as therapy, although some of Hunter's early HHM writings seem to blur this distinction. In 2014's *Shakespeare's Heartbeat*, for instance, a work that appears to have led to much of the controversy about HHM, she suggests that HHM addresses 'the processes that those on the spectrum find so difficult to achieve'.[61] Thus, she remarks, 'The games of *A Midsummer Night's Dream* . . . were the first games I made, using Shakespeare's poetic exploration of eyes and love to combat the children's autism.'[62] A recent essay, however, which includes a 'conversation' between Hunter and Robert Shaughnessy, steps back from therapeutic claims for HMM.

> In brief, HHM works with the 'pulse' of Shakespeare's iambic pentameter to create a rhythmic, sensory and immersive performance, co-created by actors and autistic participants, focusing on key moments in the plays played and replayed as interactive games. The purpose of the work is primarily artistic rather than pedagogic, therapeutic or remedial: performances

are not designed to alleviate or overcome autistic symptoms and behaviour (classically, challenges in communication, personal interaction and repetitive and stereotyped behaviours) but to create a space within to play and to dream.⁶³

This dialogue also addresses some of the issues with scientific perspectives on autism, which Hunter here distances herself from:

> Robert: one of the challenges is the idea that you're doing something to fix the autism or to provide therapy or even cure. This, in particular, is problematic from the point of view of autistic persons, if it implies imposing a neurotypical world.
> Kelly: Those problems I recognize because of the American [US] scientist, which I went along with at the time and then felt increasingly uncomfortably about and I don't like at all. The thing I've created, crucially, is not trying to change anybody, not the actors nor the people who come to play with us. Certainly it's true that some people on the spectrum struggle with anxiety and struggle with the ability to share their feelings and thoughts with another person. It's nothing to do with changing a person, it's to do with using Shakespeare to know ourselves.⁶⁴

Much of the language provoking criticism comes from *Shakespeare's Heartbeat*, and it is too early to tell whether this essay will alleviate any of the negative responses aimed at these activities.⁶⁵

The initial collaboration with OSU allowed for HHM to undergo clinical testing. It has since been cited in academic journals and has been the subject of a dissertation, markers that typically indicate efforts to establish interdisciplinary credibility.⁶⁶ The work has been presented at several theatrical venues by Flute Theatre, including the Bridge, Riverside and Orange Tree Theatres in London, at several theatres in the United States and Europe and in many countries (using the languages from those areas) over Zoom. Michael Dobson, Director of the University of Birmingham's Shakespeare Institute in Stratford-upon-Avon, is a trustee of Flute Theatre. I have attended Flute performances at several venues in England and elsewhere and I have participated in Flute HHM workshops in Indiana, Georgia, Ohio and through Zoom.

It remains unclear whether those objecting to HMM have attended any performances, but there is little indication that they have. Robert Shaughnessy from the University of Surrey, however, who co-authored the conversation with Hunter, has been to many Flute rehearsals and productions and published a positive essay about HMM in 2019's *Shakespeare Studies* that praises the use of music among other aspects of the productions, while identifying 'Shakespeare's world' as 'a third space' co-inhabited by the neurodiverse and the neurotypical, owned by neither. It is a space in which to meet, a space to play, and most of all, a space to dream.'[67] Shaughnessy is a theatrical scholar in the UK; his wife Nicola Shaughnessy, who is also a scholar, has led at least two AHRC-funded studies about the uses of theatre with autistic youth,[68] and their autistic son Gabriel has participated with HHM for many years.[69] At the *Pericles* event I attended in October 2022, all of the young people involved, including Gabriel, were experienced participants in these activities, and they were familiar with the games and the actors.

Nevertheless, while HHM has received positive attention in many venues, it concurrently attracts opposition in print and elsewhere. Sonya Freeman Loftis in *Shakespeare Survey* objects to HHM's apparent conformity with the 'medical model' of autism, which 'prioritizes treatment for autism over the need for social acceptance of autistic people'.[70] Loftis further cautions that 'the programme often employs rhetoric that casts the autistic subject as an incomplete human being waiting to be "awakened" (read civilized, humanized) by Shakespeare. Bringing Shakespeare to autistic children is a charitable impulse, but it also bears the impulse of the cultural colonizer'.[71] Loftis also acknowledges that 'there are multiple strengths to HHM's approach,' however.[72] She notes, for example, that HMM practitioners

> are enjoined to act with compassion and empathy . . . HHM teaches neurotypical educators to assume the competence of autistic children . . . Hunter's method encourages a respectful understanding of autistic sensory sensitivities . . . [and] there is some possibility for autistic collaboration in the construction of the games themselves.[73]

Because HHM was developed by an arts practitioner consulting with medical personnel, scientists, autistic youth and family members of young participants, not by a person identifying as autistic or a disabilities studies scholar, Loftis's arguments warrant careful consideration. HHM could benefit from conversations with those holding such views and relevant expertise. Some academics, however, currently seem to be using Loftis' essay to keep HHM from being discussed in professional environments.[74] Hunter was going to give a plenary address at the 2021 British Shakespeare Association (BSA) meeting, for example, but some of the BSA members objected, stating that harm would result from Hunter's inclusion.[75] A proposal that Hunter be included in a BSA panel discussion about HHM and related topics instead of giving a plenary address was rejected. As a result, Hunter did not appear on the BSA conference agenda and the sponsoring University withdrew as conference host due to institutional policies against 'de-platforming' speakers.[76]

Hunter offered a solo presentation for a Shakespeare Beyond Borders virtual panel at the Shakespeare Institute the following month,[77] but it appears as though an academic dialogue about this work remains unwelcome by those objecting to HHM.[78] I have attended numerous performances and workshops associated with HHM, but I acknowledge that it remains controversial and hope that open and respectful academic discussions of these activities becomes possible.[79] I am not a particular advocate for HHM, which, not surprisingly, has both strengths and weaknesses, but I believe wholeheartedly in the inclusion of challenging subjects within scholarly conversations and in the particular importance of respectful dialogue during our current period of widespread divisiveness.

Flute's international reach helps introduce another Shakespearean initiative involving people with learning differences, although this programme claims a place in the realm of opera rather than drama. In 2018, The World Shakespeare Project was invited by the International Opera Theater (IOT) to co-produce a newly-commissioned Italian opera based on *A Midsummer Night's Dream*: '*Sogno di Una Notte di Mezza Estate*'. IOT Founder and Artistic Director Karen Saillant describes the context for this production, which was part of a lengthy on-going series presented in Umbria,

> For the past 15 years our company, International Opera Theater of Philadelphia, has been crafting world premiere Italian operas

in Città della Pieve, a gorgeous small town high in the hills of Umbria, Italy. What started as a project to help me heal from the violent & unexpected loss of my husband through the creation of new operas based on Shakespeare, in Italy, in the Italian language, has morphed into an intercultural peace project with each opera singer and each instrumentalist coming from a different culture (75+ cultures) and each opera, when not based on Shakespeare (and so far there have been 9 operas dedicated to The Bard) sharing a social justice theme.[80]

This beautiful setting includes a renovated theatre that serves as the location for these performances that fill the streets with the diverse, international company comprising each of the IOT operas presented there. The town also includes a teaching studio devoted to working with artists with disabilities.[81] The studio provides classes, exhibits their artists' work and supplies student-decorated dinnerware for use at a restaurant in Rome. Saillant quickly found philosophical and artistic affinities with the studio. She describes her excitement about partnering with the teachers and students there,

> In the center of our Umbrian town, other abled young people happened to have been developing their artistic skills under the direction of the brilliant and innovative visionaries: Luca Sberna (sculptor) and Susana Panek (musician) in their center: Associazione Laboratorio Terrarte. The addition of the other abled culture, with their unparalleled fantasy, supported by Susana and Luca's determination to allow the artist to lead, rather than 'teaching' them, has infused our work with unimaginable and profound depth and healing potential for both artist, performer, audience and director, while giving to these young artists a new found self-esteem and release from the limitations that society, and perhaps even they themselves, might have otherwise deemed their ultimate possibilities.[82]

The artists' collaboration on this opera was lengthy and detailed, with Terrarte members ultimately designing all the costumes for this production. On opening night, I sat with them in the front row of the theatre, enjoying the crackling atmosphere of excitement. Prior to that evening, however, they had a detailed introduction to the characters and the plays and created numerous artistic models for what eventually became the costumes, which were built in Philadelphia to the artists' specifications. Saillant recalls how this process unfolded,

> In 2015 we became initiated into the Terrarte Family. Our Chinese costume & set designer, Qiang Gong, was invited to Terrarte to work with the artists there. Using discarded newspaper and other found objects, she began exploring hat and costume creations. The joyfulness and unbounding fantasy of the Terrarte creators was a thrill to experience and inspired us to ask the Terrarte artists to design all of the costumes for our next Italian premiere: *Sogno di Una Notte di Mezza Estate – A Midsummer Night's Dream*. *A Midsummer Night's Dream* was to become a healing and emancipating experience for each member of the Terrarte community, impact the artists in our production and expand and enhance the healing I experienced as a director.[83]

Saillant's typical modalities with her opera development and rehearsal practices fit well within the multisensory explorations of Shakespeare. She relies heavily on intuition, experimentation and process. She also incorporates the tactile and uncontrollable nature of awkward fabrics into the company's creative journey, often having her performers sing while interacting with large quantities of what she terms 'cheap nylon netting' that she brings with her on the airplane from the United States.[84] Her goal is to take advantage of the qualities she locates in netting.

> Net fabric: In present moment creates unpredictable obstacles that actors must deal with in front of audience, bringing them/audience into present. Free use of net fabric also allows for exploration of metaphor, rather than logic.[85]

She recycles everything, in part, so that all the artists have access to the experience of working with a wide range of physical materials. In practice, according to Saillant, this provides 'costumes, and sets from remainder fabrics, recycled water bottles, [and] repurposed materials/mundane objects turned into works of art under hands of artists'.[86]

In many ways, Saillant's artistic process, which includes an 'INTENSE NOT KNOWING PERIOD',[87] corresponds with the less conventional techniques chosen by some of the theorists and practitioners described throughout this volume. She works with several scientists, but also relies heavily on intuition and believes strongly in the power of unfettered imagination and a connection with nature. Her interest in working with artists with learning differences arose when she was invited to create a theatre piece at an Umbrian school for autistic students, most of whom did not use vocal communication.[88] The success of this undertaking helped guide her to the initial collaboration with Terrarte, which she intends to resume once the pandemic again allows in-person rehearsals and performances in Umbria.

She raved about Terrarte's involvement with *A Midsummer Night's Dream*, which corresponds with my experiences at their studio, in the theatre and in other locations around Città della Pieve. From her perspective, 'It was Fantasy which triumphed. Shakespeare's. All of Our Artists'. Our Audience's. In the line closest to the Bard was the imagination of our 4 young Terrarte artists: Camilla, Gian Paolo, Laura and Emanuele.'[89] She offers a lengthy account of some of the artists' involvement in the process,

> Camilla, for example, who lives daily in the world of the fairies, found herself truly at home. The story was hers. Her capacity for fairy costume invention was limitless. She had no previous experience with Shakespeare. For one year after the project, she was still designing fairies, but the designs had embellishing, little by little with flower flourishes and other aspects to make her designs larger than life and more fully formed with fantasy. The enthusiasm with which her work was met, both by the young sopranos who came from the US to portray her characters, as well as myself, and also visitors to the Laboratory confirmed her. That first night when she graciously entered the stage for her applause, found her beaming with pride. Camilla was confirmed. Camilla was liberated. Camilla would no longer allow instructions from well-meaning patrons of the Laboratory to influence her art making. She had a fantasy well within from which she could summon endless original works and she would no longer take 'instruction' from patrons of the laboratory.[90]

Over the course of several months, the artists engaged with the narrative, became increasingly familiar with the characters in the play, and began to create paintings, sculptures and other artistic renditions of the narrative that eventually led to their costume designs. As Saillant indicates, many of the artists quickly identified with particular characters,

> Jean Paulo immediately began to become the characters. He created an atmosphere with all of the characters of the opera and immediately began to be Puck and with his lead, everyone in the laboratory started to act out their characters – all in an operatic way. They would sing instructions to each other and respond heroically. Also, people who arrived in the laboratory participated in the world of Oberon. Laura was very interested in Bottom. She designed the animals. She was the first to design. All of the fairies and then the ass. From there she has continued to draw donkeys. They were so happy to be treated as artists. When you ask Camilla what work she does now she says artist.[91]

The costumes that resulted from this artistic experimentation were unusual and striking. The framed poster from this opera holds a prominent place on the wall in my living room where I view it often, with fond memories. Similar to the other programmes included in this chapter, the IOT's involvement of the Terrarte participants facilitated the creation of Shakespeare from newly-imagined perspectives. This kind of artistic inclusivity bodes well for our Shakespearean futures.

The programmes developed for those with learning differences are evolving, as are the other initiatives for specialized communities described herein. Many of them have been operating for several years and have built up cohorts of enthusiastic participants and supportive audiences. The physical and emotional benefits of these activities have gained accolades from many quarters, as has their ability to encourage cooperation for a common goal as well as individual senses of accomplishment. At the moment, Shakespeare is at the heart of these undertakings and many of their facilitators believe that this playwright's work is particularly suitable for such ensembles. Having spent numerous years in regular contact with many of these groups, I offer my hope for their continued successful evolution.

4

'Touch of nature'

Expanding Shakespearean sensory palates

Historically, much conventional drama relies heavily upon the senses of vision and hearing, but that tradition largely excludes or limits many people, including the d/Deaf and DeafBlind performers and audience members included here.[1] This chapter is somewhat more speculative and discusses fewer current initiatives, in part because the pandemic curtailed previously scheduled site visits and interviews, but also because increasing, though uneven, efforts to include d/Deaf actors and audience members into comparatively mainstream or broadly inclusive productions,[2] do not correlate well with the concept of 'specialized communities' being addressed here.[3]

The expansion of professional opportunities for performers with a wider range of abilities than previously common is exciting, but this volume focuses on different models of theatrical engagement.[4] Some of the practices included here feature sensory experiences that are not currently widely used in Shakespearean productions, although the growth of immersive drama may indicate that the time is ripe for broader experimentation in such realms. There is also increasing attention being paid to d/Deaf and DeafBlind audiences and others seeking theatre that emphasizes multifaceted sensory involvement.[5] Although taste, touch, smell and some other tactile experiences do not figure as prominently as vision and hearing in theatrical productions, they often play enhanced roles in the performances considered here.

Many Shakespearean productions incorporating sign language, such as Deafinitely Theatre's presentations of *Love's Labour's Lost* and *A Midsummer Night's Dream* at Shakespeare's Globe and on tour[6] or Graeae Theatre Company's joint project with the British Council and Japan's Owlspot Theatre in 2021, entitled *The Tempest: Swimming for Beginners*,[7] do not fit neatly within the concept of Shakespeare for specialized communities since they aim to perform for broad and inclusive rather than particularized audiences and their companies focus more specifically on professional trajectories than most of the other featured programmes.[8] The University of Birmingham's Shakespeare Institute, in collaboration with the RSC, however, is working on a project entitled 'Signing Shakespeare' (SS), that presents these plays effectively to d/Deaf children.

Project leads, Abigail Rokison-Woodall from the Institute and Tracey Irish from the RSC, have given several presentations about the background and progress of this initiative.[9] So far, they have created relevant performance exercises, completed a series of curricular Shakespearean films including British Sign Language (BSL) and have received a grant from the Billy Rose Foundation in order to build a corresponding set of recordings in American Sign Language (ASL).[10] In part, they are seeking to offset potential educational deficits arising from language and social developmental delays that can affect these students. Rokison-Woodall reports that 'only 30.6% achieve a strong GCSE pass . . . compared with 48.3% of children with no special educational needs'.[11] Rokison-Woodall, an actor who transitioned into academia, began her involvement with this undertaking through an interest in creating a production that could appeal to both d/Deaf and hearing audiences. As the work progresses,

> I was really struck by the clarity, the energy and the quality of the work process of translating Shakespeare into British Sign Language . . . It's a highly creative process that involves an in-depth analysis of what's being communicated. I was interested in what we could learn from the d/Deaf community about the physical nature of language.[12]

The physicality of sign language is a key feature of d/Deaf performance in the context of multisensory Shakespeare. As

Rokison-Woodall indicates, the project aims 'to show d/Deaf children that they can have ownership over Shakespeare's plays, and to showcase the brilliant, physical, and expressive potential of British Sign Language and visual vernacular'.[13]

The SS team recognizes that many common practices followed in more conventional workshops designed to immerse students in Shakespeare are not appropriate for this population. Exercises where participants engage with each other back-to-back, for instance, do not support children who need visual access to accommodate lipreading. Similarly, since the grammar of BSL differs significantly from written English, students whose first language is BSL are frequently at a disadvantage when presented with a printed copy of a Shakespearean drama. SS, therefore, chooses to 'explore ways in which aspects of the language like iambic pentameter, and personification, metaphor and scenery could be embodied in order to get children a visceral physical experience of them'.[14] These investigations encouraged the team to experiment with principles derived from embodied cognition, a theoretical framework that correlates with many of the practices discussed in this volume. The SS team suggests that

> embodied cognition is a term that captures increasing scientific understanding that far from being rational minds carried around in unruly emotional bodies, all of our thinking derives from the patterns, the associations, that are laid down in our brains from our emotionally coloured sensory contact with the world around us.[15]

The theory of embodied cognition thus supports learning through the physicality embedded in BSL.[16] As the SS collaborators acknowledge, both hearing and d/Deaf humans 'learn through sensory experiences and emotional responses of our whole bodies'.[17] Not surprisingly, therefore, Rokison-Woodall reflects, 'As the project grows, I'm increasingly convinced that a great deal of our learning from this project can inform ways of working with all students and exploring how the rhythms and metaphors of Shakespeare's language find visual and physical expression in performance.'[18] Such premises support the idea that multisensory Shakespeare offers wide-ranging benefits to an expansive population.

Throughout the sessions leading to these films, SS worked with as diverse a group as possible, including children of different ages with varying levels of experience with signing and/or speech. They also incorporate skilled d/Deaf practitioners in order to 'support the students' understanding and providing a kind of model for students to try performances for themselves'.[19] In addition, they emphasize the importance of 'explicit visual resources': 'Visual images support cognitive ease and promote understanding for all of us, but that is especially the case for d/Deaf students. So, for example, we have maps to show where places were [in *Macbeth*]. And we had sashes [and a crown] . . . that helped us indicate characters and transfer of power from one character to another.'[20] It is clear throughout Rokison-Woodall's and Irish's presentations that this initiative is a work in progress, involving colleagues and participants with a wide range of backgrounds.

Rokison-Woodall acknowledges the controversies surrounding some of their initial working models, such as theory of mind (ToM).[21] When the project began, the team approached d/Deafness from a deficit perspective, but this learning journey is continually in flux, as new information and experiences help them adjust their premises and practices and that their understanding of this work and the populations it serves continues to grow.[22]

Rokison-Woodall and Irish are accomplished professionals, have considerable experience with Shakespearean drama and are partnering with d/Deaf practitioners as well as arts and educational professionals bearing significant expertise with d/Deaf populations. They are also mindful of the importance of including a diverse cohort of d/Deaf students. Nevertheless, given concerns raised about the Hunter Heartbeat Method (HMM) connected with questions associated with ToM,[23] it seems pertinent to note that some of the theoretical underpinnings of SS, both from ToM and d/Deaf education, appear to share features with exercises offered by Flute Theatre's HMM, which has led to much of the criticism aimed at the company. Key SS partners, Jacqui O'Hanlon and Angie Wootten, for example, suggest a 'how am I feeling' game in *Using Drama to Teach Personal, Social & Emotional Skills* with similarities to Flute's 'throwing faces' game:

> Choose a word, for example, 'sad' and say or sign it. Model the corresponding facial expression. Tell the children you are going

to point to other words and say or sign them and you want them to make the corresponding facial expression.[24]

Hunter describes the 'throwing the face' game as 'an excellent warm up for acting, providing the children with a transformative challenge, without demanding that they stand up and 'act'.[25] She presents the game as it appears in Flute's adaptation of *A Midsummer Night's Dream*, 'Throwing the face is a key game and appears throughout the book in various forms. Once you have established the framework, replace the donkey face with key facial expressions using happy, sad and angry to begin with and progressing to surprised, fearful, and disgusted.'[26] For some, these games seem comparatively innocuous. Nevertheless, Hunter's explanation for the method and exercises included in her book attracts considerable criticism.[27] However, Hunter justifies the rationale for these games,

> Children with autism experience varying degrees of difficulty with communication, all of which can be understood as a disassociation of body and mind. Expressing feelings, making eye contact, accessing their mind's eye, and their dreams, keeping a steady heartbeat and recognizing faces are all poetically explored by Shakespeare. Embedding these unattainable skills within games derived from moments of Shakespeare, which the children could play and thereby benefit from, seemed like the most natural thing in the world and formed the basis of these games.[28]

These controversies suggest that a comparably divided response could arise from some of methods included in SS, since O'Hanlon and Wootten described/Deaf children in terms suggesting they suffer from deficits due to their hearing status,

> Deaf children have a need to develop PSHE [Personal, Social, and Health Education] skills as much as any other children. Some would say that they have a greater need since deafness may create a barrier to developing these crucial life-enhancing skills . . . Delayed language development in deaf children may mean that their vocabulary does not extend to everything they feel. They lack a vocabulary to describe their emotions and could

therefore be described as being less 'emotionally literate' than other children.[29]

They further contend that these children may lack social skills that needed to enhance the quality of their lives,

> Because of the communication barrier, deaf children may not have the same opportunities to know that other people have the same, and different, feelings and aspirations as themselves. Because they are less aware of this range of feelings in others, they may not always respond appropriately. This type of awareness and response is usually summed up in the word 'empathy.'[30]

Despite the potential pitfalls of these methods, the administrators of these programmes began them predominantly in order to introduce d/Deaf children to Shakespeare. Rokison-Woodall states,

> Our initial aim was to create resources to help d/Deaf children to access and enjoy Shakespeare. To access his stories, his characters and his language. A secondary aim was to use Shakespeare and the process of doing drama to aid the social development of d/Deaf children.[31]

Given the controversy potentially accompanying such perspectives, these topics warrant knowledgeable discussion, as do the potentially divisive aspects of ToM. Such conversations, inside and outside the academy, would offer considerable opportunities to practise the skills in question, that is, empathetic recognition of similarities and differences between people, as well as fostering productive discussions of difficult topics.[32]

HHM theater games frequently resemble those created for more diverse groups, such as Boal's *Games for Actors and Non-Actors* and could possibly draw less criticism if they were offered from that perspective.[33] Notably, SS already presents many of their techniques as relevant for children more broadly. As Rokison-Woodall remarks,

> As the project grows, I am increasing convinced that a great deal of our learning from this project can inform ways of working with all students and exploring how the rhythms and metaphors

of Shakespeare's language find visual and physical expression in performance.³⁴

Resembling countless theatre games devised for and shared with many populations, SS's practices emanate from the premise that drama provides opportunities to build empathy for people quite different from oneself and to practise a range of emotional responses.³⁵

During the genesis and development of the project, Rokison-Woodall and Irish worked with the aforementioned Jacqui O'Hanlon, deputy director of Learning at the RSC and Associate Fellow at Warwick University, and Angie Wootten, a teacher of the d/Deaf in Warwickshire and a regional tutor at Birmingham University on the qualification for teachers of the deaf.³⁶ Rokison-Woodall, whose young son is deaf,³⁷ tells of being invited into the RSC rehearsal room during a week-long intensive with Deafinitely Theatre and reports that 'it was one of the most inspiring weeks she has spent' as they created a version of *Macbeth* using BSL that would 'be accessible to both deaf and hearing audiences'.³⁸ Angie Wootten was the teacher assigned to work with her son, and she discovered Wootten's affiliation with both the University of Birmingham and with the RSC's Jacqui O'Hanlon.³⁹ Their subsequent conversations led to the development of SS.

As mentioned, SS thus grew from dual desires, first to 'create resources to help d/Deaf children access and enjoy Shakespeare', but also to strengthen the social skills of d/Deaf children.⁴⁰ O'Hanlon and Wootten's book, however, does not include d/Deaf children in its title. Its back-cover copy describes the contents like this:

> This innovative and successful drama programme, originally developed for deaf children, addresses personal, social and emotional needs and can benefit all children in primary schools. The interactive and lively ideas cover a variety of themes from empathy to assertiveness.⁴¹

This expansive presentation of their work, which correlates with some of Rokison-Woodall and Irish's comments about SS, may partially shield them from the kinds of criticism addressed towards HHM. While SS is clearly designed for d/Deaf children and Rokison-Woodall and Irish indicate how some of the segments address d/

Deaf children particularly, the group also outlines a potentially broader target audience.

O'Hanlon and Wootten's drama games addressing 'personal, social and emotional' development are divided into six segments, namely,

> I Can Express How I Feel
> I Know How You Feel
> I Can Make Friends
> I Can Keep Friends
> I'm Happy Being Me'
> I Can Express What I Need[42]

Their book does not focus on Shakespeare, although the games, particularly where they emphasize the development of empathy, resemble some of Colorado Shakespeare's Violence Prevention exercises mentioned in Chapter 6.[43]

SS clearly focuses on Shakespeare, however, often demonstrating goals corresponding with the tenets of O'Hanlon and Wootten's volume. They currently also draw explicitly from the previously mentioned ToM principles, which focus on children's development of empathy and their understanding of other people.[44] 'The first order of theory of mind being the ability to think about what someone else is thinking or feeling . . . Higher levels of theory of mind involve the recognition of lies, sarcasm, figurative language, idioms.'[45] Setting the controversy aside for a moment, Shakespeare seems to fit readily into such parameters. As Rokison-Woodall and Irish suggest, they find clear ways to link this drama with ToM,

> In the simplest terms in a workshop situation: to inhabit the character of Macbeth is to make decisions about how that character is thinking and feeling and to understand that the character is thinking and feeling and to understand that there are thoughts and feelings that you hopefully don't have . . . Shakespeare goes beyond this, partly due to the level of dramatic irony.[46]

This perspective corresponds with practices emerging in many of the initiatives developed for the wide range of groups presented in this volume.

As mentioned, however, it is not uncommon for ToM articles and books to address autism in ways resembling some of the HHM tenets that draw criticism, just as O'Hanlon and Wootten's work does.[47] Simon Baron-Cohen's *Mindblindness: An Essay on Autism and Theory of Mind* remarks, for instance, that 'in autism there is a genuine inability to understand other people's different beliefs'.[48] Similarly, an introductory page to Katherine Wareham and Alex Kelly's volume, *Talkabout Theory of Mind: Teaching Theory of Mind to Improve Social Skills and Relationships* indicates,

> Theory of mind is a key consideration in autism spectrum conditions and is frequently associated with social, emotional, behavioural and mental health difficulties. [This workbook] is designed to support those for whom theory of mind does not come naturally. It teaches strategies that can be used to identify other people's thoughts and feelings based on their behaviour, as well as how to adapt behaviour in order to competently manage social situations and have positive interactions.[49]

This notion that ToM needs to be taught to autistic people presumably could raise concerns about its presence in SS.

Notably, however, when Henry M. Welman introduces Shakespeare into *Making Minds: How Theory of Mind Develops*, he uses *Romeo and Juliet* to indicate ways that literature provides insight into humanity for *all* people:

> Great literature presents us human lives. Narratives, tragedies, comedies, romances all tell our stories ... a story focused on the understanding of human thoughts, emotions, desires and actions. This everyday understanding of persons as thinking, forgetful, wanting, remembering beings is known among scientists as a 'theory of mind'.[50]

While it can be difficult, if not impossible, to ascertain intentions from the written word alone, the SS team appears to be intent upon creating a programme with positive outcomes for those participating, notwithstanding any hesitations that their sources may invoke. As SS is still in development, they have significant opportunities to address the criticism directed at ToM.

As mentioned earlier, moreover, SS demonstrates embodied practices found in undertakings with other specialized communities.

Numerous rehearsal room practices, that can include many populations, closely align with principles of d/Deaf education: 'Learning by doing is a standard pedagogy principle for teachers of the deaf, and that fits very neatly with rehearsal room pedagogy where you are up on your feet, doing this relates to the principle of embodied cognition.'[51] They further indicate that

> the active embodied learning of the RSC rehearsal and pedagogy practice taps into humans' innate embodied experience, innate embodied cognition, how we learn through sensory experiences and emotional responses of our whole body . . . But we [SS] also didn't shy away from features of the language like rhythm, antithesis, metaphor. Similarly, imagery and personification, some of which sign language can express very vividly.[52]

The combined expertise of the team enables them to approach the embodiment embedded within these plays from multiple angles, including a heightened awareness of the physicality inherent in BSL.

The SS workshops led to their decision to film a number of key scenes from *Macbeth* incorporating BSL intended for classroom use. They show clips of some segments during their presentations. These materials and the workshops that led to their creation illustrate the power of multisensory explorations of Shakespeare for their intended audience. They also demonstrate how the embodied practices incorporated in their exercises and modules can apply to innumerable groups of Shakespeareans, whether they are hearing or d/Deaf.

While SS primarily targets d/Deaf students, there are additional groups dedicated to presenting Shakespeare without visual or auditory components to other constituencies. dog and pony dc, for instance, a theatrical company which may not have survived the pandemic,[53] described itself as 'an ensemble of artists who devise innovative performances that incorporate new ways for audiences to experience theater. We create productions that are visceral and unexpected with a lingering impact'.[54]

In 2017, they presented an abridged version of *Romeo and Juliet* at Gallaudet University in Washington, D.C. that included no audio or visual production elements.[55] Only a half dozen people could be accommodated for each performance since the patrons received considerable individualized attention as they interacted with actors, sets and props and because unimpeded movement is crucial in such endeavours. An announcement of the production in *DC Theatre Scene* described the production as

> Hot/Cold. Rough/Smooth. Push/Pull. Immerse yourself in a world of Capulet and Montague opposites in dog & pony dc's next sensory-centered translation of Shakespeare, *Party On*. An activation of your senses of touch, smell, and taste, *Party On* places you at the heart of the theatrical experience and stretches your concept of what defines a play.[56]

Patrons who could hear and/or see were offered ear plugs and masks in order to refocus their attention on what they would smell, taste, feel and touch, while experiencing a production designed outside familiar parameters. Those who normally rely heavily on sound and/or vision entered the performance space without many of the sensory cues they typically expect. DeafBlind patrons, on the other hand, engaged in the unusual experience of theatre created, at least partially, with them in mind.

As the name 'Party On' suggests, the production emphasized the masked ball where Romeo and Juliet first meet, although the company also referenced some other aspects of the play, such as including incense in the air in order to insinuate Friar Laurence's association with the church.[57] As they walked through the space, patrons encountered strips of rich fabrics hanging from the ceiling that they touched and interacted with, alluding to the costumes those invited to the Capulets' event would be wearing, as well indicating the elaborate room holding the ball. Piles of Mardi Gras beads set out for tactile interaction also signaled the featured festivities. These sensory engagements accompanied the regular touches exchanged between the patrons being guided and their performer hosts, including the tactile or protactile sign language (TALS or PTALS) used with DeafBlind audience members.

At one stop, while the patrons visited the set and learned the story of the play, they were offered two toothpicks: one with an olive on it, the other with a marshmallow. Patrons were invited to eat these morsels that represented the warring families of the Montagues and the Capulets.[58] Alternating savory and sweet snacks are popular on their own with many people, but most would probably agree that they do not typically complement each other well.⁵⁹ Consumers may enjoy both, but generally not at the same time.⁶⁰ This striking characterization encapsulates these families who may be noble and 'alike' in dignity, but who conventionally remain apart.⁶¹ In addition, as dog and pony dc's Rachel Grossman notes, 'Food is particularly effective at eliciting strong memories and triggering emotional responses,⁶² creating immediate performative touchstones that can be linked into a narrative journey.'⁶³ Food is sometimes, but not regularly, included in theatrical presentations. This interlude in *Party On*, however, illustrates the potential evocative power of food in such environments.⁶⁴

dog and pony dc's determination to reimagine theatre made them an apt ensemble for the kind of production they created with *Party On*. The experience was relatively short, with room for only a few participants, but the facilitated talk-back on the night I attended was uniformly positive. This production offered participants a rare opportunity to engage with a classic play through sensory experiences absent in traditional theatres. Grossman describes the idea behind the kind of experimentation they incorporate in *Party On*. The company's 'Sense-Able initiative' predates the establishment of the ProTactile Theatre (PPT) but operates with related principles, as Grossman explains,

> One of the 'unspoken' assumptions, rules, and rituals for makers and consumers of traditional theater is that stories are to be portrayed through visual and auditory elements. And yet, humans have other senses – touch, smell, and taste – that inspire just as vividly and perhaps more intimately. I started dog and pony dc's Sense-Able initiative to explore artists' and audience's biases about how theater is made and experienced, and through it we launched the 'Shakespeare without Sight or Sound' project.⁶⁵

Among the strengths of these endeavours is their expansion of many traditional conceptualizations of theatre. Only one of these projects emerged from a specific desire to create productions for DeafBlind audiences, but both of them seek to engage patrons in artistic encounters that expand the range of sensory experiences beyond the limitations accompanying theatre restricted to auditory and visual components.

In 2018, the year following *Party On: Romeo and Juliet*, Grossman joined an intensive, NEA-funded experimental week-long institute in Seattle directed by Jill Bradbury (then on the faculty at Gallaudet) and presented in conjunction with PTT.[66] Grossman and others questioned whether it was appropriate for her to be present during this project, given that she is both hearing and sighted,[67] but since the group was workshopping a multisensory *Romeo and Juliet,* she was included as a 'Theater Artist Advisor', having so recently been engaged in a related undertaking.[68]

PTT was co-founded by Jasper Norman and Yashaira Romilus, both of whom completed training with Tactile Communications LLC (TC) in 2017.[69]

> Tactile Communications is committed to maximizing the autonomy of DeafBlind people by providing necessary training in a linguistically and culturally appropriate setting. Our aim is to give DeafBlind people the tools they need to become active, productive members of society and in doing so, to improve the quality of their lives.
>
> We provide training using the ProTactile approach in the following areas: Braille proficiency and computer access using Braille display and Braille Note. Language and communication skills: Training in TASL [tactile ASL].[70] Adaptive Strategies: Proficiency in a range of adaptive strategies for daily life such as cooking and cleaning; as well as for community living, such as how to use SSPs [support service providers] and interpreters effectively. Orientation and Mobility: Learning how to travel safely and use public transportation.[71]

As these aims suggest, ProTactile learning was not developed originally for theatrical pursuits, but Norman and Romilus connected its innovative and practical approaches with their love of theatre in order to create a noteworthy new art form that has resulted in several full or partial productions, including the NEA-sponsored *Romeo and Juliet* excerpts.

PTT has not been in existence for very long, and much of this period, it has been overshadowed by the Covid-19 pandemic. Nevertheless, the group has made great strides since, until recently, 'theater for the DeafBlind [did] not exist'.[72] As the PTT website shows, in a short period of time, this group 'has hosted and affiliated numerous creative PT plays in several states and the PTT energy continues to spread like wildfire nationally and internationally'.[73] Theatre for the DeafBlind may be new, but it is gaining considerable attention.

Norman, Romilus and others discussed the PTT/NEA *Romeo and Juliet* project at length in the 2021 Emory/Folger symposium and in the documentary recounting the Institute in Seattle.[74] Romilus, for instance, indicates that

> ProTactile [is] a language based on touch. We receive our information through touch . . . For hearing people in the room, what you hear, is the way you relate to the world. How you receive information. For d/Deaf individuals, you receive information through your eyes. But individuals who are Deaf and blind, receive it through touch and that raises the value of touch.[75]

Norman adds that protactile communication differs considerably from ASL and is more of an 'international experience language'. He also notes that 'without Protactile and without having access to touch, a [DeafBlind] person would be isolated'.[76]

The duo developed PPT as a class project while they were studying protactile learning. Norman found that putting their ideas into practice with an audience and having their teacher involved was successful beyond their hopes.

> The theatre experience had been so rewarding for everyone and it was better than anything that happened with d/Deaf actors on the stage before . . . the audience was more involved through touch and [could] understand what was going on. They were able to touch the props and hair and clothing and costumes and everything to identify each character that was performing. So it gave them a boost in terms of their enjoyment of the show.[77]

Romilus remarks in a similar vein, 'I will never forget that date: October 20, 2017. October 20, 2017. That day really stands out in my mind . . . it was a beautiful start to what we were working on. Ever since that day, we have been able to connect with various, smaller groups of DeafBlind individuals.'[78] Since DeafBlind theatre is such a new endeavour, her pride in this accomplishment is understandable.

Speakers in the Emory/Folger symposium and participants in the NEA Institute comment upon aspects of Shakespeare that made this project both challenging and invigorating. Romilus, for instance, suggests that the diversity of experiences everyone involved in the project brought to bear was 'a benefit' as they investigated how to integrate their multiple backgrounds into this play.[79] Both PTT directors agree that Shakespeare's language is challenging, but they drew upon the expertise of many people as they crafted their 'translation process into Protactile'. Norman reports that 'the responses [were] amazing because we use period costumes for *Romeo and Juliet* and it is the full experience where people can get completely into the life of what it must have been like for Romeo and Juliet in their own time'.[80]

Unlike more conventional stagings of *Romeo and Juliet*, but recalling the aims of Knock at the Gate, Romilus 'wanted to make the patrons feel as involved as possible in the fight scene [with Romeo, Tybalt, and Mercutio]'.

> Our goal [was] to make the play goers feel like it was an actual fight and feel what was going on. So we did all this blocking and worked out the stage fighting. [The patrons] can feel the aggression and touch our throats and faces and feel the aggression and the whole fight scene and they were able to touch every aspect of what was going on and follow what was hitting whom and who was knocked down and who was getting hair pulled or whatever. So we tried to involve them as much as possible in the emotions and anger and aggression of the fight scene and they became into it and felt very connected to it and they were really able to follow it.[81]

While this level of immersion remains rare in many other forms of drama, the PTT's achievement in these areas illustrates the power available through multisensory experiences on stage. Through the generosity of Seattle Repertory Theatre, the group was able to include 'costumes that could provide tactile access to visual information about the early modern period'. Victoria Magliocchino indicates that they further experimented with fragrances, using

> peony for Juliet (a fruity and youthful scent), lavender for Nurse (a scent for older ladies), and men's cologne for Romeo. We

also had Tybalt drink a beer between scenes, to help the patrons understand his hot tempered and violent actions. In post-performance interviews, patrons said they noticed the scents.[82]

Like the differing musical styles associated with individual characters in Extant Theatre's *The Man Who Saw Backwards* (*King Lear*), PTT uses carefully chosen sensory signals to guide the audience through the series of complex characters and events that invariably comprise Shakespearean drama.

While this deliberate inclusion of a range of sensory experiences makes theatre for the DeafBlind possible, it can also broaden and deepen the communicative powers of performance for all people. PTT's and dog and pony dc's models for presenting Shakespeare without visual or auditory elements provide a valuable insight into ways that aspects of dramatic texts can be enhanced by sensory experimentation, just as recognition of the importance of Shakespeare's soundscapes was emphasized by the productions created for vision-impaired audiences. dog and pony dc's inclusion of incense in order to trigger associations with church, for instance, merely hints at the diffuse ways that scents can influence people.[83] Jude Stewart calls smell 'a tesseract, collapsing Space and time, it unlocks memories and grants us access to scenes we can enter only in imagination'.[84]

Similarly, A. S. Barwich contends that 'smell sits at the border of conscious and unconscious perception',[85] and Rachel S. Herz notes that 'it is clear that odors have a special propensity to become associated with events and to cue recall'.[86] Robert Muchembled disputes 'the widely held idea that the human sense of smell is weak and residual'[87] in his analysis of odors in the early modern period. As Harold McGee explains, smell is an effective conveyer of information,

> Smell is such a powerful and revealing sense because it detects actual little pieces of things in the world. These little pieces are volatile molecules, so little that they're able to break away from their source and fly invisibly throughout the air to reach our nose.[88]

Clearly, scents can activate significant cognitive and emotional responses from people, and their use in theatrical ventures could be exploited more fully.[89] Remarkably, the first olfactory scientist Barwich encountered when researching *Smellosophy*, namely Stuart Firestein, is a former theatre director, but there is no evidence that he intends to combine his two careers.[90]

Nevertheless, the conjunction of fragrance and performance is an area that could be further explored profitably. Barwich, Stewart, McGee and Elise Vernon Pearlstine, among others, write at length about the qualities of many scents with relevance to Shakespearean drama, including various woods, flowers, foods and spices. Obviously, practices developed along these lines would need to be alert to patrons with sensitivities to fragrances, but smell is an underutilized component in theatre, just as it can be essential for those without access to key elements of conventional performances. Used with creativity and sensitivity, smells could provide provocative information for many Shakespearean narratives, particularly since Shakespeare refers to scents as well as the other senses throughout his plays. Benedict's transformation into a lover in *Much Ado About Nothing*, for instance, is signaled partially through fragrance, as the Prince remarks, 'He rubs himself with civet. Can you smell him out like that?'[91] Shakespeare's sensory landscapes regularly offer opportunities to engage a wide range of human senses.

Despite the common tendency for theatre to overlook scent, however, Bob Holmes calls another sense, that is, flavor, 'our most neglected sense'.[92] Like others who write on this topic, he then both differentiates and blurs the concepts associated with 'flavor' and 'taste',[93] 'Throughout *Flavor*, I do my best to be clear about whether I'm talking about a taste or a flavor, but I fall back on the verb 'taste' for both.'[94] He makes a point that appears in such texts with relevance for the multisensory interests of this volume,

> Every one of our five senses – taste, smell, touch, sound, and even sight – contributes meaningfully to the way we perceive flavor. The best way to think about flavor is that it is the sum of all the sensations we get when we have food in the mouth. That leads to some surprising discoveries: the weight of a bowl, the color of a plate, the crunch of a potato chip, and even the choice of background music can have a direct effect on how we perceive flavor.[95]

Edmund T. Rolls describes this aspect of taste/flavor from a physiological perspective with 'how taste and smell inputs combine with each other to form flavor, how visual and oral somatosensory inputs also converge with taste and smell, and how hunger affects the representations in different cortical areas'.[96]

Given how frequently food figures prominently in Shakespeare, including the stores of corn in *Coriolanus*, Duke Senior's tempting forest spread in *As You Like It*, Katherine's unattainable neat's foot, beef and mustard in *Taming of the Shrew*, Falstaff's cakes and ale, Titus's vindictive pies and many additional beverages and comestibles, taste, mouthfeel, aroma and other sensory aspects of consumption can offer considerable additional information within dramatic environments. The use of food in PPT environments can readily be imagined. While its inclusion in other dramatic settings is relatively uncommon, it offers significant room for exploration.[97] As Ole G. Mouritsen and Klavs Styrbæk suggest, 'Taste is one of our most important senses. We depend on it to steer us away from ingredients that might be harmful or even poisonous and to guide us toward those that are palatable and nourishing.'[98] Nicola Perullo, describes the broad range of information that can be accessed through taste,

> Understanding taste as an aesthetic experience requires the knowledge of how the entire process works, if *scientifically* speaking taste is not a simple sense that can be reduced to a mere mechanical device consisting of a few basic flavors (scientists today count five: sweet, salty, sour, bitter, and umami, but new ones may join the list soon), then taste cannot be simple *philosophically* either. Rather, taste is a function of many individual, cultural, and social variables.[99]

Notably, Perullo also situates these observations metaphorically into a theatrical context. 'Taste, like theater, involves many actors and its procedural and dynamic nature comes together in scenes of particular meaning, as in a theatrical scene.'[100] While theatre often ignores taste, Holmes indicates that 'it's no exaggeration to say that the science of flavor is one of the fastest-moving and most exciting disciplines to be around these days.'[101] This excitement suggests that some interdisciplinary exploration of flavor within theatre may be overdue.[102]

In the context of PTT, however, it is particularly important to acknowledge that taste and smell are not the only senses often seen as neglected. As Matthew J. Hertenstein and Sandra J. Weiss suggest, 'The study of touch has faced strong headwinds since its inception.'[103] They cite the common perception that 'philosophers believed that vision offered the most veridical perception of the world',[104] then posit broader issues impeding appropriate study of this topic,

> A number of other relevant factors have produced challenges to the study of touch. Societal proscriptions against touch abound in most parts of the world and across domains of society (e.g., in schools, the workplace, and the healthcare system). As described in this handbook, historical, religious, and cultural variables may explain why touch is verboten in so many facets of our communication. Research about touch has also been hampered for reasons of money and infrastructure. Although many universities have entire departments dedicated to the study of vision, it is rare to find teams of faculty hired to study tactile processes and mechanisms.[105]

Constance Classon offers a similar observation, noting that 'touch lies at the heart of our experience of ourselves and the world yet it often remains unspoken, and even more, unhistoricized'.[106]

While such comments are expressed frequently, Norman's and Romilus's observations about the centrality of touch in their lives and work emphasizes the prominence of this sense in the daily experiences of DeafBlind people.[107] Part of what PTT is doing with *Romeo and Juliet* is attempting to historize early modern culture and the material aspects of the story for their audience. As an increasing number of theatres, such as the RSC, offer 'touch tours' where patrons are invited to have physical contact with costumes and sets prior to experiencing a performance,[108] the time may be ripe for expanded experimentation more broadly with touch.

Touch, of course, is crucial for all people, although it can also activate strong and challenging reactions for those responding to trauma. Richard Kearney, however, subtitles his book *Touch* with the phrase: 'recovering our most vital sense'.[109]

> Studies show a primal hunger for soothing touch and proximity overrides even the most basic needs for food and drink. We know that without repeated touch, an infant will wither away; and that

our skin – the largest organ of our body – is how we wiretap into the brain and become healthier human beings. 'Tender touch' alleviates anxiety, bolsters the immune system, lowers blood pressure, helps with sleep and digestion, and wards off colds and infections. It feed us body and soul. In short, tactile communication is absolutely vital to our physical and mental well-being.[110]

Kearney also discusses touch in a context relevant to many of the groups explored in the chapters devoted to trauma-informed Shakespeare. Citing van der Kolk's work extensively, he describes, for example, the role of touch in the healing of trauma, despite many trauma survivors' resistance to touch.[111] Appropriate touch remains key within innumerable practices described in this volume because of its significance in human experience.

Not surprisingly, therefore, Matthew Fulkerson similarly details the complicated involvement of the sense of touch in human lives,

> Human touch is a highly complex sensory modality, involving numerous interacting systems and exploratory capacities. Through touch we are able to interact directly with the world around us, feeling a wide variety of distinct properties, including warmth, solidity, roughness, and elasticity. We often incorporate tools to expand our reach and abilities. We use touch to comfort and console one another and touch is one of our primary conduits of pleasure and pain.[112]

While many Shakespearean productions successfully suggest a range of sensory experiences, such as touch, through visual or auditory means, these efforts are incompletely realized for many audience members and totally inaccessible for others. R. Murray Schafer offers a perspective about the value of touch and sound in conjunction with each other, in a formulation that seems to point the way to the importance of the feeling of sound vibrations for many people, even though Schafer appears, unfortunately, to be speaking only about hearing persons,

> Touch is the most personal of the senses. Hearing and touch meet where the lower frequencies of audible sound pass over to tactile vibrations (at about 20 hertz). Hearing is a way of touching

at a distance and the intimacy of the first sense is fused with sociability whenever people gather to hear something special.[113]

Just as Bruce R. Smith urged his readers to feel the vibrations of sound evident in their bodies,[114] Schafer reminds us that touch and sound often work in concert with each other.

Touch plays many roles in human lives that could translate well into theatrical endeavours, therefore, provided that careful attention be paid to ensure that any aspects of touch included are both voluntary and appropriate.[115] Mike McLinden, Steve McCall and Liz Hodges, for instance, investigate 'an important function of touch, namely its information-seeking role', which recalls the basis of PTT and its corresponding importance for seeing and/or hearing individuals.

> This active use of touch to seek out and acquire information has been termed haptic touch, with the term haptic deriving from the Greek word *haptikos* meaning 'able to touch.' The haptic system has been described as a distinctive perceptual system, oriented towards discriminating and recognizing objects by handling them as opposed to looking at them.[116]

While 'haptic' is not a word used in everyone's daily vocabulary,[117] its orientation towards what is experienced through touch rather than vision draws attention to a sense that is common in most people's lives, offering them considerable information that their other senses might underestimate or ignore. Architects Nathan Williams and Jonas Bjerre-Poulson, accordingly, invite the readers of their book to broaden their conscious sensory range,

> The pages of this book invite you to consider how, for example, the material palette of a Danish design showroom might compel you to reach out and touch, rather than take a photograph, how a well-tended garden outside Mumbai may smell pleasantly fragrant; how a trickle of water in a Kyoto *ryokan* may sound soothing or offer refreshment; and how the people who share all of these spaces contribute to each other's sense of self.[118]

Another architect, Steven Holl, whose work in the Klasma Museum of Contemporary Art in Helsinki and elsewhere emphasizes the importance of haptic communication, also notes, 'Similar to music, the richness of the textures, smell, and feel of materials says something without telling you exactly what it is.'[119] Delicacy might prevent inviting audience members to experience some of the scenes where touch is emphasized in Shakespeare, such as the Hostess' description of Falstaff's death in *Henry V*:

> a' bade me lay more clothes on his feet:
> I put my hand into the bed and felt them,
> and they were as cold as any stone; then I
> felt to his knees, and they were as cold as
> any stone, and so upward and upward, and
> all was as cold as any stone.[120]

Nevertheless, while handling real or recreated dying limbs might not appeal to audiences, this memorable speech reminds us that Shakespeare describes the senses often. Accordingly, more attention to 'embodied' senses could bring new vitality to the stage.

Many of the dramatic exercises undertaken by groups and individuals considered in this study could be accessible to anyone. Others are specifically pertinent to the specialized communities under discussion. Still, they share a close attention to the dual importance of mind and body in people's lives. However many senses we have, many people typically restrict their access to and use of their full range of sensory opportunities. Neither Shakespeare nor theatre, yoga, expressive arts, breathing exercises or the many other practices detailed here can fulfill all human needs and desires.

Nevertheless, these multisensory approaches to the works of this prominent playwright appear in a growing number of settings in a broad range of countries. When the old lady in *Henry VIII* asks Anne Bullen 'how tastes it?'[121] or when Claudius exclaims in *Hamlet* 'O My offense is rank, it smells to heaven',[122] Shakespeare's texts supply these characters with key human senses. As the many programmes in this volume indicate, imbuing Shakespearean encounters similarly with humanity, mindfulness and embodiment, offers many participants access to aspects of themselves that they had previously lost contact with or never fully experienced.

5

'Weight of pain'

Trauma-informed Shakespeare

Some specialized communities come to engage with Shakespeare from environments shaped by considerable trauma. The next three chapters discuss numerous such groups, ranging from programmes designed for military veterans and a number of international Shakespeare in prison endeavours, including related ensembles comprised of current or former youth offenders and at-risk youth. While these communities vary widely, the participants typically bring fraught lived experiences into their Shakespearean activities, including, for example, time in combat, struggles with addiction, repeated encounters with judicial systems, sexual abuse, violence and other experiences creating lasting trauma. While lives spent in the military and in court or detention are often distinctive from each other, they each can lead to people facing substantial challenges. Some programmes such as DE-CRUIT provide offerings for incarcerated veterans in addition to those designed for veterans living outside carceral spaces.

This chapter presents several initiatives linking Shakespeare with veterans' populations, including DE-CRUIT, Shakespeare with Veterans (Kentucky Shakespeare), the Chesapeake Shakespeare Company's Olive Branch and Laurel Crown veterans' ensemble, and Feast of Crispian (FoC) and Feast of Crispian South (FoC South) in

Milwaukee, Wisconsin and Memphis, Tennessee, respectively. There are fewer Shakespeare and veterans organizations than Shakespeare in prison efforts, but these thriving programmes regularly offer classes, presentations and/or performances in a variety of settings.[1] Many Shakespeare and veterans practitioners are also involved in Shakespeare in Prisons Network (SiPN) activities. Shakespeare for veterans is growing across the United States. There are also arts initiatives for veterans in the United Kingdom and elsewhere, with the Royal Shakespeare Company offering The Combat Veteran Players UK.[2]

Innumerable potential areas of interest for veterans appear in the Shakespearean corpus. Shakespeare spends considerable time in his plays on topics related to war, and many of his characters are current or former members of the military or have close contact with soldiers or veterans. Not surprisingly, therefore, there are numerous scholarly essays devoted to relevant topics that reflect the wide range of material that practitioners working on Shakespeare with veterans can draw from. Willy Maley, for instance, discusses 'Macbeth and Trauma' in terms that resonate with many of the themes emerging within these practical initiatives. He refers to numerous times when soldiers and veterans recognized Macbeth as a fellow soldier, from the First World War through to the early twenty-first century, including a 1947 article entitled 'Was Macbeth a Victim of Battle Fatigue?'[3] Maley also describes '*Macbeth* [as] the "Soldier's play" as well as the "Scottish play"'[4] and indicates,

> In 2004, as part of the National Endowment for the Humanities 'Bard at the Bases' project, a production of Alabama Shakespeare Festival's *Macbeth* toured US military bases, prompting the headline: 'Pentagon money is sending a stage play about a military hero who murders his commander in chief on a tour of 13 military bases.'[5]

Macbeth is frequently drawn upon in both prison and veterans programming, echoing the recognition Maley notes between this brutal play and the experiences of military personnel in a variety of current and historic conflicts. Paul Stevens offers similar remarks about *Henry V*, noting,

> [F]rom the seventeenth century to the most recent wars, from *Paradise Lost* to *Blood Meridian*, Shakespeare's drama has

played a central role in Anglophone representations of war. It is woven into the fabric of our culture; when its lines are quoted by Colonel Collins of the Royal Irish on the eve of the Iraq War or more recently by the eulogist at Senator McCain's funeral, no one has to explain where phrases like 'band of brothers' come from.[6]

Whether or not Stevens is accurate in suggesting that the general public links 'band of brothers' with Shakespeare, speeches and experiences of 'the warlike Harry', from the *Henry V* prologue, resonate broadly and lines from the play frequently appear in the work of the veterans' companies included here.[7]

Claire McEachern, moreover, suggests that Shakespeare deliberately draws upon the dramatic malleability of war. She notes,

> [War can serve] multiple dramatic functions: mere backdrop or focal point, aggravating circumstance, or crucible of manly valor and self-sacrifice. In some plays war provides the central animating conflict, and the alliance of community ... in others, it serves merely to make us realize our willingness to dismiss such abstractions as 'country' or 'sovereignty' in the face of the far more tangible – and sometimes more terrible – battles amongst family members or lovers.[8]

This acknowledgement that 'war' exists in and influences different aspects of society emphasizes the widespread ramifications of military involvement for many people beyond those directly engaged in combat. McEachern, Maley and Stevens each locate ways that Shakespearean characters face challenges corresponding to those encountered by military personnel, veterans, their families and the communities affected with conflict.[9] There are many more volumes devoted to intersections between Shakespeare and war, including a recent collection on *Shakespeare & The Ethics of War*, edited by Patrick Gray, and Ros King and Paul J.C.M. Franssen's 2008 collection *Shakespeare and War*, which help explain why Shakespeare proves valuable in these contexts.[10]

The question 'Why Shakespeare?' emerges in concert with many of the specialized communities considered in this volume. Shakespeare's texts directly help answer that query where Shakespeare and veterans are involved and these groups typically address this issue in their written or experiential material. As indicated, for instance, Feast of Crispian draws its name from *Henry V*, but its ongoing endeavours gather material from across the canon. In a workshop at Emory University, for instance, FoC co-director Bill Watson turned to *Macbeth* while answering the 'why Shakespeare' conundrum. Noting the superficiality characterizing many common societal conversations, Watson remarked on the emotional specificity frequently found in Shakespeare. Referencing Macbeth's statement to Lady Macbeth that his mind 'is full of scorpions' over the knowledge that Banquo and Fleance still live,[11] Watson emphasized the evocative power of this phrase, even though it emanates from metaphoric rather than actual experience. Shakespeare's language is often isolated as a primary reason for his longevity. As Watson suggests, Macbeth's explanation of the physicality of his mental torment illustrates how such phrases can resonate with viewers, listeners and actors despite moments of unfamiliar syntax or vocabulary.

DE-CRUIT's Dawn Stern acknowledges the power of Shakespeare in their work, but also comments that DE-CRUIT is 'keenly aware that Shakespeare was used as a colonizing tool', but that 'it doesn't have to be Shakespeare. We've had Black veterans say that Toni Morrison works for me. Anyone who writes in a rhythm. We had a veteran in Texas, a woman veteran who said "I like the Bible." Great!'[12] Wolfert also describes the utility of Shakespeare, however, in these practices.

> In English we speak in iambic pentameter, the thought continues but we grab a breath . . . I found that form of verse not only provided language for an experience that even if I had the language to articulate it, when I re-experience it and I talk about it, I retreat into my limbic system and I lose the higher function that gave me that language. On top of that, I get trapped in this breath from the traumatic events. And then the verse forces me to breath in, to reset, share this experience, using heightened language and poetry which demands more of us as a person, causes vibration in my body I didn't plan on having, which end up releasing memories and feelings I didn't plan on sharing . . . And the form helped me breath and carry me through the entire story to get to the end and feel lighter by sharing it.[13]

Wolfert further remarks that 'for most people [Shakespeare] is like learning a foreign language. We need the discombobulation. We need the obstacles that Shakespeare presents, and that in and of itself is a tool in DE-CRUIT'.[14]

This insistence on the importance of discombobulation correlates with some of the practices at Shakespeare & Company where Bella Merlin and Tina Packer argue,

> [Y]our transformative courage arises [when] your body and mind shift from their usual state of dislocation from each other into a kind of union. Indeed, a sizable time is spent in the [Acting] Intensive 'becoming observant of *your body's mind* and your "bodymindfulness" as opposed to your intellectual mind trying to figure everything out all the time.'[15]

As many of these programmes indicate, the power of much of this work emanates from such efforts to bridge the common gap separating body and mind. DE-CRUIT accordingly directs significant attention towards participants' awareness of their breath and the feelings and tensions found within their bodies.

Wolfert observes that DE-CRUIT facilitates this process by establishing a place where 'it's ok not to be ok'.

> We just leap right into Shakespeare. And the way we leap into Shakespeare is breath. Breathe in, speak a line. What do you think it means? I don't know, great. Breathe in speak the line . . . it's a room shame free above all. What we want to create is a space where people can observe for themselves where their trauma lives . . . It's usually seated near the shame. Because shame is at the root of so much trauma. And we harbor all this shame. So we're creating a room where they can share the stuff they already know, but don't normally share.[16]

Shakespeare is not the only route available for this work, but many practitioners and participants find this drama evocative. Drama opens a field to express and understand emotions in a safer manner – through the lens of the characters rather than the participants themselves – and allow for genuine healing and catharsis.

Wolfert references the work of James W. Pennebaker (who also writes under J.W. Pennebaker) and his emphasis on the interconnections between emotional and physical responses, noting that 'another problem with inhibition of thought and emotions is that suppression attempts require physiological work'.[17] Pennebaker's description of the kind of 'inhibition' afflicting many veterans helps explain why exercises by these veterans' groups can be so effective.

When individuals do not or cannot express their emotions and thoughts, they are also less likely to cognitively organize and resolve them. Indeed, the pure expression of emotions may not be a simple critical factor. If individuals can express their feelings, however, they can more easily relate to others, enhance their social support system, learn from their experiences, and adopt more healthy coping strategies in general.[18]

This observation corresponds with Linklater's contention that 'blocked emotions are the fundamental obstacle to a free voice'.[19] These writers do not all work in the same field, but they regularly come to similar conclusions about the importance of physical engagement in order to relieve emotional or psychic restrictions.

Accordingly, many of the practitioners cited here approach their endeavours from congruent perspectives. Shakespeare and veterans' programmes employ varying techniques in their work, but as these examples indicate, those involved typically demonstrate considerable knowledge of veterans, trauma studies and Shakespearean performance practices. In addition to other formal and/or practical dramatic experience, several of the practitioners have received training from Shakespeare & Co., a pioneer in social justice-oriented applied theatre.[20] Many have also studied and/or collaborated with trauma specialists such as Bessel van der Kolk and Stephen Porges.[21] Some, like Nancy Smith-Watson of FoC, have significant training and experience with somatic bodywork or other practices designed for nurturing physical and emotional well-being.

Like other Shakespearean enterprises for specialized communities, the practitioners involved in these endeavours typically avoid claims that they are engaging in therapy, although they maintain that these processes often lead to results deemed therapeutic by those involved.[22] The many collaborations between arts practitioners, trauma specialists and those experienced with the theory and practice of various bodywork modalities, however, provide these Shakespeare and veterans initiatives with a range of ways to engage beneficially with their participants.

van der Kolk, in fact, who has worked with several of the practitioners included here, came to his professional focus on trauma after working with the Department of Veterans Affairs (VA). He realized that the VA medical library did not contain the information he needed to respond appropriately to his clients, such as the Vietnam vet 'Tom', who refused medication that might help his nightmares because he believed this intervention would disrespect those who had died.

> Tom's need to live out his life as a memorial to his comrades taught me that he was suffering from a condition much more complex than simply having bad memories or damaged brain chemistry – or altered fear circuits in the brain. Before the ambush in the rice paddy, Tom had been a devoted and loyal friend, someone who enjoyed life, with many interests and pleasures. In one terrifying moment, trauma had transformed everything.[23]

van der Kolk's repeated experiences with veterans like this demonstrated that the trauma generated through combat created long-lasting ramifications that were not being addressed sufficiently.

> During my time at the VA I got to know many men who responded similarly. Faced with even minor frustrations, our veterans often flew into extreme rages. The public areas of the clinic were pockmarked with the impacts of their fists on the drywall.[24]

As van der Kolk's narrative indicates, anger was common with this population, but those afflicted also frequently felt numb in environments where feelings of connection were desirable:

> The worst of Tom's symptoms was that he felt emotionally numb. He desperately wanted to love his family, but he couldn't evoke any deep feelings for them. He felt emotionally distanced from everybody, as though his heart were frozen and he were living behind a glass wall.[25]

The research that followed such experiences in the VA led to many of the tenets now promulgated by van der Kolk and other trauma specialists and incorporated by many of those involved with Shakespeare and veterans:

> In the three decades since I met Tom . . . We have also begun to understand how overwhelming experiences affect our innermost sensations and our relationship to our physical reality – the core of who we are. We have learned that trauma is not just an event that took place sometime in the past, it is also the imprint left by that experience on mind, brain and body.[26]

Many of these practitioners engage in ongoing trauma education in order to sharpen their practice with these populations.[27]

The background and training of FoC's co-founders and directors in Milwaukee corresponds with the premises of their approach. All three, Smith-Watson, Jim Tasse and Bill Watson, have worked as actors and directors for many years, with considerable training and experience at Shakespeare & Co. and elsewhere. Tasse is also a Vietnam-era veteran. Smith-Watson has thirty years of education and practice as a Hakomi bodyworker and studied integrative somatics extensively with sensorimotor psychotherapy developer Pat Ogden.[28] Watson has also received Hakomi training. The practices embedded in FoC's work clearly reflect the convergence of these directors' backgrounds in the development and implementation of this nonprofit organization devoted to veterans and Shakespeare.

'Feast of Crispian' is immediately identifiable to Shakespeareans as a quote from the king's famous battle speech in *Henry V*. Appealing to his troops facing overwhelming odds on the battlefield, Henry looks ahead to future gatherings of veterans in remembrance of their service on the day referenced in the play. *Henry V* is only one of many Shakespearean plays featuring military figures and each of the programmes discussed here incorporate innumerable relevant passages in their endeavours. King Henry's allusion to ongoing conversations about military events, moreover, illustrates the appropriateness of this title for the activities organized by this modern Feast of Crispian. The powerful military content embedded in this play also regularly influences productions. Max Weber's 2022 *Henry V* at London's Donmar Warehouse, for instance, brought in former Royal Marines Commander Tom Leigh to instruct the cast on appropriate military movements, while *Game of Thrones*' Kit Harrington rallied the troops as England's warrior king. Its presentation soon after the 2022 war began in Ukraine heightened the audience's awareness of the topics presented in the play and conflicts often arising outside of drama.

The Hakomi method and integrative somatics approaches to psychotherapy employed by FoC may be less familiar to Shakespeareans than this well-known play, however. Ron Kurtz and a core group of trainers founded The Hakomi Institute in Boulder, Colorado, in 1981, and Kurtz directed the Institute for its first decade. The Institute offers and publicizes 'Hakomi Mindful Somatic Psychotherapy' trainings and workshops, publishes an electronic journal and helps interested individuals find practitioners in their region. According to their website, their trainings are designed 'mainly for therapists, counselors, social workers, and graduate students in these fields. The trainings have also proved invaluable for professionals in related fields (including coaching, the healing arts, organizational and group work, and other disciplines'.[29]

The name 'Hakomi' is said to be a Hopi word that asks listeners to consider 'where do you stand in relation to these many realms?' or 'who are you?'[30] It apparently emerged during a dream that a man named David Winter experienced after a series of brainstorming sessions where various potential 'umbrella' titles for these body-centered psychotherapy techniques and the newly founded Institute were being discussed. Since none of those involved in the Institute claim Hopi affiliations, the ethical implications of using this name are currently under discussion.[31]

While the provenance and appropriateness of the term 'Hakomi' attracts controversy, the multiple techniques implemented by Hakomi practitioners like Smith-Watson generally align with the principles undergirding many of the programs discussed in this study. The book cover description of Kurtz' 2015 volume details the diverse origins of Hakomi practices:

> Some of the origins of Hakomi stem from Buddhism and Taoism, especially concepts like gentleness, compassion, mindfulness and going with the grain. Other influences come from general systems theory . . . Hakomi also draws from modern body-centered psychotherapies such as Reichian work, Bioenergetics, Gestalt,

Psychomotor, Feldenkrais, Structural Bodywork, Ericksonian Hypnosis, Focusing, and Neurolinguistic Programming.[32]

These syncretic Hakomi approaches to bodywork integrate physical and emotional interventions resembling those promoted by trauma specialists such as van der Kolk, who also argues that theatre can be key in the treatment of trauma.

Describing his son's incorporation of drama into his recovery regime following a lengthy illness, he explains that theatre nurtures important connections between the body and spirit,

> Our sense of agency, how much we feel in control, is defined by our relationship with our bodies and its rhythms: Our waking and sleeping and how we eat, sit, and walk define the contours of our days. In order to find our voice, we have to be *in* our bodies – able to breathe fully and able to access our inner sensations.[33]

Theatre facilitates the kinds of sensory integration van der Kolk promotes. Similar to DE-CRUIT, therefore, groups such as FoC, which also incorporate somatic bodywork principles in their interactions with veterans, thus invoke multiple ways to support their participants' increased awareness of their minds and their bodies as part of their path towards decreasing the effects of trauma.

As noted, Smith-Watson also has considerable expertise in integrative somatics, a practice which preceded the sensorimotor psychotherapy developed and practiced by Pat Ogden and others. According to Ogden, Minton and Pain,

> Sensorimotor psychotherapy builds on traditional psychotherapeutic understanding but approaches the body as central in the therapeutic field of awareness and includes observational skills, theories, and interventions not usually practiced in psychodynamic psychotherapy. Theoretical principles and treatment approaches from both the mental health and body psychotherapy traditions are integrated in this approach.[34]

While the practitioners involved in Shakespeare for Veterans typically differentiate such work from 'therapy', the approaches taken by FoC and others often produce positive outcomes that some designate as 'therapeutic'.[35]

Those engaged with Shakespeare for Veterans frequently collaborate closely with people or organizations including licensed therapists, who can direct participants towards appropriate resources as needed. FoC, for instance, often works with veterans in an in-patient setting. Carmen Mandley from FoC South (part of Tennessee Shakespeare) notes that this group's partnership with the Memphis VA Medical Association (begun in 2017) enables their Shakespearean programmes to 'round out the therapeutic regimes' offered by the VA. Mandley, who has a background in physical theatre, trained at Shakespeare & Co. with trauma specialists, such as van der Kolk, as well as with others involved with Shakespeare and Veterans, such as Stephan Wolfert, Watson and Smith-Watson. She was also involved in Shakespeare & Co.'s Shakespeare in the Courts program, which is discussed in another chapter.[36] The work of Ogden and Fisher corresponds with the practice undertaken by both branches of FoC.

> The emotional pain of feeling hurt by people important to us, as well as physical pain, such as that incurred in trauma, is 'felt' in the body. Emotional pain may manifest physically as tightness in the throat, increased heart rate, or achiness in the chest, for example. When the sensations of physical and emotional pain are unpleasant or overwhelming, we may disconnect from them so as not to experience the hurt. A disconnection from the body can be healthy and helpful at the time of trauma and emotional stress because it allows us to distance ourselves from a painful situation while actually remaining physically present . . . However, over time, we may learn to disconnect in anticipation of hurt and discomfort . . . disconnection from the body then becomes the new norm.[37]

Efforts to alleviate this pain and disconnection underlie all of FoC's activities.

The FoC techniques draw some features from Shakespeare & Co. exercises and incorporate diverse movement and breathing exercises.[38] Combining physicality and Shakespeare, but without requiring memorization of text, which FoC practitioners find can be difficult for those grappling with PTS(D),[39] the sessions include a range of encounters with Shakespeare and with each other.

> Our techniques allow us to ensure success for our vet participants ... we stand at their shoulder and 'feed' them a line or a half line or a phrase or word – as much as they can hold onto. We ask provocative, even personal questions about the emotional content of the lines. These questions are not meant to be answered but any emotion they elicit is put on the line itself. Movement is encouraged and suggested. Full voice is encouraged. In the debrief that follows, the veterans tell us they feel a release.[40]

Smith-Watson reports that not all practitioners working with veterans support FoC's use of provocative questions, but the FoC team and their participants find this strategy effective.[41] This technique also seems to correlate with some aspects of the Hakomi method, as Kurtz describes,

> The essence and uniqueness of this method remains a simple combination of two things: the client's state of mind (mindfulness) and the therapist's ability to create experiments that trigger reactions while the client is in that state of mind. These reactions are indications of unconscious assumptions.[42]

Kurtz, who, somewhat surprisingly, did not study psychotherapy formally,[43] also refers to Hakomi as 'mindfulness-based, assisted self-study'.[44] FoC's personal questioning, in conjunction with 'feeding' Shakespearean lines, appears to correlate with this emphasis on triggering reactions that FoC participants can then transfer into their dramatic segments.[45] The practice also corresponds with the concept of 'assisted self-study', although the close proximity of therapeutic professionals helps ensure that FoC veterans are not left alone without access to help if needed. When FoC presented their workshop, a couple of the students involved appeared to experience distress at some of the 'triggering' questions asked. They all remained for the entire workshop, but their reactions suggest that practitioners in this modality need to be highly trained and that ready access to mental health assistance is ideal.

For these veterans, the speeches chosen can resonate profoundly, as Smith-Watson describes,

> When we stand at the shoulder of a combat vet and 'feed' him Brutus' lines about honor and justice (*Julius Caesar* 4.3.18–21),

he then speaks these words out loud. He says, 'remember' and 'justice', and 'touch'd his body', and 'bleed'. For veterans those are hot-button words.[46]

Smith-Watson then describes the conversation that follows this line-feeding exercise, after again differentiating it from what the veteran would encounter in therapy,

> As we sit and discuss Brutus – a man who believes that all actions, even fighting a war, must be honorably done – and Cassius – a man who believes that the purpose of fighting a war is to win, whatever it takes – a veteran 'actor' tells us that this scene feels like his own internal struggle. Once, he was a man of integrity who acted out of a sense of 'right', but alcohol has manipulated him into doing whatever it takes to get him what he wants . . . He tells us he had forgotten that feeling, and wants to feel it again.[47]

Smith-Watson further explains the bodily involvement encouraged in FoC that facilitates this veteran's movement forward,

> To have the opportunity to feel the muscles tense with strength, to feel the need for a full breath in order to shout the angry words, to be *encouraged* to shout out in anger, and to make the physical shapes of anger: clenched fists and furrowed brow, he experiences the power of his honorable self and gets a sensation of his 'better self' inside his own skin.[48]

FoC's use of breath and movement corresponds with the practices commonly undertaken by those involved with Shakespeare and veterans, for reasons van der Kolk articulates,

> Love and hate, aggression and surrender, loyalty and betrayal are the stuff of theater and the stuff of trauma. As a culture we are trained to cut ourselves off from the truth of what we're feeling. In the words of Tina Packer, the charismatic founder of Shakespeare & Company: 'Training actors involves training people to go against that tendency – not only to feel deeply, but to convey that feeling at every moment to the audience, so that the audience will get it – and not close off against it.'[49]

Each of these groups works to relieve the effects van der Kolk finds in people contending with trauma.

> Traumatized people are terrified to feel deeply. They are afraid to experience their emotions, because emotions lead to loss of control. In contrast, theater is about embodying emotions, giving voice to them, becoming rhythmically engaged, taking on and embodying different roles.[50]

Given this perspective, it is not surprising that so many theatre companies have found their way to working with populations grappling with trauma.

The Chesapeake Shakespeare Company (CSC) in Baltimore, Maryland, for instance, sponsors the Olive Branch and Laurel Crown Ensemble for veterans.[51] Formed in 2017 through a partnership with VetArts Connect to 'find ways for health and wellness through the arts',[52] the group emerged from the vision of Director of Education Ron Heneghan, who wished to include veterans in the company's community outreach programmes.[53] Drawing participants from several generational cohorts and all branches of the American military, the ensemble meets and performs regularly, although like most companies, they gathered via Zoom during the Covid-19 pandemic, a necessity that seems to have led to somewhat more cerebral explorations of Shakespeare than their in-person gatherings generate. Membership is open to former military personnel who have completed a CSC drama course for veterans, and many of the ensemble members have been involved with the group for numerous years. They perform a variety of pieces, most recently *To Be a Soldier*, a powerful production that incorporates a number of Shakespearean scenes with military resonances.

In previous years, they have explored Shakespeare through annual themes focused consecutively on war and peace, love and dreams, bravery and fear, and leadership. They have also partnered with the CSC high school ensemble on a production of *Much Ado About Nothing* and presented an original, devised piece entitled *Road to Bedlam*, which offered Shakespearean scenes involving rage, madness and despair. *To Be a Soldier*, which toured in 2022, draws from a range of Shakespearean texts, with segments devoted to 'the precursors to war', 'battlefield conflicts', 'alliances', 'betrayals', 'desertions', 'the plight of prisoners of war' and 'the adjustment back to civilian life'.[54] The performance at Classics Fest in 2022 was warmly received.[55] In keeping with CSC's dedication to the well-being of their participants, there was a PTS(D) specialist present for the audience Q&A after the show.

CSC, like other Shakespeare initiatives with veterans, works to provide safe and valuable programming for those engaged in their activities. Accordingly, their collaborators and other associates devote considerable attention to the development of appropriate workshops and productions. Their previous partner, The Institute for Integrative Health (TIIH), now Nova Institute for Health of People Places and Planet, details the ways that involvement with arts and with nature supports well-being for veterans, noting that studies indicate such engagement can decrease anxiety, reduce stress hormones, provide greater confidence and improve cognitive skills and strengthen the ability to reduce trauma, while providing better facility with facing frustration and grief. They also share observations from veterans who report that such programmes help them bond with others, provide a sense of control and a break from stress, help ease the transition to civilian life, make it easier to talk about challenging subjects and provide focus and meaning to their lives.[56] When CSC (and Nova) were involved in VetArts Connect, they drew on the experience of PsychArmor, 'a national nonprofit organization that provides education and training to improve the health and life outcomes of military-connected individuals. We create data-driven and evidence-based virtual training courses that help to enhance the level of connection between civilians and military-connected people'.[57]

In the materials available on their website, Nova provides links to several scientific studies supporting the findings that arts benefit veterans. They also include a white paper developed by the University of Florida's Center for Arts in Medicine, entitled 'Talking about Arts in Health' that further explores how arts programmes can promote better health for veterans and others. Their study reinforces the importance of distinguishing between the benefits available through the arts and clinical interventions.

> The arts provide a means of distraction and enjoyment, a sense of meaningful connection with others, and a way for participants to share who they are as a whole person rather one who is defined by diagnosis, age, or disability. This is distinct from the work

of therapists who establish and work toward specific clinical and therapeutic goals. Although artists may be called upon to work with a clinical provider, they do not themselves set or work toward treatment goals.[58]

The white paper doubles down on the differences between the distinctive professional reaches of clinical practitioners and artists, further demonstrating the reason Shakespeare and Veterans practitioners frequently shy away from making therapeutic claims.

> Terms such as 'healing' and 'therapy' have consistently been applied to this discipline [arts in health] as well. These terms are problematic in that they imply that an artist may be working beyond the appropriate scope of practice, hence violating professional boundaries . . . the term 'clinician' implies a level of training and clinical practice beyond the scope of an artist working in health.[59]

While many of the artistic practitioners involved in this work are familiar with relevant clinical studies and may refer to them in support of their endeavours, even those trained as drama therapists typically make it clear that they are working as arts practitioners, not medical or mental health professionals when they engage with veterans involved with Shakespeare. Nevertheless, they include practices that encourage better physical and mental health, and they frequently study the theory and practice of such interventions in depth in addition to their artistic training and involvement.

Heneghan offers a reflection on the CSC's veterans' programme that confirms the benefits many find in this theatrical offering, including statements by some of the participants. He cites a germane survey done by Nova that reported a 14 per cent reduction in feelings of isolation and a 21–29 per cent drop in 'feelings of depression, anger, and anxiety' among participants in CSC's veterans' ensemble. This demonstrable success led to CSC's first Creative Forces contract work with veterans at Walter Reed National Military Medical Center in 2019, where participants presented *A Midsummer Night's Dream*.[60]

Heneghan also includes a number of signed endorsements offered by ensemble members in support of Olive Branch and Laurel Crown. Richard Wirth, for instance, reports that he was surprised at age seventy, 'to be so reinvigorated at this point in my life with new ideas, experiences and creative challenges . . . to be awakened by the words of Shakespeare and to be shocked by all I have missed throughout the years'. Sharon Preator describes the ensemble as, '[P]art theatre class (history, performance), part family reunion, part support-group . . . the qualities of leadership, fidelity, commitment to mission, and service to others transition very well from the battlefield to the stage.'

David Hanauer 'did not expect' how much he 'would grow to love Shakespeare's words, style, language, and story'. He also notes that his 'moods, thoughts, emotions and life in general are far better for being a part of this program'.[61] The corps members made similar comments at 2022's Classics Fest, indicating that shared military backgrounds help cement strong partnerships despite the generational breadth of the group. As Wirth comments, 'A few short years ago we were all complete strangers. We soon became friends and cohorts. To say today that we are truly brothers and sisters is a meager understatement.'[62]

CSC has been able to work with this ensemble at military facilities, at the CSC theater site and on Zoom. The group's commitment to each other and to their Shakespearean education remains strong as the power of *To Be a Soldier* makes clear. Working closely with military personnel, clinical staff and the scientific community helps ensure appropriate practices and supports funding applications, although CSC's financial support of this undertaking, which keeps it free for participants, is striking. The Olive Branch and Laurel Crown Ensemble demonstrates that Shakespeare and veterans make formidable collaborators.

Unlike the other groups discussed in this chapter, which are largely connected with specific geographic areas (Milwaukee FoC, however, has programmes in Washington State as well as Wisconsin), DE-CRUIT leads workshops and offers performances in numerous locations.[63] Their website indicates that the programme's goal is to be widely re-creatable,

> Part of the DE-CRUIT plan is: to make it a transferable model. That means I [Stephan Wolfert] can go into Fort Worth, teach the veterans the program, then they teach it, and they teach other vets. And it's free to all the veterans. So all it requires is a commitment, from the veterans and the community members in that area.[64]

Actor and military veteran Wolfert founded DE-CRUIT, an organization designed for 'treating trauma through Shakespeare and science'.[65] As Drew Wiggins explains, DE-CRUIT is named in recognition of a perceived necessary counterbalance to the idea of 'recruitment',

> DE-CRUIT – the name of the program tells of a need for veterans who were recruited into the world of the military and 'wired up' for war, and now need to better understand the emotions roiling them as they re-enter the civilian world. The words of the great playwright are seen as a way to develop that understanding, and to help them rewire their brains for civilian life.[66]

Wolfert shares his personal story through the solo show *Cry Havoc*, a striking narrative detailing how this veteran's path ended up intertwined with Shakespeare after an abusive childhood, traumatic military experiences and battles with alcohol abuse. The National Endowment for the Arts (NEA), one of DE-CRUIT's sponsors, summarizes part of the story told in *Cry Havoc*.

> Stephan Wolfert had been in the army for six years when he saw his close friend killed during a training exercise. Wolfert 'lost it,' as he put it, hopped a train, and went on a drinking binge that lasted quite a while. He ended up in Montana and wandered into a theater where *Richard III* was being performed. Wolfert saw in the title character a veteran like himself who did not fit in and who spoke directly and eloquently to the audience about his anger and contempt for those that did. Wolfert's life was transformed. He left the army, went to graduate school to study acting, and immersed himself in Shakespeare. He quickly saw that Shakespeare populated his plays with soldiers and veterans who faced their own bloody losses and seemed to speak directly to the trauma Wolfert was facing.[67]

Wolfert's feelings of affinity with veterans, their families and associates presented in Shakespeare led him to create this meaningful dramatic rendition of his life. They also provide the building blocks for DE-CRUIT, which facilitates reduced trauma for veterans through Shakespeare in conjunction with a range of physically and emotionally restorative techniques.

Course materials compiled in 2015 for a DE-CRUIT workshop begin with a quote from van der Kolk that signals DE-CRUIT's associations with trauma studies:

> [We learned] that traumatized people have a tendency to superimpose their trauma on everything around them and have trouble deciphering whatever is going on around them.[68]

Inside the course packet are Shakespearean materials from *Macbeth* to be used in a 'breath and shared lines scene', followed by some lines 'to compare' *Macbeth* to *Julius Caesar*, *Henry V* and *Coriolanus*.[69] Participants are instructed to 'try vowels as emotion' and 'consonants as action'. Attention then turns to an edited version of Lady Percy's monologue from *Henry IV, part one*,[70] which is analyzed in conjunction with PTS(D) symptoms in an exercise drawn from Jonathan Shay's *Achilles in Vietnam*,[71] a text that also links classic literature with the experiences of former military personnel.[72] This section highlights correspondences between Shakespearean lines and PTS(D) symptoms, such as Lady Percy's observation that her husband is 'alone', and that he is missing his 'golden sleep', which correlates with the social withdrawal, isolation and insomnia associated with PTS(D). This segment also draws parallels between this poignant monologue and other signs of trauma in veterans, such as anorexia, somatic disturbances and anhedonia.[73] Stav Dimitropoulos describes some participants' responses to DE-CRUIT,

> [Frank] Lesnefsky was diagnosed with post-traumatic stress disorder (PTSD) and, after experimenting with different therapists, he learned about DE-CRUIT, a program that combines theater and psychotherapy to treat trauma in veterans. DE-CRUIT completely transformed his life, Lesnefsky says.
>
> It is healing, he says, to share his "hidden 'voices' through Shakespeare and DE-CRUIT." Lesnefsky has come to learn that he is 'not the only one who struggles with trauma like this'.[74]

Wolfert has gathered twenty-two Shakespearean monologues in readiness to use in DE-CRUIT's workshops, in recognition of the twenty-two American veterans who take their own lives each day, but turns to other passages as needed to match a particular veteran's emotional needs.[75]

Dimitropoulos also details the close partnership DE-CRUIT has established with scientific researchers at NYU, including DE-CRUIT's lead researcher, Alisha Ali, an associate professor of applied psychology. The NYU team has designed and implemented studies that confirm the positive reports emanating from anecdotal responses to these undertakings, demonstrating that 'the 24 veterans [in the study] experienced significantly decreased PTSD and depression, and increased confidence in themselves'. As Dimitropolulo reports, Ali suggests that 'Shakespeare's heightened language has long reflected the soldier's internal struggle'. DE-CRUIT trainers 'also note Shakespeare writes about the common experience of veterans. And remind them how iambic pentameter and breathwork ground a person, stimulating their vagus nerve (the longest of twelve cranial nerves, whose stimulation helps regulate physiological responses to strong emotions)'.[76] This reference to the vagus nerve draws attention to a neurophysiological theory that informs the work of DE-CRUIT and of many of the Shakespeare practitioners assisting populations contending with extensive trauma.

Polyvagal theory emerged from the research of Stephen W. Porges, PhD. While some of Porges's writings are dense and difficult for non-scientists to understand, as the author acknowledges,[77] he has also published his findings in arenas designated for broad audiences and several other mental health and bodywork practitioners have developed practical ways to apply polyvagal theory which they detail in publications sanctioned by Porges. As Porges explains, 'Polyvagal Theory emphasizes that evolution provides an organizing principle to identify neural circuits that promoted social behavior and two classes of defensive strategies, mobilization associated with fighting or fleeing and immobilization associated with hiding or feigning death.'[78]

According to this research and the practices that draw from it, the physical aftermath left by trauma often requires bodily interventions. The breathwork and physicality associated with the drama exercises introduced by Shakespearean practitioners, therefore, can be fashioned in accordance with the tenets of polyvagal theory. Deb Dana summarizes several pertinent facets of polyvagal theory that can be adapted to Shakespearean enterprises for specialized communities. There are three segments of this theoretical structure, which Dana describes,

1. Autonomic hierarchy: The system is organized around three building blocks that work in a certain order and come with preset pathways.
2. Neuroception: The system has a built-in surveillance system that watches for signs of safety and warnings about danger ahead.
3. Co-regulation: Having moments of safety connecting to others is a necessary ingredient for well-being.[79]

Dana elaborates on the role these systems play in daily life, indicating that 'autonomic hierarchy . . . provides a pathway to health and well-being and the place where life feels manageable. We connect and communicate with others or [can] be happy on our own'.[80] 'Neuroception', which Dana notes is a word coined by Porges,

> follows three streams of awareness: inside, outside, and between. Inside listening happens as neuroperception attends to what's happening inside your body – your heartbeat, breath, rhythms, and muscle action – and inside your organs, especially those involved with your digestion. Outside listening begins in your immediate environment (where you are physically located) and then expands out into the larger world to include neighborhoods, nations, and the global community. The third stream of awareness, listening between is the way your nervous system communicates with other systems one-on-one or with a group of people.[81]

She then indicates that 'co-regulation', the 'third principle of polyvagal theory is the need for finding connection with others in the experience of co-regulation'.[82] She further suggests that 'in order to co-regulate, I have to feel safe with you, you have to feel safe with me, and we have to find a way to come into connection and regulate with each other'.[83]

Stanley Rosenberg describes the evolution of polyvagal theory, with a particular emphasis upon the discovery of two distinct vagus nerves, which he indicates were mistakenly seen as one for a considerable time.[84] The consequences of this confusion, he maintains, has undermined therapeutic responses to individuals afflicted by trauma. In his clinical practice, he notes,

> Many patients who come to my clinic with a diagnosis of post-traumatic stress are not stressed in their nervous system (via spinal sympathetic chain activation) but are actually in a chronic dorsal vagal state. They are not mobilized into fight or flight but immobilized into fear, apathy, and hopelessness. Trying to treat them as if they are stressed can therefore be confusing and counterproductive.[85]

In response to these circumstances, Rosenberg recommends that 'we get a clearer and more useful picture by differentiating between post-traumatic stress and post-traumatic shutdown'.[86] As part of this suggestion, he describes a difference in treatment that clarifies the potential role for dramatic engagement in this work,

> When treating post-traumatic stress, therapists tend to focus on the trauma itself rather than the psychophysiological fixation that followed the event. Recalling the experience and telling someone about it is certainly one way to ease post-traumatic stress, but it is not the only way and it can often backfire, as the person can become re-traumatized by recounting it. In many cases, it is easier and more effective for a therapist to bypass recall of the event, and work with exercises or hands-on treatments to restore a state of social engagement.[87]

DE-CRUIT furthers this work, by guiding participants to focus on their breathing and their physical and emotional feelings, and by emphasizing that they are operating in a space free from value judgements.

The perceived benefits of drawing from classic literature and applied polyvagal theory in work with veterans become sharply evident in discussions throughout Shay's two volumes that link Homer's epics with the experience of those afflicted with combat trauma.[88] Shay, who holds both an MD and a PhD, served as a long-term staff psychiatrist in the Department of Veterans Affairs Outpatient Clinic in Boston, working with Vietnam veterans contending with severe combat trauma. Shay details 'the strengths, skills, and capacities acquired during prolonged combat' as the following:

Control of fear.
Cunning, the arts of deception, the arts of the 'mind-fuck.'
Control of violence against members of their own group.
The capacity to respond skillfully and *instantly* with violent, lethal force.
Vigilance, perpetual mobilization for danger.
Regarding fixed rules as possible threats to their own and their comrades' survival.
Regarding fixed 'rules of war' as possible advantages to be gained over the enemy.
Suppression of compassion, horror, guilt, tenderness, grief, disgust.
The capacity to lie fluently and convincingly.
Physical strength, quickness, endurance, stealth.
Skill at locating and grabbing needed supplies, whether officially provided or not.
Skill in the use of a variety of lethal weapons.
Skill in adapting to harsh physical conditions.[89]

As Shay notes, this list of acquired skills is 'chilling'.[90] In his earlier volume, Shay summarizes the concurrent 'key symptoms of PTSD and of the personality changes that mark its severe forms'[91] as the following:

Loss of authority over mental function – particularly memory and trustworthy perception
Persistent mobilization of the body and the mind for lethal danger, with the potential for explosive violence
Persistence and activation of combat survival skills in civilian life
Chronic health problems stemming from chronic mobilization of the body for danger
Persistent expectation of betrayal and exploitation, destruction of the capacity for social trust
Alcohol and drug abuse
Suicidality, despair, isolation, and meaninglessness[92]

Shay further remarks that 'unhealed PTSD can devastate life and incapacitate its victims... The painful paradox is that fighting for one's country can render one unfit to be its citizen'.⁹³ Shay's two volumes, which offer innumerable first-person and composite accounts of the long-term struggles afflicting those endeavouring to recuperate from combat trauma, detail the kind of intractable mental and physical challenges addressed by Shakespeare for veterans initiatives.

The frequent collaborations established between trauma specialists, such as van der Kolk and Porges, with these programmes illuminate the strength of practices incorporating physical, emotional, cognitive and cooperative engagements. Shakespeare is not the only path towards success, but there is substantial evidence to suggest that the multisensory involvements associated with Shakespearean performance help facilitate the mental and physiological shifts necessary to reduce PTS(D).

The testimonials from participants in these groups regularly praise the efficacy of such undertakings. On Kentucky Shakespeare's website, for instance, one member of their Shakespeare with Veterans group reports 'This group has helped me to gain control over what my emotions do. It's also helped me relate to civilians better' (US Army veteran, Vietnam War). Another notes, 'We can just let our guard down here. Shakespeare pushes things to the surface that we need to deal with' (US Air Force veteran) and an Indiana Army National Guard soldier indicates, 'The group is accepting and I feel comfortable here. While we're here we don't feel like we're broken. We know these are normal reactions to experiences we've had.'⁹⁴

In a 2022 interview, Kentucky group facilitator Amy Attaway remarks that these gatherings are 'different from therapy. They are not there to talk about their problems, they are there to talk about Shakespeare, but if they want to voice their experiences and feelings: great. If not: Great.' She also indicates that participants comment that 'Shakespeare often says things we're not able to say. He lets us express what we're feeling but cannot say.' Like other Shakespeare and veterans gatherings, this ensemble uses theatre games and warm-up exercises to build camaraderie, encourage movement and eye contact and to spark the bountiful laughter that often infuses these sessions.⁹⁵

While there are many activities that can support veterans, drama often leads to impressive results as van der Kolk learned many years ago,

> In 1988 I was still treating three veterans with PTSD whom I'd met at the VA, and when they showed a sudden improvement in

their vitality, optimism, and family relationships, I attributed it to my growing therapeutic skills. Then I discovered that all three were involved in a theatrical production.[96]

The skills needed to perform on stage as part of an ensemble correlate with activities that support those facing the challenges associated with PTS(D). None of these groups demonstrate what Todd Landon Barnes terms 'the Perils of Redemptive Performance'.[97] Instead, they encourage the breathwork, the bodily and communal engagements, and the challenges that help offset the trauma faced by many veterans. While Shakespeare may not resonate for everyone, the participants in these groups often find that 'the play's the thing' that facilitates their personal growth.[98]

6

'The rich advantage of good exercise'

Physicality, art and mindfulness in prison Shakespeare

Shakespeare in prison programmes thrive in several countries. While the Covid-19 pandemic halted in-person engagements, many practitioners, participants and alumni remained closely engaged in this work. During both abnormal circumstances and more typical times, individual groups vary in their design and implementation, but mutual respect, commitment, flexibility, collaboration and integrative approaches to their endeavours characterize the most successful Shakespeare programmes in prisons.[1] While I will focus largely on the recognizably sensory aspects of these undertakings, the congruent cultivation of less tangible qualities such as kindness, caring, humanity and the community-building resonate throughout these carceral and alumni gatherings and often result from sensorial activities. Laura Bates makes it clear how prevalent sensory deprivation can be in carceral environments, particularly in solitary confinement, where she did much of her Shakespearean work,

> Like other supermax units across the country, the SHU [Secured Housing Unit] was designed as a unit of sensory deprivation . . .

It's not that there are no senses engaged, but the sensations are monotonous: the same few voices you hear across the range every day, the same gray concrete walls. Those who are lucky enough to have a TV say that, over time, staring at the same programs day after day becomes every bit as monotonous as staring at the gray walls. The only human touch is the cold steel and leg chains placed on you by the officers. Even the meals are required by law, to be bland. Forget about spices; any identifiable flavors are prohibited.[2]

For many of those involved in these carceral Shakespearean activities, such theatrical-based interactions helped them maintain and rediscover a sense of humanity eroded by the sensory deprivation and other harsh aspects of prison. Asia and Sharie from Shakespeare in Prison (SIP), for instance, each remarked in similar words that unlike most prison interactions, this programme allowed them to 'be who they are', even when 'the person they thought they were was gone'.[3] They also discovered 'new sides' to themselves and found themselves to be 'new human beings'. Sharie explained that SIP provided the opportunity 'to be yourself for five hours, not who you need to be to get through prison'.[4] Such comments are common among those involved in these undertakings, even those who join them hesitantly. Kelly, for instance, reported that she was angry for her first year in SIP and planned to drop out, but later apologized for her behaviour and remained involved both within prison and after release.

A desire for continuing education is also a key factor guiding those involved in these programmes, whether as facilitators or participants. Typically, those leading and teaching in Shakespeare in prison programmes have considerable theatrical training, education and experience. Many of them pursue additional education in related fields.[5] Some of the incarcerated participants also attain degrees or further education either while in prison or after their release. Since Shakespeare is often new and challenging for many of those engaged in these initiatives, grappling with these plays often leads to a sense of accomplishment for all involved. Additional 'why Shakespeare' questions frequently emerge in these endeavours and some of the answers will be presented here.[6] Curt L. Tofteland addresses the complexities of connecting Shakespeare with incarcerated actors in his 2023 STA Master Class materials,

Each day in our work sessions, we ask ourselves, 'Why Shakespeare now?' We engage Shakespeare's plays with questions that reflect our priorities, confusions, uncertainties, and urgent concerns. We produce Shakespeare that is fully alive in this present moment and rich in meaning for ourselves and our contemporary audiences. We do not foist on our marginalized communities the host of negative western values that have accumulated around Shakespeare.[7]

Regardless of the understandable challenges directed at Shakespeare currently, the physical and emotional benefits for the diverse participants in these groups figure prominently in testimonials, studies and other evaluative markers applied to Shakespeare in prison undertakings. Given the levels of trauma encountered in carceral environments and in the life experiences of those incarcerated, there are significant overlaps with the circumstances and practices for Shakespeare and veterans programmes, but there are also important differences.

SIP has worked with both male and female prisoners and brings both groups together in their alumni events, which began in 2018. When I met with SIP alumni members in 2022, Erric joined both the electronic and virtual conversations. He spoke at length about his preparation for playing Gloucester in *King Lear*, which included wearing a blindfold throughout the day, except while eating.[8] Remarkably, Erric discovered a cane in the prison which he used to help acclimate to Gloucester's status after being blinded. At the Detroit gathering, everyone insisted that 'finding' such an item randomly in a carceral setting was unprecedented. Erric's personal decision to embody Gloucester's physical limitations as much as possible illustrates one of the ways that these Shakespearean endeavours encourage participants to explore a variety of physical and emotional circumstances and facilitate a better understanding of distinctive viewpoints. While not everyone would agree, Erric finds Shakespeare particularly helpful in as an inspiration for SIP, 'At a party, Shakespeare would be the DJ, who would have the rhythm and beat we march to. No better way of finding the beat we dance to. He would also bring the cookies. Everyone enjoys all the different cookies Shakespeare brings.' Not surprisingly, from this perspective, several SIP alumni reported that Shakespeare 'got them through covid'.

Several SIP alumni indicated that they could (perhaps) focus on rapper Kendrick Lamar instead of Shakespeare, but Randy, who has performed with both SBB and SIP, believes that the 'intellectual challenge' of Shakespeare provides critical thinking skills, 'deep diving' and 'brain exercises' that are difficult to find in a carceral environment. Others, such as Nick and Jay, found that the group's theatre games, ice breakers, performances and honest discussions, showed sides of their fellow inmates they never saw otherwise. Jay added that 'you haven't done Shakespeare until you've helped a man into a dress'. Within SIP, some of these participants were actors, while some worked on sets and costumes. Regardless of their contribution, everyone had an equal voice.

SIP is currently preparing a volume about their work on *Richard III* for publication, which they hope will reach a broad audience.[9] In their proposal for the book, one SIP member states, 'We get to make these plays our own because we bring our own perspectives to 'em. No one has to tell us the answers, because we take 'em from our own lives.'[10] Jean Trounstine, one of the pioneers of Shakespeare in prison makes a related point; she always based her programs on 'classic texts', so that her incarcerated actors could take ownership of material often wrongly seen as out of their grasp.[11]

As with Shakespeare initiatives in other communities, carceral Shakespearean practice includes breathwork. There are many such practical commonalities among these diverse groups – theatrical practice typically involves considerable physicality and that is true in these instances as well. At least two Shakespeare in prison facilitators, Hulugappa Kattimani in Mysore, India, and Scott Jackson in Indiana, integrate yoga extensively into their carceral engagements.[12] Jackson has also offered in person and Zoom yoga practice techniques to members of the Shakespeare in Prisons Network (SiPN), the Shakespeare Theatre Association (STA) and the Shakespeare Association of America (SAA). Since yoga focuses on breath, mindfulness and attention to the integration of body and spirit, it develops practices associated with addressing trauma as well as a range of the goals sought through Shakespeare in prison programs.[13]

Claire Szabo-Cassella explicitly links Shakespeare and yoga in her 2016 volume *Shakespeare's Yoga*.[14] Szabo-Cassella, who has experience as an actor as well as a yoga instructor and practitioner,[15] maintains that these two spheres intersect significantly, 'Thanks to my yoga practice I better comprehend the crucial importance of Shakespeare's core themes and spiritual wisdom, especially his recurring reminder on the integrity of self.'[16] Much of her writing elaborates on the correlations she finds between Shakespeare's plays and the tenets of yoga found in the works of Pantanjali, whom she terms the 'father of yoga',[17]

> Each Shakespearean play, like every yoga practice, is an open-ended opportunity to encounter the story of our life as just a play unfolding. The ego-directed self, with its panache for theatricality and drama, makes being true to the higher Self noble work, just the opposite of self-serving. Because when we're true to who we really are, we act with a heightened awareness of our every thought, word, and action and their effects on our lives and others . . . our interconnectedness.[18]

Szabo-Cassella's thematic emphasis on correlations between Shakespearean drama and yoga incorporates references to many plays, including, tragedies such as *Hamlet*, *King Lear* and *Romeo and Juliet*; comedies such as *Twelfth Night*, *As You Like It* and *Much Ado About Nothing*, and a representation of the histories, namely, the first Henriad tetralogy. Each chapter links one or more plays with a yogic principle, as these chapter titles demonstrate: 'Bramacharya as Reflected in *Romeo and Juliet*' (she defines Bramacharya as 'Moderation and Balance'); 'Shakespeare's Use of Violence to Highlight Ahimsa' ('ahimsa' denoting 'nonviolence'); and 'Aparigraha [or nonpossessiveness] as Reflected in *Macbeth*'.[19] While there is much in this book that might appeal to those with prior knowledge of yoga and/or Shakespeare, the author insists this is not a prerequisite.

> Shakespeare and yoga both offer benefits to even the absolute beginner on the very first encounter. Our bodies and minds are hardwired to benefit from all forms of yoga: conscious movement (*asana*), breathing exercises (*pranayama*), and the self-improvement that comes from exploring the human experience from a spiritual perspective (*svadbyaya*). And as with Hamlet (a yoga philosopher in the extreme), asking ourselves the big questions – Who's there? What if? Who Am I? To be or not to be? – comes naturally when given the inspiration, time, and space to do so.[20]

While there is room to question how one determines what is 'hardwired' and 'comes naturally', the queries and physical practices she mentions frequently come into play during Shakespeare in prison gatherings. SBB creates its 'restorative circles of reconciliation', sometimes referred to as circles of truth, around principles emerging from four central questions: 'Who am I?' 'What do I love?' 'How will I live my life knowing I will die?' and 'What is my gift to humankind?'[21] SBB also spends significant time focusing on breath, heartbeat, and diverse kinesthetic activities.[22] Many prison groups raise similar questions, whether or not they connect them directly with yoga or the physical practices they incorporate in their sessions.

Jackson has studied yoga within an Anglo-American environment,[23] while Kattamani lives and works in Mysore, a traditional yoga center.[24] Kattamani incorporates yoga and studio arts into his dramatic regimen,[25] and Jackson brings yogic breathing, movement and focus into his Shakespearean practice. At Westville Correctional Facility, where Jackson has been convening Shakespearean gatherings for several years, he also guides many of the same participants through Kundalini exercises. Breathing, movement and mindfulness work effectively to reduce the effects of long-term trauma while facilitating participants' exploration and development of new habits and practices, whether connected with yoga or in other areas. Encouraging participants to imagine and test out new beliefs, understandings and ways of being, in conjunction with a range of physical, artistic and intellectual activities, holds a central place in theatrical projects for incarcerated individuals.

Registered yoga teacher David Emerson and licensed clinical psychologist Elizabeth Hopper from the Center for Trauma & Embodiment (CFTE) at the Justice Resource Institute (JRI) in Massachusetts discuss their work incorporating yoga into trauma treatment in a book containing forewords by trauma specialist Peter A. Levine and psychotherapist and yoga teacher Stephen Cope[26] as well as an introduction by trauma specialist Bessel van der Kolk.[27] In their book, they describe the ways that yoga can be a central component in the treatment of trauma:

> At the Trauma Center at Justice Resource Institute (JRI), a world-renowned center for the research and teaching of trauma, we have introduced trauma-sensitive yoga as an adjunctive treatment for

trauma survivors. We view trauma-sensitive yoga as a way to make peace with your body, to learn through experience that your body can be effective again, and to reclaim your body as your own. We also believe that the lessons learned through trauma-sensitive yoga can translate into a more generalized acceptance of, and trust in, one's own self.[28]

They also recognize that practitioners need to be respectful of the needs and boundaries of those recovering from trauma,[29] including a common discomfort with touch and the necessity for both gentleness and self-determination.[30]

> Trauma survivors need to find ways to be in their bodies in a gentle, nurturing way. What trauma-sensitive yoga offers that is distinct from many other physical practices is a structured, supportive, and self-paced medium for survivors to make choices in relation to their bodies and their experiences that are kind, gentle, and caring – all of the things that were missing during the trauma.[31]

While neither Jackson or Kattimani are associated with JRI, their practices draw from congruent principles and help illustrate why many practitioners, like Lisa Danylchuk, who works simultaneously with yoga and trauma studies, believe that these realms 'balance' and 'complement' each other in ways that are 'sustainable, skilled, and embodied' by 'combining a deep focus on the mind with movement'.[32]

As the collaboration between Emerson and Hopper and other partnerships between scientists and theatrical practitioners suggest, there is considerable interest in determining the best way to integrate scientific understanding with the kinds of physical and emotional practices being offered to trauma survivors. Ann Swanson, for example, completed a Master's degree in yoga therapy at the Maryland University of Integrative Health and published *Science of Yoga*,

> to spark more curiosity and discussion about the science of yoga, and lead to more inspired yoga practitioners and professionals, more rigorous research, [and] more public policies that encourage yoga in schools and healthcare.[33]

Swanson's detailed, illustrated guide to the anatomical, physiological, cognitive and emotional facets of yoga helps explain why some Shakespearean practitioners include such practices in their dramatic endeavours in prison. In an extensive question and answer section, she provides information that is pertinent to such undertakings, such as, 'How can yoga help my mental well-being?'[34] In her response, she describes how people can 'get stuck in a rajasic (the energy of agitation) or a tamasic (the energy of resistance) slump'.[35]

While Swanson is careful to remind readers that 'yoga alone is not enough to manage a serious mental health concern', she does argue that 'it can be an effective supplement to your medical and psychological care'.[36] She differentiates between 'the 'instinctual brain' (brain stem), which asks 'Am I safe?' the 'emotional brain' (limbic system), which asks, 'What am I feeling?' and the 'thinking brain' (frontal cortex), which asks 'What does this mean?'[37] She also makes observations similar to others found in the trauma studies used by practitioners involved with veterans and the incarcerated, for instance,

> Researchers believe that **somatic practices** (or movement practices that emphasize **perception** such as yoga asanas) are useful for helping people to **process trauma** without retriggering because they help us **release tension** held in the body.[38]

Swanson is also careful to acknowledge limits to our understanding of yoga in current scientific environments. Accordingly, for the question, 'Is there scientific evidence to support yogic concepts such as prana and the chakras?'[39] she responds that these yogic energetic phenomena do not figure in many of today's medical understandings of the body.

> Yoga research tends to focus on specific health conditions and practical benefits, rather than subtle energetics, as prana and chakras represent a way of knowing that doesn't necessarily translate directly to a straightforward analysis of biology. Some people, for example, claim that the flow of prana is in alignment with the nerves and the chakras with the glands, but there is no scientific evidence to support this. It may be that before dissection showed us where these structures were, yogis felt them working in their bodies. It is also possible that we are still limited by our

current instruments and will one day have the tools to locate and measure prana.[40]

Despite such uncertainties, Swanson's book serves as a valuable guide for those seeking more information about the way yoga interacts with the body and demonstrates how practices integrating mindfulness and physicality can be beneficial in the Shakespeare in prison context.[41]

In a related field, psychologist Michael A. West has a number of publications regarding mindfulness and meditation, including an edited volume that suggests that meditation can be beneficial for many, including those living with the repercussions of trauma.

> The practice of meditation is a way of coming to experience more fully our moment-by-moment existence by encountering the mind directly. Meditation involves increasing awareness of the body (sensations), emotions, thoughts, the mind, and mental qualities (e.g. turgid, clear, focused). Through practice, the aim is for this awareness to be increasingly non-reactive, though more acute to events and experiences . . . It offers a means of opening to or connecting with all experience, whether positive, negative, or neutral, in a (relatively) unprocessed way . . . The aim is also to reduce suffering as a consequence of this greater openness, through reduced reactivity to experience, and increasing well-being.[42]

Providing heightened access to sensory experiences and reducing reactivity supports the aims and outcomes of the prison programmes considered here. Including meditation and/or yoga offers participants pathways towards changing their awareness of and response to their minds, bodies and emotions, while encouraging non-reactivity. Such practices can help redirect the residue left by the many traumatic experiences leading to and resultant from incarceration. Later, in the same volume, psychologist Antonio Raffone describes a range of germane cognitive and affective results emanating from meditative engagements,

> Meditation can be conceptualized as a family of practices regulating cognition and emotion, in which mental and related somatic events are influenced by a specific directing of attention

and awareness. As promulgated in several contemplative traditions, mental training based on meditation leads to enhanced cognitive and emotional regulation and to mental states characterized by reduced negative emotions and motives, and enhanced positive features and attitudes such as serenity, joy, acceptance, and compassion.[43]

Numerous additional studies confirm these results. Thus, while many Shakespeare in prison practitioners implement other kinds of physical and emotional activities in their programmes, there appear to be substantial potential benefits for those incorporating these practices in their theatrical work with incarcerated populations.

Additional facets of Kattimani's programme correlate with some recommendations in trauma studies and with practices included in some other prison initiatives. His prison drama contains a number of activities that precede and supplement theatrical exercises. His incarcerated thespians devote considerable time to studio arts. They have created an extensive body of material that they share with visitors to their carceral space in Mysore.[44] Occasionally, alumni from this drama group establish themselves as professional artists upon leaving confinement, but such occupational pathways are not the central objective of these activities. Instead, Kattimani recognizes the value inherent in the creative and sensorial aspects of these artistic endeavours, as well as the opportunity for those contending with incarceration to feel pride in accomplishing something individual and tangible that can be shared with family members and the community. Some of those involved in drama also devote themselves to producing and performing the music accompaniment for the group's theatrical presentations. In short, there are multiple avenues for creative expression explored by various members of the ensemble.[45]

Related opportunities are embraced by many of the participants in the various prison groups associated with Rowan Mackenzie and Shakespeare UnBard. Mackenzie, who decided to devote herself full-time to her Shakespearean engagements with incarcerated and other specialized populations after finishing her PhD at the University of Birmingham's Shakespeare Institute, now works closely with groups at several prisons and serves as a co-chair for the Shakespeare Institute's Shakespeare Beyond Borders initiative. Mackenzie is involved with Shakespeare groups at a number of institutions under the Shakespeare UnBard 'umbrella'. In each instance, the ensembles embrace a model of shared governance, whereby Mackenzie provides one voice among many. All decisions are made collaboratively, with equal voting rights shared between all. The programme notes for the 2021 production of *Othello* indicates the value of this structure:

> We are a collaboratively owned theatre company where each and every one of us has an equal voice, an opportunity to make suggestions and a contribution to make not only our own role but to the play and the theatre company itself. This provides a few hours a week where those in the company can feel like they are not imprisoned and that they are valued actors.[46]

During the autumn of 2021, I was able to visit an *Othello* rehearsal and then a performance by the Emergency Shakespeare ensemble, housed within HMP Stafford, a facility designated for men convicted of sexual offenses. In addition to the many members of the acting company, there were a number of more broadly artistic and musical contributors to the production. The heavily illustrated programme lists a number of participants involved with creating sets, props, posters, costumes, programmes and music. It also includes the score for 'Adesio for Des' attributed to 'DKM' and 'DRM' in August of 2021. One ensemble member, Stuart, indicates that he 'came to the group to help out with the artistic side of things', but discovered that this creative 'journey' became 'an adventure: one that has set my sights beyond these walls'[47] Cal, another member of Emergency Shakespeare, speaks to how critical this ensemble has been to his life,

> I never thought I would come to prison and many of the directions my life was going in were shattered by my sentence. I lost my opportunities to flourish and my means for creativity and self-expression. I also lost my family and many friends. What I found was a group of people in similar circumstances who were willing to give time, space and attention – to help me translate some of my traumas and emotions into theatre. To create something together that speaks a little about life, love and loss and the journeys we go on and the stories we tell together.[48]

Cal offers a vision whereby others in need can share similar experiences for their own benefit and for those who experience these artistic and theatrical creations,

I hope that more people are blessed with the opportunity that I've had and that more of us can work together to create these spaces and enable the voiceless and those who never had a chance to turn some of their past and potential into art. For all of our sakes. I hope that you enjoy your stay in our prison and as a part of our little theatre, our sanctuary and our canvas.[49]

The participants I encountered on my two visits made similar comments.

As indicated, some scholars have expressed concerns about the potential harm caused by what Todd Landon Barnes terms 'redemptive' Shakespeare practices within what he calls the 'white Christian Shakespeare complex'.[50] Courtney Lehmann asks whether 'Shakespeare is a coercive force in prison programs',[51] while Barnes suggests that these endeavours can 'serve or reflect larger projects of neoliberalism'.[52] I have never heard such sentiments shared by participants or alumni of these programmes. Rob Pensalfini, who has extensive experience with prison Shakespeare in Australia, discusses the potential for harm or coercion in such circumstances, but concludes that these kinds of problems are 'rare'.[53]

Participation is, of course, voluntary, so any incarcerated people with hesitation about these endeavours can readily distance themselves from involvement. Many of the programmes included here have participated in formal studies to determine their effectiveness. Pensalfini devotes an extensive chapter to 'The Claims of Prison Shakespeare'.[54] On their website, SIP provides a 2016–17 case study and 2020 Follow-up Report on their activities.[55] These assessments indicate long-term benefits associated with SIP, mirroring the results reported by similar groups.[56]

Neither Kattimani nor Mackenzie describes themselves as art or music therapists (and are not trained or licensed). Nevertheless, when they include such creative activities in their prison initiatives, they align their activities with practices suggested for those working in therapeutic relationships with traumatized individuals.[57] Cathy A. Malchiodi, for example, encourages art therapists to include a range of art forms in their work, such as 'drawing, movement, sound, improvisation, play, and storytelling'.[58] She asserts that 'it is this integrative experience that can make a difference in clients' ability to more quickly and effectively address traumatic stress and engage their own healing processes', and she offers her book as a 'framework for arts-based approaches to traumatic stress that are based not only in neurobiology, but also in our growing understanding of culturally relevant healing practices that are found only in the arts'.[59] Jamie Marich's book *Process, NOT Perfection: Expressive Arts Solutions for Trauma Recovery* makes similar claims, as do other expressive arts practitioners.[60]

Lukasz M. Konopka, senior executive director of Illinois' Spectrum for Integrative Neuroscience explains the scientific basis for the success of integrative approaches for many types of learning, including those activities that help redress trauma,

> Spatial summation indicates that cellular learning occurs most efficiently with converging multisensory input, which, from the standpoint of human behavior, can be used to understand memory establishment. For instance, when we learn using only one sensory modality, such as vision, it takes more time and effort to master the task and form a memory; however, if we have learned using two modalities, such as vision and audition, the converging sensory will expedite our learning.[61]

Konopka further explains these phenomena, relating it to the way that people learn to ride a bicycle,

> The brain initially requires multiple networks when leaning [sic] novel cognitive tasks, but eventually it trims superfluous networks, focusing its activity and optimizing its performance. One of the best examples is learning to ride a bicycle, a task that initially requires significant brain effort, but over time becomes simple and natural. Although most of us have learned to ride a bike, we would find it nearly impossible to describe the individual steps that led to our success because our learning resulted from numerous unconscious structural and biochemical changes, i.e., neuroplasticity.[62]

Art therapists Vija J. Lusebrink and Lisa D. Hinz further delineate how different parts of the brain respond to varying stimuli, using these variations in support of what they term the expressive therapies continuum (ETC), 'with its conceptual approach to the multilevel nature of visual expression [which] facilitates the individualization of art therapy treatment strategies with trauma patients'. They divide the therapeutic experience into four domains: 'Kinesthetic/Sensory (K/S) Level', the 'Perceptual/Affective (P/A) Level', the 'Cognitive/Symbolic (C/Sy) Level' and the 'Creative (Cr) Level' of visual expression. This conceptual model describes how the brain uses sensorimotor, formal visual, autobiographical and abstracted cognitive processing, as well as the synthesized product of these, to heal from trauma through art.[63] In somewhat less technical language, Johanne Hamel describes somatic art therapy as something that

> provides access to soma [physical reality as it is experienced from within the person] through two-dimensional or three-dimensional representations (drawing, painting, clay, etc.) of the physical sensation felt subjectively. This access makes one aware of intense emotional states embedded in one's sensations, allows catharsis and facilitates communication of these experiences.[64]

From this perspective, there are innumerable reasons why the physicality of art can help facilitate the alleviation of trauma.

While Kattimani, Mackenzie and other Shakespeare in prison practitioners do not present themselves as therapists of any kind, it can be helpful to understand how facilitating movement, music and art can be beneficial within such environments.[65] Tofteland identifies as 'an artist who does work that is therapeutic and not a therapist who does work that is artistic. I never forget the difference',[66] and most of those I have met who are working in carceral settings concur.[67] At the same time, the positive results emanating from the incorporation of diverse artistic activities into these dramatic spaces suggest that such practices strengthen the ability of these programmes to support their participants in multiple ways. Since these endeavours simultaneously incorporate breath, movement and mindfulness exercises, numerous avenues are available for reducing trauma and developing new habits of mind, body and community-forming.

During the Covid-19 pandemic, when in-person meetings became impossible for an extended period, the commitment and resourcefulness of these arts practitioners and their respective communities demonstrated itself in innumerable ways. The 2020 SiPN conference (SiPC 4), originally scheduled for an October in-person gathering sponsored jointly by Shakespeare at Notre Dame and the Folger Shakespeare Institute, transformed into a weekly virtual gathering running from early November 2020 until late April 2021. The sessions included an extensive array of speakers from all aspects of these projects. They were recorded and remain available online,[68] now forming an invaluable archive for those interested in germane topics.[69]

SiPN was founded in 2012 by Curt L. Tofteland of Shakespeare Behind Bars (SBB), in partnership with Shakespeare at Notre Dame's Peter Holland and Scott Jackson, in order to bring together prison practitioners and participants who typically worked in isolation from each other, often not even knowing who else was involved in similar work. Prior to the pandemic, the group met in person biennially, most recently at the Old Globe Theatre in San Diego. Separately during lockdown, Jonathan Shailor, of Wisconsin's Shakespeare in Prison Project, held weekly virtual play readings with far-flung SiPN participants for several months, until highly publicized shootings in Kenosha diverted the attention of many of those involved. These virtual activities ensured that practitioners and alumni from many of these programmes were able to keep in touch and remain focused on their goals during the pandemic's curtailment of in person activities.

In addition, some SiPN members were able to distribute materials to incarcerated participants, who spent the pandemic in comparative isolation, typically in environments where the virus remained a continual threat. Frannie Shepherd-Bates and her team from SIP, for example, mailed written materials to the incarcerated Shakespeareans who were unable to meet in person,

> Though we cannot work with incarcerated ensemble members in person at this time, we have found a way to sustain our connection by sending ensemble members Shakespeare-based activity packs to help alleviate their isolation, boredom, and fear. Each activity pack consists of a piece of Shakespeare's text and prompts for intellectual stimulation, creative expression, and self-reflection.[70]

Erric, the SIP alumnus who described playing Gloucester, indicated that these packets were the equivalent of 'manna from heaven' during the 'nuclear bomb' of the pandemic, helping the performers continue to practice, but on their own terms, despite the isolation forced by Covid-19.

Mackenzie also created packets designed for inmates of different skill levels that were able to reach these populations during the constraints associated with the pandemic, a project which attracted significant attention and resulted in these materials being distributed throughout the British prison system, as reported in the Birmingham press,

> In response to the crisis she created a series of Shakespeare distance learning packs which are allowing inmates to continue the education programmes she has established, as well as widening participation to many more prisoners. As Rowan confirmed, 'providing our inmates with activities to keep their minds occupied is crucial to their mental health, now more so than ever.' So successful have Rowan's initiatives been that Her Majesty's Prison and Probation Services have made her activity packs a formal part of their 'In Cell Activity' resources [including artistic prompts] available to all prisons, and her work forms a key part of the Prisoner Learning Alliance COVID-19 response resources.[71]

Mackenzie also received numerous accolades for this work, which was honored by several groups across the UK,

> Following an Award for Best Provocation for her lecture about her pioneering work, delivered at the Teaching Early Modern Drama conference at the University of Warwick, Rowan won an Outstanding Individual Award from the Prisoner Learning Alliance in 2019, following 11 separate nominations from HMP Gartree (the largest ever number of nominations for any single winner). Further recognitions were not long in coming. The Worshipful Company of Educators created a new category of award to honour her work, identifying her as Highly Commended Prison Educator of the Year 2019. The Company quickly followed this up by awarding her the Trust's main prize, the 2020 Inspirational Educator Award for 'Teaching Shakespeare in Challenging Settings'.'[72]

SiPN pandemic gatherings made it clear that practitioners' inability to meet in person with their incarcerated participants was stressful and disheartening to all involved. Those attending the virtual conference activities and its corollary anti-racism sessions gained invaluable knowledge while strengthening this far-flung community, but the strain of being excluded from the carceral bases of these programmes took a deep toll on everyone.

Some in-person meetings have resumed by 2022, while other groups continue to prepare for future gatherings inside these facilities. In certain environments, Shakespeare in prison alumni have been able to convene, even though practitioners cannot directly support those currently incarcerated. In some locations, 'outside' meetings for those formerly involved in Shakespeare in prison programs are not allowed after release. Participants and facilitators are barred from contacting each other. In Michigan, however, SIP and other groups, including SBB, have permission to continue their work in person and electronically once participants have returned to the community.[73] SIP reports that this opportunity has not only supported ensemble members who are adjusting to their new lives, but that this continued communication also has allowed staff to hear about the value of the materials that were sent inside during the pandemic,

> We are not able to be in direct communication with incarcerated ensemble members, but SIP alums who received activity packs and have since been paroled are enthusiastic about the project. The packs, they say, are fun and engaging. Simply receiving them in the mail reminds them that they are still part of the SIP ensemble – and that we on the outside have not forgotten them.[74]

Notably, while inside their respective prisons, the male and female SIP ensemble members never meet each other. In a recent outdoor gathering in Detroit, however, a group of alumni reported that they were very aware that these different groups were engaged in similar activities and often felt themselves in congenial competition with each other.[75]

SBB alumni also frequently interact with each other, and several of them have attended SiPN events in person and online. While the pandemic forced many Shakespeare in prison activities to stop, it also facilitated many new, virtual activities. SBB, for example, presented numerous installments of their juvenile program over Zoom.[76] Tofteland was also able to keep many SBB alumni involved with each other through the Zoom-based Shax BEYOND Bars network. Those who have participated in SBB programs now often live widely distant from each other, but Shax BEYOND Bars enables them to keep in touch and continue their work together. As Tofteland also notes, life after incarceration frequently makes 'prison look like a cakewalk', so regular electronic communication offers needed support during what are often challenging times.[77] Accordingly, while prison practitioners deeply regret their inability to meet with incarcerated Shakespeareans during the pandemic, these conditions opened time and space for this online community which has been deeply beneficial for many SBB alumni.

Tofteland has also been working closely with SBB alumnus Sammie Byron before and during the pandemic. I am fortunate to be able to host Byron on Emory University's campus regularly, in collaboration with my faculty colleagues from Oxford College at Emory University, namely, prison educator and Common Good Atlanta co-founder Sarah Higinbotham and prison theatre practitioner Nick Fesette. Byron has given a number of public talks at Emory and makes frequent visits to my classroom, sometimes in conjunction with Tofteland and/or Jackson. Several of my undergraduate and graduate students were able to join both Byron and Tofteland at an SBB training workshop sponsored by the Rome, Georgia Shakespeare Festival. More recently, Byron and Jackson met with my students in class and during a series of weekend events featuring Byron's autobiographical show *Othello's Tribunal* and a conversation between Byron and actor Harry Lennix at the Atlanta Shakespeare Tavern.[78]

These events have been revelatory and memorable. They enable students to learn more about the ways that SBB transforms lives and leads students to become more familiar with issues surrounding the prison industrial complex. Byron engages closely with the students, performs monologues, encourages their participation and frankly discusses his tumultuous life journey and SBB's role in his pathway back into society. Byron's wife frequently accompanies him to class and students report that these visits are highlights of their college careers. Two of the graduate students who studied with Byron and Tofteland in Rome cite that experience as a turning point in their own professional engagement. Along with another graduate student colleague, they formed the Shakespeare-based Puck Project for children experiencing homelessness, that is discussed in another chapter, after witnessing the power of SBB.

Byron has moved into employment counseling at-risk young adults following his experiences with Emory students and he continues to share the power of SBB with other communities. In addition to his teaching, dramatic and professional engagements, he mentors other SBB members who have been released from prison.[79] Continuing to work closely with Tofteland on *Othello's Tribunal* and other endeavours, Byron quotes Shakespeare regularly when confronting decisions and questions in his life and credits SBB with his ability to thrive despite being incarcerated for several decades.

Scott Jackson's work with and on behalf of currently and previously incarcerated Shakespeareans also continues to evolve. His capstone project at the University of London's Royal Central School of Speech & Drama, for instance, focused on prison Shakespeare, and he concurrently completed his Kundalini yoga teacher certification which he now employs, in conjunction with Shakespeare, at Indiana's Westville Correctional Facility. His capstone plots his journey of discovery as a producer, practitioner and educator during the evolution of the Shakespeare in Prison conference from its beginning in 2013 through to the lengthy electronic meetings spanning from November 2020 until late April 2021 and continuing with an ongoing monthly series of Zoom conversations and workshops about anti-racism. Grounding his analysis in theoretical discussions by writers such as Paulo Freire,[80] bell hooks, Ibram X. Kendi, David Takacs and adrienne maree brown, Jackson describes how his educational pathway was crafted to ensure that his work concurs with harm-reduction principles[81] and that he carefully avoids practices often associated with 'the dreaded White Saviour' [who upholds] supremacist systems and validates 'white privilege'.[82] In concurrence with Takacs' pedagogical perspectives regarding 'individual epistemology' and 'collective social action', Jackson situates his current work within his professional and educational trajectory,

> [Takacs'] words resonated with me as I am a believer in the power of the arts as a catalyst for positive social change, and their unique ability to foster the untapped potential found in overlooked and often traumatised spaces, most notably within the adult and juvenile correctional facilities in which I teach.[83]

He further remarks on his long-lasting belief in the transformative possibilities of artistic engagement,

> In fact, [my] impetus for embarking on a career in the performing arts, first as a practitioner and later as a creative producer and pedagogue, was my core belief in the inherent value of the arts as a tool for self-actualisation, community-building, and creative expression[84].

Jackson gives an unflinching analysis of his role in the development of SiPC 1–4 and readily admits times he and other members of the planning committee 'were wrong', such as when initially resisting a new schedule to keep the conference from coinciding with the polarizing 2020 US presidential election and when being comparatively slow to recognize and increase the BIPOC, female and returned citizen representation among the speakers and attendees at the conference.[85] As indicated, the electronic archive of the conference provides a remarkable record of a series of invaluable presentations from multiple perspectives, an accomplishment which led to the conference coordinators being honoured by the Shakespeare Association of America.[86] Jackson's capstone analysis of this endeavour, moreover, offers a humbling and insightful look at the ways that Shakespeare in prison work can transform the facilitators as well as those involved as participants, funders, and audience members.

Kate Powers also provides a powerful and provocative account of her theatrical involvement in the criminal justice system as part of her Master's degree work at the University of Idaho.[87] Powers has a lengthy history of facilitating Shakespearean performances at Sing Sing and other carceral institutions. Some of her masters writing details her efforts in support of the Redeeming Time Project (RTP), a new prison programme she started in Minnesota that was eventually stalled by the pandemic and by intensive caregiving responsibilities that led to her relocation. Powers aptly labels her experience as 'Exit, Pursued by a Pandemic'.

Like many fellow SiPN practitioners, Powers crafts an inclusive environment, as she describes,

> In the prison, we use a circle process, borrowed from restorative justice and indigenous practices, to explore and then collectively

make decisions about how we work together and what we want to do next; we work to ensure that we hear from every voice in the room. It takes more time than issuing a directorial fiat, but it's not that difficult; it's beautiful, inclusive, empowering, and restorative. Let's try. Let's fail. Reflect, reflect again, reflect better.[88]

Powers has honed her practice with considerable training in acting, directing and social justice, including courses with Shakespeare & Co. and the Shakespeare Institute, as well as engagement with RTA's prison programing. In conjunction with the SiPN conference, she partnered with Jackson and Melinda Cooper to begin a regular anti-racism group, which met monthly, starting in June 2020. In Powers' words, this undertaking

> has allowed me to test drive my deeper understanding around structural racism ... we have focused our attention on the various components of the criminal justice system, from differential policing through racial bias in prosecution to the racism embedded even in the process of re-entry for a returned citizen. We invited returned citizens into the conversation as we spoke about racism behind prison walls, how prison theatre practitioners may need to revise their curriculum, and the differential impacts of COVID-19 on the incarcerated population, from the impossibility of social distance inside maximum security, to the deprivations inflicted by denying parents visits with their children to the suspension of all activities and higher ed programs behind the walls during this fraught moment.[89]

The combination of a pandemic and broad calls for racial reckoning in society at-large has led to considerable reflection on behalf of those engaged in these activities, particularly since in-person gatherings were curtailed. At the same time, some of Powers' words preceding lockdown still resonate with the ongoing goals of these initiatives, whether taking place in person or virtually. Her description of the beginning of RTP, for instance, conforms with the precepts guiding many of these programmes both before and after the pandemic,

> I introduce myself to the men. I tell them the work is not about turning convicted felons into actors, though occasionally that

happens.⁹⁰ The work is about using the arts as a tool for social and cognitive change, leveraging theatre to improve communication skills, critical thinking, spur robust debate, self-reflection, stress release, discipline, teamwork, delayed gratification, thoughtful criticism, and most importantly to me, play. So many of the men with whom I have worked behind the walls had their childhoods stolen or interrupted by neglect, abuse, abandonment, deprivation. This work is art giving people tools with which they can change their lives and head in new directions, skills that they can take 'over the wall'.⁹¹

Like other practitioners, Powers shares stories about the gratitude expressed by those who participate in these activities, even those who enter with hesitation. She recounts the story of one such reluctant Shakespearean,

Remember Bob, who was sure the workshop would kill him? He forgets a word in his soliloquy from *Hamlet*, but substitutes a word with the same number of syllables, so that he holds the rhythm of the verse even as he stumbles . . . Afterwards, he approaches me, his eyes moist, to tell me that the class has changed his life: 'People keep asking me what happened to the grumpy old man'.⁹²

Such narratives are common. People behaving like 'white saviors' are difficult to identify in these settings, but the commitment of the practitioners here, who are consistently learning, engaging and reflecting on what is working and what needs adjustment, remains prominent. Like Bridget McCarthy, who studied with SBB, then trained as a certified trauma and resilience practitioner by acquiring skills she shares with theatrical professionals across the United States, and Kate Kenney, who supplemented her extensive drama training and experience with an MS in criminal justice, Jackson, Powers and others continually sharpen and reassess their practices.

These practitioners often emphasize Shakespeare, but also include other dramatic pieces. Powers, for instance, provides a packet of monologues including material from Edgar Lee Masters' *Spoon River Anthology*, August Wilson's *Fences* and *Jitney* and James Baldwin's *The Fire Next Time* in conjunction with speeches from Shakespeare.⁹³ Many of these programmes draw from a breadth of dramatic pieces, including texts created by the participants themselves. Others encourage participants to bring other artistic creations into their practice, such as music, drawing, painting, clay and woodwork. Shakespeare in prison takes many forms, but those involved typically work from congruent perspectives.

To conclude this chapter, I will quote from SBB's 'Core Values/ Creed Statement' that sums up the goals of many Shakespeare in prison endeavours:

1. Develop a lifelong passion for learning, especially those participants who are at high risk of not completing or continuing their education;
2. Develop literacy skills (reading, writing, and oral communication), including those Participants who are classified as learning disabled and/or developmentally challenged;
3. Develop decision making, problem solving and creative thinking skills;
4. Develop empathy, compassion and trust;
5. Nurture a desire to help others;
6. Increase self esteem and develop a positive self image;
7. Take responsibility for the crime/s committed;
8. Become a responsible member of a group, community and family;
9. Learn tolerance and peaceful resolution of conflict;
10. Relate the universal human themes contained in Shakespeare's work to themselves, including their past experiences and choices, their present situation, and their future possibility;
11. Relate the universal themes of Shakespeare to the lives of other human beings and to Society at-large;
12. Return to society as a contributing member.[94]

From the accounts of many who participate in these activities, these goals are regularly met.

7

'The Open Ear of Youth'

Shakespeare through physical and expressive arts

Many of the Shakespeare groups described here are designed for children and young adults facing challenging circumstances. Some are deemed 'at risk', some have become entangled with the juvenile justice system, and others are experiencing homelessness. Some of these ensembles are long-standing initiatives, either as parts of larger organizations or as theatrical entities in their own right. They share common features in their incorporation of a variety of physical and creative forms into their practice and use these activities as ways to encourage self-knowledge and expression while providing the participants with opportunities to craft safe, healthy and productive paths for their lives. Shakespeare is only one part of these journeys and none of those included here present Shakespeare as a panacea for difficult life situations.

The newest is the Puck Project (PP), a summer initiative for children associated with Nicholas House, an Atlanta facility offering services to families contending with homelessness, notably without the common practice of separating family members. PP was created, designed and implemented by three Emory University English Department graduate students: Kelly Duquette, Mary Taylor Mann and John Gulledge. As they describe in an essay in *Early Modern Culture Online*, this programme, which began in 2018, emerged from their collective skills and experiences.[1] Duquette spent several years as an elementary educator with Teach for America, Mann holds an advanced degree in bioethics and Gulledge has a background in Shakespearean performance. After a series of talks and workshops by Tofteland and Byron of Shakespeare Behind Bars (SBB), the trio became interested by intersections between Shakespeare and social justice work.

Accordingly, they submitted several grant proposals in order to bring the Feast of Crispian (FoC) veterans' program leaders to campus for an intensive workshop. The FoC project attracted eager faculty and students from two of Emory's undergraduate colleges, one of which (Oxford College of Emory University) has a campus 40 miles from Atlanta and serves exclusively first- and second-year students. It is comparatively rare for Oxford students to come to the Atlanta campus for such a lengthy commitment, which suggests that the PP creators were tapping into an active interest at the university.[2]

After investigating possible community partners for their own emerging project and considering different potential populations to engage with, the PP team initially offered a four-week engagement at Nicholas House in 2018, followed by a 2019 intensive workshop, partially facilitated by Shakespearean scholar (and Emory PhD) Justin Shaw. Their desire to lengthen the session in subsequent years was thwarted due to the pandemic. In 2022, they were able to book a week-long residency, but a Covid-19 outbreak among the staff moved it to the shorter week encompassing the Independence Day holiday.

I was able to attend half of these most recent sessions, so here report firsthand, in addition to including information drawn from conversations, presentations and written material. While these sessions are shorter than many of Shakespearean initiatives in other domains, they provide valuable programming and give the leaders important experience, so the time commitment that is often key for some other populations is neither expected nor manageable. These Nicholas House young Shakespeareans would not be available for longer periods.

The programme, which has received funding from Emory's Jones Fund for Ethics and other internal sources, focuses on ethical engagement as well as Shakespearean involvement, teamwork, expressive arts and increased confidence. PP aims towards developing empathic imagination.³ As they describe this goal, they indicate,

> The purpose is not to instruct campers towards a certain kind of moral thinking, nor is it to pore endlessly over the many ethical conflicts that occur during Shakespeare's plays. Instead, we seek to create a space in which children are invited to address the ethical questions that surface in the act of performance.⁴

In practice, the group works through various modalities that engage cognitive, affective and sensory learning. Participants sing, paint, write, run, laugh, choose costumes, learn lines and discuss issues connected with the play (usually *A Midsummer Night's Dream*, but scenes from other plays creep in as well).

Connections between the drama and their own experiences often factor into the discussions and provide material for devised segments. Some exercises have the children on their feet, other times they are journaling, creating art or engaging with the play's story through exercises modeled after the popular word game Mad Libs.⁵ In 2022, most students presented Shakespeare scenes for their final performance piece, but one group offered a devised skit that emerged during their writing sessions. The leaders incorporate 'recent studies in psychology [that] elucidate the profound link between physical movement and emotional sensitivity':⁶

> The body experiences emotions via various physical sensations, postures, gesture, and expressions . . . From this body of research, Fuchs and Koch define and describe the phenomenon of embodied affectivity, or the circular relationship between emotion and physical motion.
>
> [. . .]
>
> The skills and capacities children acquire during the process of engaging and performing a play – building a community – collaborating to create and express ideas, using voice and body to communicate, acknowledging and addressing other's emotions, and managing one's own emotions – may be translated into emotional intelligence and recognition capacities that have ethical implications. Empathic imagination requires close attention to the lived experience of another person, the position of the self

in relation to that person, and the differences in perspective or point of view.[7]

PP's collaboration with Nicholas House has been successful during its initial iterations. As the graduate student leaders receive their doctorates and move on towards the next stages in their lives, they are hoping to continue work in this vein wherever they reside.

PP is not the only Shakespearean program in Atlanta designed for children who are currently experiencing or have previously experienced homelessness, however. Laura Cole, Education and Training Director at the Atlanta Shakespeare Company (ASC), reports two partnerships facilitating such endeavours: a five-year relationship with the Boyce L. Ansley School, a tuition-free private school for students in these circumstances, and a newly initiated collaboration with the Atlanta Children's Center, which provides services for children and families without stable accommodation. Both venues offer significant support for these children and their families, including trauma relief services, therapy, speech and language assistance and help with the underlying circumstances undermining their stability.[8]

In these two programmes, the ASC works with pre-K through early elementary students. Their modules draw from many impressive predecessors in this kind of engagement, such as Shakespeare & Co. Cole indicates that there are numerous goals for these partnerships, including demonstrating empathy by emphasizing language from the plays that shows empathy or lack of empathy; strengthening course skills, such as following directions; providing a more physical experience of language than a teacher might have time for; and modeling the long-term benefits of devoting structured time to a multifaceted project, in this case, reading and hearing the story, creating scenes and experiencing the pleasure of having teachers and family members enjoy their presentations. Cole suggests that Shakespeare lends itself to social, emotional learning, although she also remarks that introducing costumes into their sessions can be disruptive and raise issues about sharing.[9]

ASC strives to meet every child where they seem to be. Cole tells of one young Ansley student who only communicated by meowing during the first year of their residency there, but a couple of years later, the same child is comfortable participating more fully. They typically draw from *The Tempest* or *A Midsummer Night's Dream* for these sessions, with the Ansley students becoming more familiar with the plot and characters each year. They interweave physical exercises with vocal work and reading children's versions of the plays, although Cole finds that juvenile Shakespearean adaptations rarely include BIPOC characters.

Through *A Midsummer Night's Dream*, they engage the children with the magic, but they also introduce real-life issues, such as kids' struggles with their parents or adults arguing with each other. They include a lot of games to keep the children moving and spark their imaginations as they explore how the different characters in the play would walk, talk or be dressed. They feed the words to the children, who are not expected to memorize, and they encourage them to craft scenes incorporating the language, the songs and the actions they encounter in the story and in the lines provided to them.[10]

The ASC ensemble is always careful with their own language, so that they don't make promises they cannot definitely keep. 'See you next week', for example, may raise impossible expectations for children whose life experiences remain subject to possible changes.[11] ASC is a well-established company in Atlanta, however, so it is plausible that they will be able to continue in such endeavours with this population for many weeks – and years – to come, even if their student population inevitably changes.

Another noteworthy set of Shakespearean youth programs takes place through the Robinson Community Learning Center in South Bend, Indiana (a sister organization to Shakespeare at Notre Dame).[12] The Robinson Center is significant in its community engagement and considerable socio-economic, racial and religious diversity. It offers onsite programmes year-round as well as weekly classes in a range of Title 1 schools in the region.[13] Approximately 72 per cent of the youthful Shakespeareans who participate onsite qualify for free or reduced-price school lunches, while many other ensemble members are the children of University faculty or staff, who are often more financially secure.[14]

Drawing from such disparate sectors of the community leads to unexpected levels of diversity in these Shakespearean undertakings that are open to children from grades 3 through 12. The yearlong onsite programme costs $100 per student and no one has ever been turned away for the inability to pay. Christy Burgess, the talented actor, director and educator who oversees the Robinson Center's

Shakespeare programs, believes that theatre is one of the few 'equalizers' in life, 'When you are on stage it doesn't matter who your parents are, how much money they make, what school you go to, everyone is equal: public speaking is people's number one fear.'[15] While this optimistic evaluation may not always be true, the ongoing success of Robinson Shakespeare warrants attention.

They present at least two productions a year; younger students enact a shortened version of the play offered by the older actors. They learn a number of scenes and monologues, enter Shakespearean speech competitions, and participate in a 24-hour Shakespeare marathon for fundraising. In 2017, the older students' troupe was invited to England after they led warm-up exercises at the Shakespeare Theatre Association annual conference and attracted the attention of the Shakespeare Birthplace Trust. After raising the necessary financial resources, they were able to perform in Stratford-upon-Avon and enjoy theatre games on the stage at Shakespeare's Globe Theatre in London.[16] In this instance, the integration of participants across the socio-economic spectrum and the group's association with an affluent university helped support a memorable opportunity for a team of dedicated thespians.

When this programme began in 2008, critics voiced their skepticism about its prospects for success, but contrary to their expectations, it has thrived for many reasons. Both in the schools and at the Robinson Center, the Shakespeare group engages with students across multiple age cohorts, with different activities associated with each level. In the schools, for instance, younger children watch their older siblings present scenes and plays, so when they receive their opportunity to join in during the third grade, they are ready and excited. Similarly, since the smallest Shakespeareans do not stay overnight during the Shakespeare marathon, they are thrilled when they reach the age where they can remain involved throughout the event.

The older children guide and support the youngest ensemble members and the casting reflects the age and experience of the actors. In 2022's *Richard II*, for instance, enthusiastic fourth graders took on the roles of the gardeners, while the narcissistic king was played by an older member of the troupe, who energetically 'unboxed' a number of sweaters and other items emblazoned with his image, encompassing many poses. This allowed the young group to incorporate images from their own experiences with popular culture that corresponded with aspects of the text. The troupe performs plays from across the canon, but student requests to present *Titus Andronicus* have not yet been successful, due to concerns that parents might object to their child playing Lavinia.

The activities introduced to the Robinson company helps support what Burgess terms 'sneaky' pedagogy. One of their partner teachers, for example, requested that her students practice writing drawn from facts. Accordingly, the Robinson group made a list of the true things they could ascertain about Juliet from *Romeo and Juliet* and created a series of improvisational dialogues where various characters tried to dissuade the young woman from the life choices that lead to her death. The students had a lot to say when asked to write something about the experience. Typically, the children are not told (and do not ask) how long their written pieces should be, but since they become caught up in their roles, they generally produce lengthy pieces of prose, drawn from the 'facts' of the play. The concomitant physicality of acting further supports the more cognitive goals of many classrooms, in concordance with what award-winning educator Susan Hrach argues in her volume on *Minding Bodies: How Physical Space, Sensation, and Movement Affect Learning*.[17]

When asked the inevitable 'why Shakespeare?' question, Burgess contends that plays written by many classic authors, such as Eugene O'Neill or Arthur Miller, bring attention to the perspectives of those playwrights, but that Shakespeare is more malleable and introduces children to a range of possibilities on the stage and in life, 'I try to explain to the kids, it's like a blank coloring page where you can pass out the same coloring page to 100 different people and when they color it, it's all going to be different.'[18] For these groups of students, Shakespeare provides an extended experience of ensemble-building, growing confidence and multisensory learning through physicality, reading and collaboration. Burgess rejects any intimation of 'white savior' activities in this work with diverse participants, instead insisting on the equalizing quality of dramatic experience and the breadth of interpretation facilitated by Shakespeare. Burgess also works to shake up many common societal stereotypes, for example, by casting young women into 'tough guy' parts.

These children do not fit as easily into categories of endangerment as some other groups, but for many, their socioeconomic circumstances make their potential for academic success more precarious than some of their peers. Burgess, however, welcomes all comers with the same care, enthusiasm and high expectations. Whenever a teacher warns her about a particular student, she immediately asks that they be brought into the fold as quickly as possible. Shakespeare, in this environment, often leads to multifaceted success and community.

London's Intermission Youth Theatre predominantly serves teenagers and young adults, a slightly older population than PP or the Robinson Shakespeareans, but uses similar strategies and shares many goals.[19] Like the Robinson company, Intermission was founded in 2008, when Darren Raymond, who had already encountered various bumps in his life, was invited by Bishop Rob and Janine Gillion to become Intermission's artistic director at a church theatre in Knightsbridge.[20] The ensemble's website notes,

> We use Shakespeare as a mirror to young people's lives, tackling issues that are relevant and challenging, such as knife crime, gang violence, peer pressure, jealousy, rage, and relationships. Using IYT's techniques of re-imaging Shakespeare, the programme promotes literacy, improves behaviour, builds confidence, self-awareness, and communication skills.[21]

Intermission now engages with diverse young people, including those perceived as 'at risk', and youth offenders. In addition to their intensive ten-month-long ensemble, they also work with schools and pupil referral units (PRUs).[22] They use a variety of multisensory activities, mentoring and 'conversations regarding the young people's thoughts interests and issues they face'[23] in order to achieve the objectives they seek,

> Increased engagement with learning
> Improved literacy and communication skills
> Increased self-confidence & positivity
> Ability to demonstrate learnings in the form of a performance
> Increased knowledge of drama, theatre & Shakespeare
> Improved behaviour and self-awareness
> Greater understanding of empathy and understanding of others
> Links made with Intermission to provide ongoing support in order to build skills & reduce the risk of re-offending
> Willingness and confidence to sit Functional Skills for English 1 or 2[24]

Social justice is at the core of their activities, as their public statements make clear,

> Intermission Youth helps to transform disadvantaged young people living in deprivation and experiencing high levels of anti-social behaviour, family breakdown, dependency, and criminality. We believe that constant support, nurture, and care in a young person's life can give them the confidence and believe [sic] to make positive choices and change the course of their lives.[25]

Part of their techniques involve sometimes changing the plays in deliberate ways, such as in 2021's production of *Juliet and Romeo*, as the programme notes indicate,

> This evening you are going to be treated to an Intermission retelling of Shakespeare's most famous tragedy, *Juliet and Romeo*. The play, as the title suggests, has been reversed. Juliet has Romeo's lines and he has hers. Transposing them in this way adds something really interesting to this ancient text. We see Juliet exploring a more dominant side, connecting with her masculinity. Romeo is able to tap more into his vulnerability and express his emotions. As always, it was fascinating to hear the conversations and watch the improvisations during our weekly Saturday workshops, gaining a fresh perspective on what it's like to be young women and men in today's changing world.[26]

This role reversal appears to have sparked considerable enthusiasm among the cast and animated discussion by the audience.

Intermission's *M.S.N.D: A Shakespeare Remix* (2022) similarly presented segments of *A Midsummer Night's Dream* in a modern, urban context.[27] The characters, who bear Shakespearean names, begin speaking the lines from this play, as well as *Romeo and Juliet* and *Macbeth*, after ingesting a fictitious drug called MSND. They then adapt the original text with additional perspectives on addiction, parenthood, misogyny and sexual consent. The fairies serve as malicious enablers, but also help deflect some of the play's more uncomfortable moments, such as Helena offering herself as Demetrius's 'spaniel'.[28] This production also omits any intimation of sex between the drugged Titania and Bottom, although the queen does express her love for Bottom while the weaver is wearing an ass's head.

Like many of the adaptations described in this volume, this production involves considerable dance, movement and popular music, including several clips from Sam Cooke's song 'Cupid'.[29] It also plants Puck and Oberon in the audience at key moments in the drama to highlight their role as voyeurs on the young lovers' escapades. In the talk-back after the performance I attended, the cast emphasized the long-term involvement of many of Intermission's alumni in their ongoing activities, which clearly pleased all participants.

Raymond's friendship with Sir Mark Rylance led to the Oscar-winning former artistic director of Shakespeare's Globe serving as a trustee of the ensemble, a role he has taken on enthusiastically. This connection supported the development of an online Shakespearean monologue slam by members of the group, with feedback from a number of prominent British actors.[30] The ensemble created 'Shakespeare on Smartphone' videos for the London Short Film Festival. Intermission presents their Shakespearean endeavours in ways that can lead to both personal and professional advancement.

From Raymond's perspective, this work puts self-discovery at the center of the training and enables the participants to strive towards the 'best version of themselves'. They gain experience in acting, directing and writing. Using an eclectic set of dramatic techniques drawing from Meisner, Stanislavski and many others, the ensemble works to 'demystify Shakespeare's language [and] their own lives . . . seeking diversity, inclusivity, and change'. Raymond believes that 'Shakespeare's characters are really cool' and that ensemble members learn a great deal about themselves and the world by engaging with them. He does note, however, that he started with Shakespeare because that's where his own actor training focused; 'Shakespeare is so important in school curricula'. He believes that arming young people with Shakespeare gives them more hope of infiltrating those in power and igniting change.[31] At the same time, Intermission's account of the ensemble's history indicates that company's pathway 'actually started four years earlier (2004), when Darren discovered Shakespeare's *Othello*. He was a character he recognized. Someone like him, who was vulnerable, isolated, who needed to belong, find out who he was. Someone who was black'.[32] This narrative of Raymond's journey towards the Intermission Youth Theatre illustrates how this desire to connect self-knowledge with dramatic understanding eventually led to their 2021 performance that North West End UK calls 'an exciting and urgent production' commenting on contemporary society.

IYT's *Juliet & Romeo* at the Chelsea Theatre is a stunning example of how the bard's timeless love story might find a place in today's increasingly fractured political scenario without being reduced to merely an academic or a nostalgic indulgence.[33]

Intermission's ensemble invites applications for their ten-month programme from youth in challenging circumstances, with the hope that participants will gain substantial life skills and help them move in productive directions. There are a number of other Shakespearean initiatives, several sponsored by grants from the National Endowment for the Arts (NEA) and Arts Midwest in the United States, that work with young people involved with the juvenile justice system. One long-running programme, 'Shakespeare in the Courts' was initiated in 2001 when a local judge, the Honorable Paul E. Parachi, partnered with Massachusetts' Shakespeare & Co. in the hope that youth offenders could benefit from Shakespeare & Co's 'gold-dust learning' by

> learning to articulate their thoughts and feelings; respecting other people's feelings; committing to and collaborating with each other; and bolstering each other's achievements within a group. And perhaps one of the direct ways in which S & Co's education artist can help them is in *making better choices* . . . Acting is all about making choices.[34]

The initiative has found considerable success and sentencing policies incentivize participation; those joining the programme receive lower community service sentences.[35]

As Shakespeare & Co.'s Kevin Coleman notes, most of the participants begin the programme wishing they were 'anywhere else'.[36] Unlike the Shakespeareans in many other initiatives, those involved in some of these juvenile justice endeavours often begin reluctantly, but, as Merlin and Packer observe,

> The stakes are high: If the students succeed in the program – by showing up, showing respect and participating in the rehearsals

and performance – they could finish their probation early. And if they fail to participate – they could get jail-time.[37]

Those 'sentenced to Shakespeare' are often hesitant, but more nervous about the alternative of physical detention.

Accordingly, Coleman indicates that the programme has to take 'baby steps' in moving forward with this skeptical bunch. Shakespeare & Co. enacts an embodied practice that engages the emerging ensemble physically, emotionally and intellectually. Following this methodology, Coleman insists that this work is done best outside of a classroom, where the actors can scream, shout and whisper the lines. He maintains that conventional classroom Shakespeare does not allow the group to breathe deeply enough to wake them up physically and that within a classroom, no one is meeting Shakespeare on 'his' embodied terms. In our conversation, Coleman alluded to neuroscientific research supporting the idea of this drama's particular power.[38] Shakespeare & Co.'s active approach of engaging with Shakespeare's dynamic, emotional stories, Coleman suggests, more quickly leads the actors towards emotional responses, where the participants 'learn something new, listen to each other, risk saying something real, realize that they are being listened to and can express a thought, then a feeling, speak more, risk more'.[39]

Judge Parachi has observed that involvement with stage combat helps the students 'manage their anger'.[40] Coleman adds that the drama programme often enables these actors to look again at the traumatic situations that led to their encounters with the justice system and realize that they can 'change themselves'. They 'fall in love with Shakespeare's words', but also realize that they can love 'what is awakening within themselves'. Since many of the practitioners involved in programmes detailed throughout this study have trained or worked with Shakespeare & Co., the practices developed by Coleman and others figure prominently in these realms.

While Shakespeare in the Courts diverts juvenile offenders from detention, many Shakespearean juvenile justice programs take place in residential settings, where the various ensembles face differing levels of confinement. Argentinian Sergio Amigo works on Shakespeare with youth offenders at Marcos Paz Penitentiary Centre in the province of Buenos Aires, following several years of teaching at Wandsworth Prison and Morley College in London.[41] Amigo's stint in England arose because he wanted to engage with Shakespeare in English, so he learned the language and relocated to the United Kingdom in middle age.[42] He is thus able to bring his experience as an actor, director and comparatively recent English speaker into his work with the Marcos Paz Shakespeareans. He also relies heavily on exercises adapted from Augusto Boal's *Theatre of the Oppressed*, which has inspired numerous practitioners.

Amigo became involved in prison education as a volunteer after an encounter with a pair of prison instructors who told him of their need for a drama teacher. He subsequently was hired by Wandsworth and later by Marcos Paz after he returned to Argentina. One of his first productions at Wandsworth was Tom Stoppard's *Dogg's Hamlet* in 2008. The response of the incarcerated star of this production encouraged him to continue with Shakespeare in carceral settings,

> It was so moving for me. The guy playing Hamlet, when it finished, burst into tears and said 'Well, I never thought I was going to say this, but at last I found a reason I came to prison. I have learned Shakespeare.' I [Amigo] was offered paid work after that. I started work not only with vulnerable prisoners but within the main prison.[43]

Amigo shifted away from Shakespeare for some time, but has returned to those plays and sonnets at Marcos Paz.

Education is compulsory in Argentinian prisons for those who have not completed primary or secondary school.[44] Amigo's students at Marcos Paz are ages eighteen to twenty-one and generally have little to no competency in Shakespeare or English. When he began teaching there, Amigo translated the 'Seven Ages of Man' speech from *As You Like It* into Spanish and introduced the students to King Richard II's remarks about his life in imprisonment: 'This Prison Where I Live.'[45] Initially, he feared that the students would resist these texts, but he soon discovered that they preferred the most challenging material he could bring them.

As his prison practice with young adults evolved, he expanded his long-term practice of focusing on the physicality of performance by bringing his actors speeches in English and guiding them to physicalize the rhythms, without initially worrying about their inability to understand the words. Through his guidance, these young men learn to turn words into action. Amigo finds that Shakespearean language typically loses rhythm and pitch when not presented in English, but he believes that his students can learn the lines the way people learn a song or their national anthem or how religious people learn a prayer even when they do not speak the language. He maintains that it is easier and more enjoyable to learn the words through clapping, stomping and other physical activities while leaving the decipherment of meaning for later sessions. In his view, words are performative and that other than space, little is needed to bring Shakespeare to these prison populations.

Official metrics in Argentina assess levels of recidivism to determine how successful such educational projects are. Amigo's students meet such measures, but they also demonstrate success by other outcomes: some alumni, for instance, have gone on to become writers and movie industry professionals.[46] Other students request the complete works of Shakespeare. While some prison educators view themselves as 'Florence Nightingales' who are there to save people, Amigo says he is there to teach. The man Radha Spratt calls an 'inspirational theatre director' appears to be a talented teacher as well.[47]

Some of the NEA-funded juvenile justice Shakespeare initiatives also rely on the rhythm of Shakespeare's writing to align with the interests of this population and to engage with them physically. Shakespeare Behind Bars/Illinois, for example, offers a Juvenile programme in Chicago with Curt L Tofteland (Producer and Spoken Word Poet), Jason Boulware (Videographer) and Devon Glover (The Sonnet Man) that incorporates spoken word, poetry, hip-hop, rap, music and film into their encounters with Shakespeare.[48] Last year, SBB/Illinois initially planned for their group to rewrite the seven *Hamlet* soliloquies but the participants requested that they spend more time linking what Shakespeare wrote in that play with their own lives, so the direction of their sessions together shifted.

Glover is a talented performer, who is skilled at bringing out correspondences between Shakespeare, rap and hip-hop.[49] He performs regularly and often visits schools and colleges.[50] In addition to being a highly experienced theatre professional both inside and outside carceral environments, Tofteland is also a spoken word poet. Throughout the juvenile justice sessions, Tofteland writes alongside the students and regularly shares his work, which helps develop a strong sense of trust in the gathering. Glover acknowledges that he is the facilitator closest to their age, but these young men still consider him old. Apparently, they refer to Tofteland as 'the cool old head' who connects with them in part through their shared writing.

The participants in Chicago also find connection with situations and characters in *Hamlet*. Many of them report that revenge tales like the ones related in *Hamlet* are familiar to them since revenge narratives often lie at the heart of the circumstances that led them into confinement. The play's themes of jealousy, revenge and loyalty also resonate with them, and they believe that these characters and situations align well with the experiences of ordinary people. In these sessions, they learn that many modern rap and hip-hop artists like Tupac Shakur have drawn from Shakespeare, and they find many Shakespearean resonances in Eminem, J. Cole, Kendrick Lamar, Jay-Z, Wu-Tang Clan and other performers from Devon's generation of listening, while also addressing intersections with more recent artists, such as Lil Baby and Lil Durk. As The Sonnet Man suggests, these performers, like Shakespeare, tell innovative stories with messages that many can relate to. He tells the students that Shakespeare's work is so pervasive that 'you know him even if you don't know you know him'.[51]

During the 2020 pandemic, when the group could only gather by Zoom, they were unable to incorporate music successfully into the sessions, so they focused on poetry and spoken word. When back in person, in 2021, they used a lot of music, video and computer technology. They are also able to guide the participants through the processes of writing and of producing video. Tofteland and Glover believe that sessions went well over Zoom, but they express a clear preference for face-to-face gatherings. In person, the group is able to share their accomplishments with invited family and friends after spending several sessions revising and rehearsing. These Arts Midwest/NEA grants are part of their 'Shakespeare in American Communities' program; this correctional facility in Illinois definitely forges a community with significant Shakespearean associations.[52]

SBB's incorporation of rap and hip-hop in their sessions not only emphasizes Shakespearean associations with these modern musical and movement genres, but also aligns with a growing body of material about the benefits of rap and hip-hop in education and mental health for young people, particularly those in challenging circumstances. Ian Levy, for example, has written and co-edited volumes devoted to 'Hip-Hop Ed' and 'Hip-Hop and Spoken Word Therapy'; Susan Hadley and George Yancy have edited a volume on *Therapeutic Uses of Rap and Hip-Hop*; and Raphael Travis has written *The Healing Power of Hip Hop*.[53] These volumes detail how this genre of music can make education and school counseling practices more culturally relevant and therapeutic. The authors offer both personal and empirical evidence to support their contentions that these musical cultures are beneficial. Levy, for instance, describes his introduction to this aspect of hip-hop,

> As a soul-influenced hip-hop beat boomed through the amplifier on top of a desk, I nervously prepared to share a verse about self-doubt and not feeling supported. These are feelings I had not disclosed to others, as they are connected to my being diagnosed as dyslexic, being academically tracked to take remedial classes during my middle and high school years, and then developing low academic efficacy. Despite my reservation to open up about these thoughts and feelings, the rhymes spoken through the music are met with emphatic slaps on the back, and words of encouragement.[54]

He then speaks of how hip-hop regularly invites such responses and describes how 'research on hip-hop based strategies in therapy' or Hip-Hop and Spoken Word Therapy (HHSWT) have been explored in social work studies for over twenty years.[55] Yancy and Hadley also describe how it makes sense for these musical traditions to operate well in such environments,

> That rap provides this important alternative, functioning as a site of emotional release, speaks to the deeper ways in which rap functions as a site of counter-nihilism and counter-destructiveness. Rap does give voice to feelings of meaninglessness and dread, but the power of giving voice to such feelings creates an important psychological distance from such feelings.[56]

Raphael Travis makes a similar point, suggesting that this trend towards intermingling these expressive forms into Shakespeare programs for youth are likely to expand.

> Hip Hop changes lives. It brings into expression the soul's yearning for meaning and connection. At its core, a raw power

pervades the culture of Hip Hop – celebrated through its beats, art, movement, analysis, lyrical dialogue, rhythm, overall musicality, and style. With this sense of urgency, Hip Hop has had a forty-year history of giving voice to the voiceless, allowing people a renewed freedom of cultural expression, and giving people tools to liberate themselves from a belief that their external conditions define them.[57]

While there are many years separating Shakespeare from these current modes of expression, their goals resonate clearly with the aims of Shakespeare for specialized communities.

Several of the other NEA-sponsored Shakespeare and juvenile justice programs also rely heavily on these forms of music, rhythm and physicality, while locating correlations between Shakespeare and modern art forms and experiences in their activities. Keith McGill of Shakespeare Behind Bars/Kentucky recounted that his group watches rapper Akala's TEDx talk, which begins with audience members being asked to identify whether a series of quotes come from Shakespeare or hip-hop – and they frequently get it wrong.[58] Like other SBB programs, the Kentucky group often approaches Shakespeare through visual and musical arts and they write sonnets of their own.[59] They watch Shakespearean films when physical classes are cancelled for snow days or similar interruptions.

Unlike many of these gatherings, SBB/Kentucky's programme is mixed gender, although most of those in the circle identify as male. They spend time enacting and discussing the lessons found in Shakespeare. Approaching *Othello*, they talk about being marginalized, trusting the wrong people, racism, betrayal and being blind to others' actions. They recognize that King Richard III remains focused on revenge and that no one cares if he dies. They watch Antony gaslight the crowds at Caesar's funeral and discuss similar experiences from their own lives. They understand what it might feel like for Romeo to be banished.

McGill finds that Shakespeare does not 'get in the way', and he always tells participants that 'Shakespeare is tricky, but we'll do this'. He finds that Shakespeare facilitates a range of skills, including emotional literacy. Like many facilitators of such groups, McGill encourages people not to make unwarranted assumptions about the backgrounds, intelligence and educational levels of those in detention. Many of those involved in these programmes, even those who begin reluctantly, take on leadership positions and demonstrate growing insight, maturity and self-understanding. While much of the evidence he provides is anecdotal, his long-term experience with the group has been encouraging.[60]

Delaware Shakespeare's juvenile justice program began when a local judge approached the company about the possibility of such an endeavour, according to facilitator Eric Mills.[61] Their sessions typically revolve around whatever play the professional company is presenting that season and the young people are either taken to a show if they are in one of the groups transitioning towards release, or the play is performed within the residential facility. This initiative largely focuses on acting, but the students also use music and art to approach the plays, which the Delaware Company also encourages in the community with their "Beyond Shakespeare" project.[62]

In the juvenile programme, participants make comic book versions of the scenes or experiment with rap and hip-hop renditions of the stories. Some of the students have no prior experience with Shakespeare or drama altogether, some have engaged with these texts and activities before, and some remain in resistance throughout the programme. Like many such initiatives, the Delaware Shakespeare offering maintains that Shakespeare is 'for everyone', but some of the young people in detention may disagree. Most, however, express a sense of accomplishment at achieving something often considered elitist.

Like the majority of Shakespeare programs described here, Delaware Shakespeare's multifaceted, often physical, approach furthers their ability to attain productive results. Hrach focuses in depth on the ways that engaging students' bodies effectively increases their ability to create and process knowledge and emphasizes why such programmes often succeed,

> The field of embodied cognition draws from phenomenology and brain science to explore how the body shapes human perception. A general summary of its shared assumptions starts from the position that our brains are not in charge in the sense that we previously thought, issuing orders to various systems and parts of the body. Rather, the brain acts as a site for hosting and curating conversations; bodily organs like the heart and lungs and brain communicate and respond to each other as part of

a dynamic ecosystem through a variety of channels, including electrical, hormonal, and mechanical.[63]

Hrach's account of embodied cognition offers an explanation of how undertakings like Delaware Shakespeare's juvenile justice program and similar endeavours can be so effective. Acting involves the engagement of all our senses, which Hrach suggests corresponds with our body's most effective modes of learning,

> We know from the principles of embodied cognition that a productive learning experience involves asking students to move – and stand if possible – as they process ideas. Because movement is integral to perception and expedites the circulation of neurochemical signals, human beings literally think better on their feet.[64]

In conjunction with corresponding evidence from trauma studies, breathwork and other sensory modalities considered elsewhere in this volume, the importance of the physical body in the kinds of work involved in Shakespearean juvenile justice programs appears to be irrefutable.

Colorado Shakespeare's long-running school-based programme takes a different tack. Working in collaboration with the University of Colorado Center for the Study and Prevention of Violence, they send a small group of actors/teaching artists into classrooms to present an abridged version of a play, followed by an interactive workshop. The schools vary widely; they visit populations representing the diversity of the region's inhabitants. In 2021–2, they offered a thirty-minute version of *Twelfth Night* for grades three through five and a forty-five-minute *Julius Caesar* for grades six to twelve. In 2022–3, they did a thirty-minute *Tempest* and a forty-five-minute *Merchant of Venice*. There is always one member of the cast who delivers their lines in Spanish and the study guides produced for each performance/workshop are available in both English and Spanish.[65] The troupe travels to schools across the state of Colorado, but the pandemic postponed their goal of presenting at one or more schools in every Colorado county. During this period, they produced filmed versions of the plays and offered the workshops over Zoom instead.

Drawing in part from the expertise of their partner organization and in consultation with the teachers whose classrooms they visit, they devise sessions where the students enact improvisational scenes associated with the play they will have just seen. With *Twelfth Night*, they revisit Malvolio's imprisonment in the 'dark place' and identify what happened, how it could have been prevented, and what someone in the area could have done to prevent or reduce this bullying. While the abridged plays are presented in the original text, the student scenes use the pupils' ordinary language. Since many students in Colorado speak Spanish, having a bilingual production broadens accessibility. The teaching artists are careful never to guide the students' responses as they address the problematic behaviours being witnessed. Instead, they ask questions about what they saw, who could help and what might make a difference in the outcome. They also discuss what is happening in the students' own environments and what it takes to move towards 'upstanding' behaviour rather than remaining as a bystander.

Colorado practitioner Amanda Giguere believes that Shakespeare's plays raise many of the issues found in violence prevention curricula and that theatrical practices support the lessons being presented. The connectedness that can come from forming an ensemble resonates with the students. Giguere also contends that the power of the voice and the power of words in Shakespeare encourages students to use their voices, even when they are not speaking directly. Bringing issues to the attention of a trusted adult, she suggests, is another way of speaking up. Theatre also encourages empathy, because playing a role helps students

> put themselves in someone else's shoes and see the world from someone else's perspective. If we see the full humanity of another human we're more likely to watch out for them and see that we're connected to them and that their fate is caught up in their fate. I think Shakespeare does that really well.[66]

While the company is looking forward to being able to fund a formal study of their practice and its outcomes, surveys from students and teachers indicate a high level of success. In the eleven years since the programme began, they have reached over 120,000 students, with many schools inviting them back annually. Collaborating with the Center for the Study and Prevention of Violence has been key in the development and assessment of their programme, but when Colorado Shakespeare first approached this group, they anticipated that they would be handed an article about bullying rather than encounter an eager team of partners, who wholeheartedly understand the importance of the arts in education. These and other violence prevention workshops emphasize physical activity and mediate discussions connecting Shakespeare's plays to the students' own lives. In contrast to some of the other initiatives, they focus on individual workshops rather than an extended engagement.

These programmes engaging youth with Shakespeare underscore the value of embodied learning. By incorporating their Shakespearean exercises with music, movement, art, writing and personal expression, they offer innumerable ways to help these participants survive and thrive in the challenging circumstances facing many youths and adolescents. Whether taking place in Argentina, Chicago, London or Colorado, they offer opportunities for their participants to succeed in new and complicated ventures even while they are simultaneously contending with difficult personal situations. Like the other initiatives discussed throughout this volume, embodied and multisensory Shakespeare appears to be central to the success of these diverse programmes.

NOTES

Introduction

1 Shakespeare in Prison (SIP) refers to the Detroit group discussed in this volume. With the hope of reducing confusion, I will refer to other prison programmes as Shakespeare in prison (lowercase p) when I am speaking about them more generally.
2 As my work on this book has progressed, I have become increasingly less comfortable noting misspellings and other signals of non-academic writing found in these ventures emphasizing diversity. As noted in my introduction, therefore, I am not marking these in the works written by participants in these programmes.
3 Transcript of pre-Covid-19 prison session of Shakespeare in Prison, Detroit Public Theatre's Signature Community Programme, provided by Frannie Shepherd-Bates, with permission of the author.
4 All SIP quotes here come from the in-person and Zoom meetings I had with SIP alumni in May 2022.
5 Frannie Shepherd-Bates, 'Michael Chekhov Technique as a Trauma-Responsive Practice in Shakespeare in Prison' (Unpublished Manuscript, 2022). I appreciate Shepherd-Bates's generosity in sharing this and other unpublished materials in support of this volume.
6 Graeae is a prominent theatre company that includes many d/Deaf actors and others with physical differences. I have seen them perform numerous times, but have not seen them present Shakespeare. For more information, *see* https://graeae.org/.
7 Information about *The Taming of the Shrew Drag Show* comes from a Zoom conversation with John Handscombe on 29 November 2022. I appreciate his willingness to share his experience of this show with me.
8 The Weather Girls, 'It's Raining Men', recorded in 24 January 1980, track 9 on *Two Tons O' Fun*.

9 Assistant director, Lewis Penfold, for example, sometimes offers cues on his ukulele. Site visit, 21 November 2022.

10 Such programmes are often referred to as 'applied theatre', a term with a number of complex, intertwined meanings. I am not typically using that name here, but Rowan Mackenzie discusses the implications of labeling such initiatives in this way in *Creating Space for Shakespeare: Working with Marginalised Communities* (London: Arden Shakespeare, Bloomsbury Publishing, 2023), 2. Mackenzie's book is the first in this Arden Shakespeare and Social Justice series. I am extremely grateful that she gave me access to her page proofs in advance of publication so that I could cite her book, which is in conversation with my own at numerous points. Working with Rowan (and Emergency Shakespeare) over the years has been a delight and I look forward to our future encounters.

11 Laura Bates, for instance, was interviewed by NPR. *See* 'Teaching Shakespeare in a Maximum Security Prison', interview by Michel Martin, *Tell Me More*, NPR, 22 April 2013, https://www.npr.org/2013/04/22/178411754/teaching-shakespeare-in-a-maximum-security-prison. Shepherd-Bates was also interviewed by NPR in 2013, audio, 14:43. See Kyle Norris, 'Shakespeare Helps Prisoners Change', *Arts & Life*, NPR Michigan Radio, 18 April 2013, audio, 3:39, https://www.michiganradio.org/arts-culture/2013-04-28/shakespeare-helps-prisoners-change. Agnes Wilcox, who died in 2017, was heard by innumerable people when she appeared on Ira Glass's *This American Life* on NPR, 1 September 2017, audio, 21:28, https://news.stlpublicradio.org/show/st-louis-on-the-air/2017-09-01/remembering-prison-performing-arts-founder-agnes-wilcox-who-died-unexpectedly-while-vacationing. There is a new Shakespeare in prison film in 2022, featuring Johnny Stallings' production of *A Midsummer Night's Dream* at Oregon's Two Rivers Correctional Facility. Bushra Azzouz, dir., *A Midsummer Night's Dream in Prison*, Vimeo. I watched it through SiPN.

12 *Shakespeare Behind Bars*, directed by Hank Rogerson (Philomath Films, 2005).

13 Due to the pandemic, I had to cancel an extended research trip to Africa, for example, where there are several pertinent programmes, including one for people experiencing homelessness in South Africa. Caryn Edwards, 'Homeless Actors in Jo'burg take Shakespeare to the Streets', *The South African*, 12 June 2017, https://www.thesouthafrican.com/lifestyle/homeless-actors-in-joburg-take-shakespeare-to-the-streets/.

14 Tom Bishop and Alexa Alice Joubin, eds. With special guest editors, Ton Hoenselaars and Stephen O'Neill, *The Shakespeare International Yearbook*: *Special Section, Shakespeare and Refugees* 19 (London: Routledge, 2021).

15 There has been considerable attention paid, for instance, to Gregory Doran's casting of an actor with limb differences in the title role of the RSC's 2022 *Richard III*. See, for example, Emma Saunders, 'Arthur Hughes: First Disabled Richard III is "Big Gesture" from RSC',– *BBC News*, 17 June 2022, https://www.bbc.co.uk/news/entertainment-arts-61549419.

16 I wrote these words before I realized that Regan Linton is on the advisory board of this series. A fortuitous coincidence.

17 Regan Linton, 'Actor Training and Instruction for Wheelchair-using Artists', in *Inclusivity and Equality in Performance Training*, ed. Petronilla Whitfield (London: Routledge, 2022), 25–42. Linton was a splendid Don John in *Much Ado* but I did not see her as Titania/Hippolyta. Bill Rauch, who was Artistic Director of OSF when *Much Ado* was presented, told me that Linton's experiences as a performer in a wheelchair was a significant factor in the redesigns of all their spaces as part of the OSF 'Access for All' initiative. For information about the development of this *A Midsummer Night's Dream*, scroll down on the Apothetae website, 'Body of Work', *The Apothetae*, http://www.theapothetae.org/body-of-work.html. I am grateful to Apothetae founder Gregg Mozgala for sharing this material with me and to Lue Douhit for introducing me to Gregg a couple of years ago. This production of *Dream* included actors with a wide range of physical and intellectual differences.

18 See, for example, '"Being Here Together": Global Partnerships in Higher Education', *Contingencies: A Journal of Global Pedagogy* 1, no. 1 (Spring 2021), https://doi.org/10.33682/m6hx-0wnd;

Steve Rowland, 'Shakespeare in and out of Prison: The World Shakespeare Project and Shakespeare Central', in *Reimaging Shakespeare Education: Teaching and Learning Through Collaboration*, ed. Liam Semler et al. (Cambridge: Cambridge University Press, 2023). '"Make New Nations": Shakespearean Communities in the Twenty-First Century', in *Handbook of Shakespeare and Global Appropriation*, ed. Christy Desmet, Sujata Iyengar and Miriam Jacobsen (London: Routledge, 2021), 195–226. '"Come, and Learn of Us": Shakespeare in An Age of Global Communication', *CEA Critic* 78, no. 2 (2016): 242–55. '"All Corners of the World": The Possibilities and Challenges of International Electronic Education', *Journal of Interactive*

Technology and Pedagogy 6 (2014), http://jitp.commons.gc.cuny.edu/. '"The World Together Joins": Electronic Shakespearean Collaborations', co-written for special edition 'Digital Shakespeares: Innovations, Interventions, Mediations', *The Shakespearean International Yearbook* (2014): 117–32. London; '"All Great Neptune's Ocean": iShakespeare and Play in a Transatlantic Context', in *Digital Shakespeare*, ed. Christie Carson and Peter Kirwan (Cambridge: Cambridge University Press, 2014), 87–99; '"The World's Common Place": Leveling the Shakespearean Playing Field', *Borrowers and Lenders: Journal of Shakespearean Appropriation* 8, no. 2 (2014), http://www.borrowers.uga.edu/. 'The Curiosity of Nations: Shakespeare and International Electronic Education', *Journal For Early Modern Cultural Studies: The Digital Turn* 13, no. 4 (2013): 121–5. New York. Shakespeare Theatre Association, 'The World Shakespeare Project', *Quarto* (2013) Digital.

19 Ron Henergen, for example, from Chesapeake Shakespeare Company, offers a stock answer that 'Shakespeare is our middle name'.

20 Ashley E. Lucas, *Prison Theatre and the Global Crisis of Incarceration* (London: Methuen Drama, 2020), 3–28.

21 Sonya Freeman Loftis, 'Autistic Culture, Shakespeare Therapy, and the Hunter Heartbeat Method', in *Shakespeare Survey* (Cambridge: Cambridge University Press, 2019), 256–67.

22 Madeline Sayet, 'Interrogating the Shakespeare System' in 'Reimagining Shakespeare's Legacy with Madeline Sayet', Howlaround Theatre History Podcast #46, produced by Michael Lueger, 2017, https://howlround.com/theatre-history-podcast-46. Sayet's powerful autobiographical play, *Where We Belong*, details her complicated relationship with Shakespeare. It has been widely performed, at Shakespeares's Globe in London and elsewhere.

23 Jenna Dreier, 'Decolonising Pedagogies in Prison Performance Programmes: Making Shakespeare Secondary', *Ride: The Journal of Applied Theatre and Performance* 26, no. 3 (2021): 477–93. Routledge. Essay abstract.

24 Jenna Dreier, '"As You from Crimes would Pardoned Be": Prison Shakespeare and the Practices of Empowerment' (PhD dissertation, University of Minnesota, 2020), 8.

25 Labels often create conflict or misunderstanding. Some people refer to the communities involved in these endeavours as 'marginalized'. To my ear, that term introduces the potential of unwelcome value judgments. 'Specialized' is intended to communicate that these

groups share qualities or circumstances that may gather them together in communities, but without any suggestion that they are outside any concept of 'normality'. Linguistic controversies emerge regularly in these discussions, and many will be noted in this volume. I aim to be respectful and appropriate and apologize sincerely for any mistakes. They are unintentional. I understand and respect Michael W. Twitty's observation that 'Nomenclature and self-definition do not constantly change among marginalized and oppressed people for fun––they are there for safety, power, and comfort.' For his expanded discussion of this topic, see Michael W. Twitty, *Koshersoul: The Faith and Food Journey of an African American Jew* (New York: Amistad, Harper Collins, 2022), 42. Questions about appropriate language in this regard occur regularly, as a recent question submitted to *Smithsonian* magazine about the difference between 'American Indian' and 'Native American' indicates. 'Ask Smithsonian', *Smithsonian* (September 2022): 92.

26 'Shakespeare in Prisons', Shakespeare at Notre Dame, https://shakespeare.nd.edu/service/shakespeare-in-prisons/.

27 The recordings from these sessions can be found on the Shakespeare at Notre Dame YouTube Channel, 'Shakespeare in Prisons Network', https://www.youtube.com/playlist?list=PLF2QbT7cszC4rAQl4cSx0lqy3yUdBvAP4.

28 DE-CRUIT website, https://www.decruit.org/.

29 Flute Theatre website, https://flutetheatre.co.uk.

30 Mackenzie discusses these packets and includes examples of what was distributed. See Mackenzie, *Creating Space*, 133–147.

31 Mackenzie was also honored by the Shakespeare Association of America with their inaugural Shakespeare Publics Award (SAA, 'Award Winners', https://shakespeareassociation.org/saa-archives/grant-and-award-winners/) and by the Worshipful Company of Educators who named her Highly Commended Prison Educator in 2019, then gave her the Inspirational Educator Award for 'Teaching Shakespeare in Challenging Settings' in 2020.

32 'Rowan Mackenzie (HMPs Gartree & Stafford)', Butler Trust UK, https://www.butlertrust.org.uk/rowan-mackenzie/.

33 'Shakespeare in Prison: Detroit Public Theatre's Signature Community Program', Detroit Public Theatre, http://www.detroitpublictheatre.org/shakespeareinprison/.

34 Mackenzie also talks about these issues. See, for example, *Creating Space*, 6.

35 Todd Landon Barnes makes a number of claims from this perspective, but he is focusing on various documentaries made about such programmes and does not appear to have any firsthand experience with Shakespeare in prison groups. The documentaries he cites vary widely, as films even by the same directors can differ. *Shakespeare Behind Bars* (SBB), for example, films participants, rehearsals and performances from Curt L. Tofteland's long-standing initiative in Kentucky, although Tofteland operated separately from the filmmakers. The same group later produced *Still Dreaming*, which focused on a group of retired actors who were not actually involved in a formal Shakespeare group. It is no surprise that SBB resonates more honestly and powerfully than *Still Dreaming*, where none of those involved engaged in such practices in 'real' life. In this study, such documentaries are not conflated with their subjects.

36 Scott Jackson confirmed that the organizers use 'SiPN for the network and SiPC1 (or 2, 3, 4 etc.) for the conference', email to author, 30 October 2022.

37 The organizers (several of whom have since changed affiliations) were Freedome Bradley-Ballentine, then Associate Artistic Director and Director of Arts Engagement at the Old Globe in San Diego; Melinda Cooper, then an independent project manager and activist living in Virginia; Karen Ann Daniels, then Director of the Public Theater's Mobile Unit in NYC; Scott Jackson, the Mary Irene Ryan Family Executive Director of Shakespeare at Notre Dame; Curt L. Tofteland, Founding Director of Shakespeare Behind Bars; and Praycious Wilson-Gay, Coordinator of the Public Theater's Mobile Unit in NYC.

38 Many prison practitioners refer to those who have been released from custody as 'returned citizens' in order to emphasize these individuals' identities as community members rather than labeling them by their carceral history.

39 In addition to the conference sessions, Scott Jackson, Melinda Cooper and Kate Powers organized monthly Zoom meetings to discuss anti-racist practices.

40 Mackenzie also discusses some of the issues surrounding terminology with such groups. *Creating Space*, 3, 14.

41 Aristotle, *On the Soul*, translated by Edwin Wallace, Digireads.com, 38.

42 Willi Aeppli, *The Care and Development of the Human Senses: Rudolf Steiner's Work on the Significance of the Senses in Education* (London: Floris Books, 2021), 28–9.

43 Rob DeSalle, *Our Senses: An Immersive Experience* (New Haven: Yale University Press, 2018), vii.
44 Ibid., vii–viii.
45 Ibid., ix.
46 Ibid., 202.
47 Ibid., 232.
48 Ibid.
49 A fascinating new book about the senses appeared as I was completing this manuscript. The work is intriguing, but I can only reference and recommend it here. Ashley Ward, *Sensational: A New Story of Our Senses* (London: Profile Books, 2023).
50 'Proprioception' refers to people's awareness of the placement and movement of their bodies.
51 Jackie Higgins, *Sentient: What Animals Reveal about our Senses* (London: Picador, 2021).
52 Susan Hrach, *Minding Bodies: How Physical Space, Sensation, and Movement Affect Learning* (Morgantown: West Virginia University Press), 85.
53 DeSalle, *Our Senses*, 108.
54 Ibid.
55 Shari Tishman, *Slow Looking: The Art and Practice of Learning Through Observation* (New York: Routledge, 2018),139.
56 Mark M. Smith, *A Sensory History Manifesto* (University Park: Penn State University Press, 2021), 35–62.
57 Ibid., 62.
58 There are, of course, exceptions to this tendency. *See*, for example, Philip A. Andersen, 'Tactile Traditions: Cultural Differences and Similarities in Haptic Communication', in *The Handbook of Touch: Neuroscience, Behavioral, and Health Perspectives*, ed. Matthew J. Hertenstein and Sandra J. Weiss (New York: Springer Publishing Co., 2011) 351–69; Emily Wilbourne and Suzanne G. Cusick, eds, *Acoustemologies in Contact: Sounding Subjects and Modes of Listening in Early Modernity* (Cambridge: Open Book Publishers, 2021); David Sterling Brown and Jennifer Lynn Stoerer, 'Blanched with Fear: Reading the Racialized Soundscape in *Macbeth*', *Shakespeare Studies* 50 (2022): 33–43; Carolyn McCaskill, Ceil Lucas, Robert Bayley and Joseph Hill, *Hidden Treasure of Black ASL: Its History and Structure* (Washington, D.C.: Gallaudet UP, 2011); and Michael W. Twitty, who describes the cultural differences

associated with the senses through varying cultural backgrounds, Twitty, *Koshersoul*, 195–6. Deirdre Mask, in her fascinating book about the evolution of addresses, describes the 'multisensory maps' of ancient Rome, where people could 'navigate by ear.' *See* Deirdre Mask, *The Address Book: What Street Addresses Reveal about Identity, Race, Wealth, and Power* (New York: St. Martin's Press, 2020), 66. In a related vein, cultural issues in dramatic practice, including in Shakespeare, are not always closely considered. For a racially informed perspective on acting, *see* Sharrell Luckett and Tia M. Shaffer, eds, *Black Acting Methods: Critical Approaches* (London: Routledge, 2016).

59 I had a number of electronic conversations with Arts Access Aotearoa personnel during the pandemic and appreciate the generosity extended by many, particularly Chris Ulutupu.

60 Eli A. Wolf and Mary Hums, '"Nothing About Us Without Us" -- Mantra for a Movement', *Huff Post*, 5 September 2017, https://www.huffpost.com/entry/nothing-about-us-without-us-mantra-for-a-movement_b_59aea450e4b0c50640cd61cf.

61 See, for example, 'Uncovering the Spectrum of Insider-Outsiderness', in *Questions in Qualitative Social Justice Research in Multicultural Contexts*, ed. Anna CohenMiller and Nettie Boivin (New York: Routledge, 2022), 73–95.

62 Ibid., 78.

63 Jenna Dreier notes that some prison practitioners, such as Jonathan Shailor and Curt Tofteland, call themselves 'facilitators', in contrast to Agnes Wilcox, who claimed 'The theatre is a benign dictatorship and I'm the dictator.' Dreier, '"As You from Crimes would Pardoned Be"', 37. During a Zoom conversation, Shailor indicated that he was increasingly drawn to a shared governance model. Jonathan Shailor, Zoom interview, 28 July 2022.

64 Frequently, however, even those with training in drama therapy or other pertinent areas are not engaged in this work under the auspices of those credentials. Suraya Susana Keating, the Shakespeare for Social Justice Director for Marin Shakespeare, for example, is a licensed marriage and family therapist, a registered drama therapist, a yoga teacher and adjunct professor at California Institute of Integral Studies where she teaches in the Master's programme for drama therapy. She clearly brings all of this expertise to her prison work, but she is not practicing there as a therapist. Keating and others presented a session at SiPC 4, discussing the role of drama therapy in their work: 'Approaches to Drama Therapy (SiPC4)', YouTube, Shakespeare at Notre Dame, 18 February 2021, https://www.youtube

.com/watch?v=azEh2f-pToM&list=PLF2QbT7cszC4rAQl4cSx0lqy3y UdBvAP4&index=17. In July, 2022, Feast of Crispian's Nancy Smith-Watson announced on Facebook that she is beginning formal drama therapy study in support of her work with veterans and others.

65 I am grateful to Tofteland for directing me to Baim's work and for his numerous contributions to my understanding of Shakespeare Behind Bars and other relevant undertakings. I also appreciate his willingness to read some of my chapters prior to publication.

66 Cited in Lawrence Shapiro, *Embodied Cognition* (New York: Routledge, 2019), 64.

67 Francisco J. Varela, Evan Thompson, and Eleanor Rosch (first edition published in 1991), *The Embodied Mind: Cognitive Science and Human Condition* (revised edition), (Cambridge, MA: MIT University Press, [1991] 2016); Rick Kemp, *Embodied Acting: What Neuroscience Tells Us About Performance* (New York: Routledge, [1991] 2012); and Experience J. Bryon, Mark Bishop, Deirdre McLaughlin and Jess Kaufman, eds, *Embodied Cognition, Acting, and Performance* (New York: Routledge, 2018).

68 Kemp, *Embodied Acting*, xv.

69 Ibid., xv.

70 Ibid., 15.

71 Hrach's book focuses on the importance of embodied cognition in the classroom, in contrast to what she terms the 'brains on sticks' approach to teaching. *Minding Bodies*, ix.

72 Cheryl Pallant, *Writing and the Body in Motion: Awakening Voice through Somatic Practice* (Jefferson: McFarland & Company, 2018), 72.

73 McLaughlin, 'Embodiment: A Cross-Disciplinary Provocation', in *Embodied Cognition, Acting, and Performance*, ed. Experience J. Bryon et al. (New York: Routledge, 2018), 36.

74 Ysabel Clare, 'Stanislavski's System as an Enactive Guide to Embodied Cognition?' in *Embodied Cognition, Acting, and Performance*, ed. Experience J. Bryon et al. (New York: Routledge, 2018), 45.

75 Kemp, *Embodied Acting*, 5.

76 Ibid., 7.

77 Thanks, as always, to Scott Jackson, who directed me to work exploring links between Stanislavski and yoga. I deeply appreciate his willingness to read and comment upon many of my texts in advance of publication.

78 Sergie Tcherkasski, *Stanislavsky and Yoga* (New York: Routledge, 2016), 18–19.
79 Steiner's philosophy contains racial perspectives denounced by many contemporary Waldorf institutions, as the Waldorf School of Atlanta acknowledges: 'Diversity, Equity, and Inclusion', The Waldorf School of Atlanta, https://www.waldorfatlanta.org/dei-2.
80 Chekhov spent a couple of years (1936–8) offering actor training at Dartington Hall in Devon. While my own residency at Dartington was not connected with Chekhov, I thank the remarkable, late Brad Brown for hosting me and the sorely missed Shakespearean Kate Belsey for driving me there from Wales. This venue is inspiring.
81 Charles Marowitz, *The Other Chekhov: A Biography of Michael Chekhov, the Legendary Actor, Director, and Theorist* (New York: Applause Theatre & Cinema Books, 2004), 51.
82 Ibid., 13–14.
83 Ibid., 12.
84 I am grateful to Frannie-Shepherd-Bates and Scott Jackson, who each spoke at length about Chekhov with me over Zoom in June 2022.
85 Sheila T. Cavanagh, '"In India": Shakespeare and Prison in Kolkata and Mysore', *Shakespeare Survey* 74 (2021): 98–110.
86 Paolo Freire, *Pedagogy of the Oppressed* (London: Bloomsbury Academic, [1970] 2020),1–2.
87 See Augusto Boal, *Games for Actors and Non-Actors* (New York: Routledge, 1995). *The Rainbow of Desire: The Boal Method of Theatre and Therapy* (New York: Routledge, 1992); and *Theatre of the Oppressed* (New York: Theatre Communications Group, 1985).
88 Mackenzie discusses Jackson's prominent role with the theatrical ensemble Cardboard Citizens, which includes people who have experienced homelessness. *Creating Space*, 2–3, 22–3.
89 Boal, *Games*, xxi–xxii.
90 Ibid., 60.
91 Cited from Dani Snyder-Young, *Theatre of Good Intentions: Hopes for Theatre and Social Change* (New York: Palgrave Macmillan, 2013), 7. Heritage's account appears in 'Stealing Kisses', in *Theatre in Crisis? Performance Manifesto for a New Century*, ed. Maria M. Delgado and Caridad Svich (Manchester: Manchester University Press, 2002), 166–79.

92 Cited in Snyder-Young, *Theatre of Good Intentions*, 7. The citation comes from Tim Prentki and Sheila Preston, *The Applied Theatre Reader* (New York. Routledge, 2009), 13.

93 I have, however, heard about and witnessed varying levels of support for such programmes from officials in prison environments. Practitioners generally need to tread cautiously, in order to enable their initiatives to survive and thrive.

94 Todd Landon Barnes, *Shakespearean Charity and the Perils of Redemptive Performance* (Cambridge: Cambridge University Press, 2020).

95 In a brief discussion with Flute's Kelly Hunter about some of the objections raised in academic contexts about that company's work, for instance, Hunter insisted that she is an actor, not an academic, and that her practices come from that artistic realm. Conversation with Kelly Hunter at Riverside Theatre, London. 25 October 2022.

96 These organizations and events can be found at their relevant websites: Shakespeare Association of America: https://shakespeareassociation.org; Shakespeare Theatre Association: https://www.stahome.org; British Shakespeare Association: https://www.britishshakespeare.ws/; Armenian Shakespeare Association: https://www.armenianshakespeare.org/; Shakespeare Association of India: https://tsaind.com/; European Shakespeare Research Association: https://www.um.es/shakespeare/esra/; American Shakespeare Center Blackfriars Conference: https://americanshakespearecenter.com/education/educationhomepage/blackfriars-conference/; Wooden O Symposium: https://www.bard.org/about/education/wooden-o-symposium/; University of Waterloo/Stratford Shakespeare Festival Conference: Waterloo/Stratford: https://uwaterloo.ca/english/shakespeare.

97 I am especially grateful to those who read parts (or all!) of my text in preparation for publication, including John Watkins, Stephen Unwin, Tina Packer, Curt L. Tofteland, Tom Magill, Scott Jackson, Kate Powers, Sammie Byron, Esther Ruth Elliott and Frannie Shepherd-Bates.

98 See Anne Cushman and Lizette Montgomery, 'Yogi Desai Resigns from Kripalu', *Yoga Journal* (February 1995): 40–2 and Jennifer Davis-Flynn, 'A New Report Details Decades of Abuse at the Hands of Yogi Bhajan', *Yoga Journal* (15 August 2020), https://www.yogajournal.com/yoga-101/abuse-in-kundalini-yoga/.

99 Liz Kowalczyk, 'Allegations of Employee Mistreatment Roil Renowned Brookline Trauma Center', Boston Globe, 7 March

2018, https://www.bostonglobe.com/metro/2018/03/07/allegations-employee-mistreatment-roil-renowned-trauma-center/sWW13agQDY9B9A1rt9eqnK/story.html. My understanding is that van der Kolk won his own lawsuit related to these events, but an NDA keeps the details private.

100   Brian Dunning's critique of Porges's work is mentioned as follows. For an overview of questions raised about van der Kolk's research, *see* Scott Alexander, 'Book Review: The Body Keeps the Score', review of *The Body Keeps the Score*, by Bessel van der Kolk, *Slate Star Codex*, https://slatestarcodex.com/2019/11/12/book-review-the-body-keeps-the-score/.

101   Porges' website does not include his educational background: 'About Dr. Stephen Porges', Stephen W. Porges, PhD personal website, https://www.stephenporges.com/about. Wikipedia indicates that he studied at Michigan State, but does not identify which degrees were earned there. 'Stephen Porges', Wikipedia, https://en.wikipedia.org/wiki/Stephen_Porges.

102   Polyvagal theory is not without its critics, however. Brian Dunning, for instance, in his notably named 'Skeptoid' podcast, raises serious questions about the theory and its uses and offers a bibliography containing other works critical of the theory as well as some of Porges' texts. 'The Dark Side of Polyvagal Theory', Skeptoid Podcast #816, 25 January 2022, https://skeptoid.com/episodes/4816#:~:text=The%20dispute%20arose%20in%201994%20when%20Stephen%20Porges,dorsal%20branch%2C%20active%20when%20you%27re%20in%20immobilized%20mode.

103   Unfortunately, I have not been able to confirm this information apart from its inclusion on Wikipedia: 'Cathy Malchiodi', Wikipedia, https://en.wikipedia.org/wiki/Cathy_Malchiodi.

104   Cathy Maldiochi personal website, https://www.cathymalchiodi.com/.

105   'Meet Jamie', Dr. Jamie Marich, https://www.drjamiemarich.com/meet-jamie.html and 'Jamie Nicole Marich, CDCA', Dr. Jamie Marich, http://www.drjamiemarich.com/uploads/3/0/2/4/3024486/jamiemarichcv2011.pdf.

106   Pallant, *Writing and the Body in Motion*, 17–18.

107   Given that the pandemic has made it clear that many people deride science today, I hasten to add that I am personally 'pro-science', but recognize that differing modalities can potentially offer us new insights when they are not themselves exploitative of people's insufficient knowledge or gullibility. The incorporation

of acupuncture into some Western medical practices, for instance, demonstrates how formerly incompatible theories can coalesce. The somatic work used by many working on Shakespeare with survivors of trauma, moreover, often appears to lead to positive results.

108 Mackenzie discusses Emergency Shakespeare, including the participants' pseudonyms, in *Creating Space*, 60–3, 107–17.

109 My university is undertaking significant work into relationships between modern science and contemplative traditions. His Holiness, the Dalai Lama, holds a faculty appointment at Emory and has been involved in a lengthy project designed to present modern scientific theories to Tibetan monks, while exploring the contributions Tibetan practices offer to the West. This partnership has been illuminating. *See*, for example, Kim Severson, 'A Bridge Between Western Science and Eastern Faith', *New York Times*, 11 October 2013, https://www.nytimes.com/2013/10/12/us/seeking-a-bridge-between-western-science-and-eastern-faith-with-the-Dalai-Lama.html.

Chapter 1

1 Thanks to Frannie Shepherd-Bates for confirming that a participant provided this quote.

2 While this chapter includes written material from a number of influential theatrical and trauma specialists, it is important to note that those involved in Shakespearean work with specialized communities tend to draw from an eclectic range of sources. Those cited here are significant and their work is widely influential, but the practices individual groups engage with typically emanate from multiple intertwined readings, teachings, trainings and rehearsal experiences.

3 Aristotle, *De Anima* (*On the Soul*), 425a2–3.

4 John Calapinto, *This is the Voice* (New York: Simon and Schuster, 2021), 18.

5 Stephen Unwin discusses his son Joey, who uses minimal spoken language, in an essay about Joey's participation in *A Midsummer Night's Dream* at his school. See Stephen Unwin, 'Joey's Dream', in Forum: Specialized Performers and Audiences, *Shakespeare Studies* 74 (2019): 31–7.

6 Several of the groups included in this volume contain participants who do not use verbal speech. Breathwork is often used for purposes

other than speech, however. Some of the vocal theorists discussed here do not address such circumstances, but these specialized communities typically work effectively with broadly diverse ensemble members.

7   Linklater was one of the foremost voice theorists and teachers in Shakespearean acting until her death in 2020. She described herself, however, as an 'Oxfordian', who believed that the Earl of Oxford wrote the Shakespearean canon. Nevertheless, her assertion does not appear to be relevant in this context. Kristin Linklater, *Freeing Shakespeare's Voice: The Actor's Guide to Talking the Text* (London: Nick Hearn, 1993), 209–14.

8   Linklater, *Freeing Shakespeare's Voice*, 4.

9   Patsy Rodenburg, *Speaking Shakespeare* (New York: St. Martin's, 2019), 8.

10 Ibid., 40–1.

11 Ibid., 8.

12 Linklater, *Freeing Shakespeare's Voice*, 11.

13 Bloom's works can be found widely. See, for example, Benjamin S. Bloom, *Taxonomy of Educational Objectives, Handbook 1: Cognitive Domain* 2nd edn (Boston: Addison-Wesley Longman, 1969) and David R. Krathwohl, Benjamin S. Bloom and Bertram B. Massia, *Taxonomy of Educational Objectives, Handbook II: Affective Domain (The Classification of Educational Goals)* (Philadelphia: David McKay Publishers, 1956).

14 Steve Rowland and I discuss cognitive and affective learning in a prison/university partnership in Sheila T. Cavanagh and Steve Rowland, 'Those Twins of Learning": Cognitive and Affective Learning in an Inclusive Shakespearean Curriculum', *Critical Survey* 31, no. 4 (2019): 54–64. This essay is being revised and expanded in a book (due out in 2023) edited by Rowan Mackenzie and Robert Shaughnessy.

15 Linklater, *Freeing Shakespeare's Voice*, 5.

16 Ibid.

17 Ibid., 6.

18 Unlike most of the books included here that are published by practitioners and offer insight into their methods, Simpson does not believe that her programme should be taught by anyone except for the teachers listed on her website. It remains unclear whether people are simultaneously being discouraged from attempting the exercises listed in the book without professional assistance. Fay Simpson, *The*

Lucid Body: A Guide for the Physical Actor (New York: Allworth Press, 2020), x.
19 Simpson, *The Lucid Body*, 87–8.
20 Linklater, *Freeing Shakespeare's Voice*, 4.
21 According to the back book cover, The Expressive Actor is a non-profit arts organization committed to integrated methods of actor training. Michael Lugering, *The Expressive Actor: Integrated Voice, Movement, and Acting Training* (New York: Routledge, 2019).
22 Lugering, *The Expressive Actor*, 110–11.
23 van der Kolk, *The Body Keeps the Score*, 267–8.
24 Ibid., 265–78.
25 Stephen W. Porges, *The Pocket Guide to The Polyvagal Theory: The Transformative Power of Feeling Safe* (New York: W.W. Norton, 2017), 170.
26 Ibid., 176.
27 Many sessions associated with the 2020–1 SiPC 4 included trauma specialists, such as van der Kolk, and work derived from related research. SiPC 4 also sponsored an intensive workshop on Mental Wellness for Creative Professionals, led by Atlanta Artist Relief Executive Director Bridget McCarthy. These sessions incorporated information about trauma interventions including concepts from vagal theory such as those presented by Stephen Porges and others. McCarthy made it clear that these workshops were not credentialling sessions, but she offered a wide range of materials for practitioners interested in expanding their expertise in working with traumatized individuals.
28 Cicely Berry maintains, however, that athletic breath training differs from, and can conflict with, breath training for actors. Cicely Berry, *Voice and the Actor* (New York: Wiley, 1973), 21.
29 Michael J. Stephen, *Breath Taking: The Power, Fragility, and Future of Our Extraordinary Lungs* (New York: First Grove Atlantic, 2021), xiii.
30 Ibid., xii.
31 van der Kolk, *The Body Keeps the Score*, 265–6.
32 Calapinto, *This is the Voice*, 82–3.
33 James Nestor, *Breath: The New Science of a Lost Art* (New York: Riverhead Books, Penguin, 2020), xix.
34 Calapinto, *This is the Voice*, 58.
35 Nestor, *Breath*, xxi–xxii.

36 Ibid., xx.
37 Ibid.
38 Bella Merlin and Tina Packer, *Shakespeare & Company: When Action is Eloquence* (London: Routledge, 2020), 116. I would like to take this opportunity to thank Tina Packer for her encouragement and help with the preparation for this volume. I have enormous respect for her accomplishments and greatly appreciate her support of my endeavours. I am also grateful that the pandemic enabled me to take movement and breathing classes at Shakespeare & Co. through Zoom.
39 Ibid., 117. Later chapters make mention of participants in some programmes who prefer not to be touched. These ground rules acknowledge that physical contact is typically part of these trainings, but that actors can ask that teachers 'find another way to reach you'. 117.
40 Ibid., 128. The first part of this citation includes a quote from V. Sanders, 'The Passion of Tina Packer', *The Boston Globe,* 17 August 1997.
41 Merlin and Packer, *Shakespeare & Company*, 123.
42 Berry, *Voice*, 18.
43 Ibid., 22.
44 Giles Block, *Speaking the Speech: An Actor's Guide to Shakespeare* (London: Nick Hern, 2013).
45 Ibid., 14.
46 Ibid., 15.
47 Ibid., 23–4.
48 Ibid., 30.
49 Ibid., Kelly Hunter, among others, also emphasizes such correspondences between our physicality and Shakespeare's lines. Her book about Shakespeare games for those on the autism spectrum thus is titled *Shakespeare's Heartbeat: Drama Games for Children with Autism* (Abingdon, Oxfordshire: Routledge, 2014).
50 There is not room to include this here, but he offers a compelling account of the breakdown of Hermione's breathing and speech patterns as the tragedy builds in *The Winter's Tale*. Ibid., 60.
51 Ibid., 40–1.
52 Ibid., 41.
53 Rodenburg, *Speaking Shakespeare*, 30.

54 This information was shared during a Zoom conversation on 8 October 2022.
55 *Shakespeare Behind Bars*, directed by Rogerson.
56 Byron also indicates that these exercises expanded inclusivity among the ensemble, allowing one dyslexic participant to join in freely without their typical fear of activities involving reading.
57 These previously were referred to as 'Circles of Trust'.
58 Byron's regular visits to Atlanta have been a tremendous gift. I am extremely grateful for Sammie's and Barb's willingness to share their lives and experiences with the Emory community.
59 Berry, *Voice*, 25.
60 Tara McAllister-Viel, '"Embodied Voice" and Inclusivity: Ableism and Theater Voice Training', in *Inclusivity and Equality in Performance Training: Teaching and Learning for Neuro and Physical Diversity*, ed. Petronilla Whitfield (New York: Routledge, 2022), 190.
61 Ibid., 188.
62 Ibid., 188–9. In addition to her determination for voice training to accommodate a wider range of bodies, McAllister-Viel also argues strongly in favor of voice curricula that incorporate more multicultural perspectives than are now common in western contexts. See Tara McAllister-Viel, *Training Actors' Voices: Towards an Intercultural/Interdisciplinary Approach* (London: Routledge, 2018). Additional important work in this realm is also found in Virginie Magnat, *The Performative Power of Vocality* (London: Routledge, 2020). Given this recent expansion of understanding about voice training, it seems likely that revised practices will become more evident in a number of Shakespearean environments.
63 *Timon of Athens* 1.2.121.

Chapter 2

1 Not surprisingly, given the large number of people involved, there are diverse and shifting preferences regarding the vocabulary associated with individuals belonging to the communities included in these chapters. I always aim for inclusive language, but not everyone agrees about the parameters of such designations. Some of those discussed here describe themselves as 'vision impaired', for example, although 'hearing impaired' is frequently not a preferred term for individuals in germane circumstances. Elliott reports that the actors she has

worked with wish to be called 'actors with vision impairments' rather than 'vision impaired actors', so that their status as actors remains primary. Hunter confirms that 'vision impaired' is widely used by actors at Extant and that he is ambivalent about which term is applied. He has had a lengthy acting career and only recently was told he fit the government category marking 'severe' impairment, even though he has significantly more vision than the fully blind people also included in this governmental designation. Such linguistic controversies are common among the groups included in this study. News reports in India, for example, often refer to incarcerated Shakespeareans as 'jailbirds', which is not a term congruent with the perspective typically shared by the Shakespeare in Prisons Network. In addition, a number of words historically used for some of the people discussed here would now be seen as offensive, inaccurate or otherwise inappropriate. The vocabulary included in these chapters is chosen out of respect, with the recognition that diverse individuals may choose to describe themselves in other ways and that what are considered 'best practices' regarding word choice remain in flux. For general guidance, as noted elsewhere, my Atlanta editor, Madeline Long and I rely on the American Psychological Association's 'Bias-free Language Guide', https://apastyle.apa.org/style-grammar-guidelines/bias-free-language.

2 Shanti Das and Gabriel Pogrund, 'Literary Elders in Shock as Mary Feilding Guild Retirement Home Written Off', *The Times UK*, 14 March 2021, https://www.thetimes.co.uk/article/literary-elders-in-shock-as-mary-feilding-guild-retirement-home-written-off-mtwqmxljz; Francis Beckett, 'London Care Home Residents Given Three Months to Leave', *The Guardian*, 16 March 2021, https://www.theguardian.com/society/2021/mar/16/london-care-home-residents-given-three-months-to-leave?fbclid=IwAR2dE_bOx0bPlQFJNeaE0c7fTR7CZEDaA5w11cGJDa1RdygzqpT48WHS3pk.

3 Extant commissioned a study of audio access which resulted in a book addressing the philosophical and technical aspects of this practice at length. *See* Louise Fryer and Amelia Cavallo, *Integrating Access in Live Performance* (New York: Routledge, 2022).

4 'Extant Stage States of Mind as Part of Bloomsbury Festival 2021', Theatre. London, https://www.theatre.london/news/extant-stage-states-of-mind-as-part-of-bloomsbury-festival-2021; 'States of Mind', Extant, https://extant.org.uk/project/states-of-mind/.

5 Hunter presented his solo version at the 2017 Edinburgh Fringe Festival. I am grateful that he provided me with a Vimeo version of that strong performance, which was reviewed in the *London Times*,

among other venues: Allan Radcliffe, 'Edinburgh Theatre Review: Venus and Adonis at C Primo', *London Times*, 26 August 2017, https://www.thetimes.co.uk/article/edinburgh-theatre-review-venus-and-adonis-at-c-primo-ldx65ss8p.

6 Audio access and other aspects of accessibility are currently being discussed widely. *See*, for example, Anna Matamala and Pilar Orero, eds, *Researching Audio Description: New Approaches* (London: Palgrave Macmillan, 2016).

7 Maria Oshodi, Zoom interview, 17 November 2020.

8 Shona Louise, 'Meet the Visually Impaired Performers Reimagining Shakespeare', 11 October 2021, http://www.shonalouise.com/2021/10/meet-visually-impaired-performers.html#.YZYrk73P3CU.

9 RADA, the Royal Academy of Dramatic Arts, is a prominent actor training venue in London.

10 In October 2021, disabilities and theatre blogger Shona Louise addresses this issue in 'An open letter to the commercial theatre industry about accessibility and disability representation,' Shona Louise, 'An Open Letter To The Commercial Theatre Industry about Accessibility and Disability Representation', 19 October 2021, http://www.shonalouise.com/2021/10/an-open-letter-to-commercial-theatre.html#.YZYsdb3P3CU.

11 'About Us', Extant, extant.org.uk/about-us.

12 Oshodi, Zoom Interview.

13 The Vision Statement at Survivors UK promotes 'A society that acknowledges, supports, and advocates for men and non-binary people who have been affected by rape or sexual abuse,' Survivors UK, 'About us', https://www.survivorsuk.org/about-us/.

14 Oshodi prefers the term 'inclusive' rather than 'specialized communities'. I welcome her suggestion, but 'inclusive' does not address what is distinctive about the groups considered here. As noted, such vocabulary choices remain difficult and need to remain open for emendation.

15 'GUIDELINES FOR ENGAGING INTIMACY DIRECTORS FOR LIVE PERFORMANCE', Intimacy for Stage and Screen, https://www.intimacyforstageandscreen.com/uploads/1/3/1/5/131581092/guidelines_for_engaging_an_intimacy_director_in_live_performance_v8.pdf.

16 Hunter met with me for a lengthy conversation at London's Royal Society for the Arts (thersa.org) in November 2021, with subsequent, invaluable, electronic exchanges. I appreciate his willingness to share his creative process with me and I am grateful to Esther Ruth Elliott for introducing us.

17 William Shakespeare, *The Norton Complete Works,* third edition, edited by Stephen Greenblatt, Walter Cohen, Jean Howard, Katharine Eisaman Maus, Gordon McMullan and Suzanne Gossett (New York: Norton, 2015). *Venus and Adonis*, 431.

18 'Circles' are common physical configurations in the theatrical spaces considered here, with many of the prison troupes, for instance, creating what Shakespeare Behind Bars terms circles of truth.

19 Conversation with Hunter at the RSA, November 2021.

20 Conversation with Esther Ruth Elliott, October 2021.

21 Louise, 'Meet the Visually Impaired Performers Reimagining Shakespeare'. In these interviews and elsewhere, I often diverge from academic convention and rarely mark places where typical spelling or punctuation is not included. The demand for such practices is attracting increased attention as many people are revisiting the ways that such conventions have contributed to inequities. Many disabled people, for example, use technologies that may not readily accommodate the creation of text conforming to such strictures. These conversations are ongoing, but it seems likely that changes in what constitutes 'standard' or 'proper' writing will emerge from these dialogues. *See*, for example, work on the related issue regarding racial or socio-economic language expectations by Katrina Bartow Jacobs, '"I Believe in Home Language, but the Tests don't": Addressing Linguistic Diversity within Assessment Practices across Literacy Teacher Preparation and Classroom Practice', *Teachers' College Record* 121, no. 7 (2019): 1–42, https://journals.sagepub.com/doi/abs/10.1177/016146811912100705.

22 Louise, 'Meet the Visually Impaired Performers Reimagining Shakespeare'.

23 This chapter features two former RSC actors facing increasing visual challenges. In 2019, visually blind actor and voice coach Karina Jones performed in the RSC's productions of *Measure for Measure* and *As You Like It* as the company's first blind performer on stage. More information is available at In Touch, 'A Blind Shakespearean Debut', *BBC Sounds*, 9 July 2019, https://www.bbc.co.uk/sounds/play/m0006m40.

24 Esther Ruth Elliott, 'The Man Who Saw Backwards', Extant Theatre Podcast #7 (2018), https://extant.org.uk/media/podcasts/.

25 Esther Ruth Elliott, 'Reflections on "Social Dreaming" with Shakespeare', *Shakespeare Studies* 47 (2019): 61–70.

26 According to their website, 'Pathways is Extant's pioneering four-year-long programme that aims to influence, embed and improve

greater awareness of and accessibility for blind and visually impaired practitioners across the theatre industry', extant.org.uk/artist-development/pathways/.

27 In Touch, 'A Blind Shakespearean Debut', https://www.bbc.co.uk/sounds/play/m0006m40. Featuring, in part, RSC actor Karina Jones.
28 Louise, 'Meet the Visually Impaired Performers Reimagining Shakespeare'.
29 Ibid.
30 For a description of foley techniques, *see* Jodie Francis, 'Foley Sound: What Is Foley Sound In Film & How Can I Make It?' 25 January 2021, https://www.musicgateway.com/blog/how-to/foley-sound. Foley artist Alison Craig's podcast is found at https://alisonsdiary.com/.
31 Esther Ruth Elliott, Interview with the author, November 2020.
32 Many of Synetic's award-winning wordless Shakespeare productions are now available for streaming through their website, https://synetictheater.org/.
33 Susan Bennett, *Theory for Theatre Studies: Sound* (London: Methuen Drama, 2019), 72.
34 Ibid.
35 'The Mary Feilding Guiid', Time of Their Lives, http://timeoftheirlives.com/biogs/mary-feilding-guild.
36 This information comes from an interview with Elliott in October 2021.
37 See Catherine West MP, 'Mary Feilding Guild Scandal Highlights Appalling Insecurity for Elderly Care Home Residents', Spring 2021, https://www.catherinewest.org.uk/latest-news/2021/03/23/closure-of-mary-fielding-guild/.
38 The origin of the term soundscape remains uncertain, although R. Murray Schafer seems to have brought it into wider attention after it was either coined or used earlier by city planner Michael Southworth in 1969. For an account of Schafer's discussion of Southworth, *see* Carlotta Darò, *Avant-gardes Sonores en architecture [Avant-garde in sonic architecture]* (Dijon: Les Presses du Réel, 2013), 185.
39 Emory recently acquired John Moore's Bram Stoker archive; consequently, I have become immersed in that realm. The Shakespearean soundscape quickly becomes evident in this context, since one of Thomas Edison's first recordings (which survive) were of Henry Irving reciting excerpts from the plays. See Michael Kilgarriff, 'The Voice of Henry Irving: Henry Irving and the Phonograph: Bennett Maxwell', *The Irving Society*, https://www

.theirvingsociety.org.uk/the-voice-of-henry-irving/. Only one of the recordings, from *Richard III,* is widely believed to be by Irving, but the Irving Society offers it as well as a less certain excerpt from *Henry VIII* at https://www.theirvingsociety.org.uk/king-richard-iii-act-i-scene-1/.

40 The idea that audiences would go to 'hear' a play has been commonly reported over the past few years, by Bridget Escolme and others. See Bridget Escolme, 'Costume', in *The Cambridge Guide to the Worlds of Shakespeare*, vol. 1, ed. Bruce R. Smith (Cambridge: Cambridge University Press, 2016), 105–12. Shakespeareans have begun to question this belief, however. For detailed discussions of this topic, see Tiffany Stern, 'Theatre'+ 'Play + House': Naming Spaces in the Time of Shakespeare', in *Playing and Playgoing in Early Modern England: Actor, Audience, and Performance*, ed. Simon Smith and Emma Whipday (Cambridge: Cambridge University Press, 2016), 186–204 and Gabriel Egan, 'Hearing or Seeing a Play: Evidence in Early Modern Theatrical Terminology', *Ben Jonson Journal* 8 (2001): 327–47. I appreciate Tiffany Stern's willingness to share her essay with me while it was in page proofs.

41 Predictably, 'sound studies' is a contested term. Mark Grimshaw-Aagaard, for instance, suggests 'auditory culture,' a preference he proffers in *The Routledge Companion to Sound Studies*, 16.

42 While working on this chapter, I learned of the death of sound specialist, Ian Rawes, who documented London's soundscape: https://soundsurvey.org.uk/. His career corresponds with the growth of sound studies and his contributions are greatly appreciated. Tony Harrington, 'Ian Rawes (26 February 1965–19 October 2021)', *The Wire*, https://www.thewire.co.uk/in-writing/essays/ian-rawes-26-february-1965-19-october-2021.

43 Michael Bull, ed., *The Routledge Companion to Sound Studies* (New York: Routledge 2019), xvii.

44 Jonathan Sterne, ed., *The Sound Studies Reader* (New York: Routledge, 2012), 1.

45 Ibid., 2.

46 Bennet, *Theory for Theatre*, 2.

47 Ibid., 27.

48 Elliott, '"Social Dreaming"', 64.

49 Ibid.

50 Wes Folkerth, *The Sound of Shakespeare* (New York: Routledge, 2002), 9.

51 Smith's current work is also based on sound and promises to be as illuminating as his previous publications. It gives me particular pleasure to cite Smith's body of significant scholarship, because I have known him since I was seventeen. As a freshman in college, I was not enrolled in his course, but knocked on his office door in pursuit of a book I thought he might own, even though the Georgetown library did not. He graciously provided the book and has subsequently served as a generous and thought-provoking colleague. I am very appreciative of his contributions to the world of Shakespeare studies and to my travels through this realm.

52 Bruce R. Smith, *The Acoustic World of Early Modern England: Attending to the O-Factor* (Chicago: University of Chicago Press, 1999), 3.

53 Ibid., 4.

54 Ibid., 25.

55 Ibid., 29.

56 The use of regional accents is increasing in mainstream productions and other entertainment media currently. Renowned actor David Tennant, for example, did not alter his Scottish accent in 'Good,' a recent production at London's Harold Pinter Theatre, that will be shown at international cinemas through National Theatre Live. *See* Holly O'Mahoney, 'David Tennant in "Good," Harold Pinter Theatre Review', *Culture Whisper*, 13 October 2022, https://www.culturewhisper.com/r/theatre/david_tennant_good_play_london/15181#:~:text=One%20of%20them%20is%2C%20of%20course%2C%20TV%20star,make%20Cooke%E2%80%99s%20confusing%2C%20overtly%20intellectual%20production%20wholly%20engaging; and National Theatre Live, 'Good' Synopsis', National Theatre Live, https://good.ntlive.com/synopsis/. Martin Compston, who captured wide acclaim for his role in *Line of Duty*, apparently startles viewers who hear him speak in his Scottish accent, something he also does in his current television series, *The Dig*. See 'Line of Duty fans shocked to hear Scot Martin Compston's real accent after years of playing Southerner Steve Arnott.' *See* Henna Sharma, 'GREAT SCOT! Line of Duty Fans Shocked to Discover Scot Martin Compston's Real Accent after Years of Playing Southerner Steve Arnott', *The Sun*, 2 May 2021, https://www.thesun.co.uk/uncategorized/14831585/line-of-duty-martin-compston-real-accent/ and Alex Moreland, 'The Rig: Amazon Prime Release Date, Trailer, and Cast with Martin Compston, Iain Glen, and Emily Hampshire', *The Scotsman*, https://www.scotsman.com/culture/television/the-rig-amazon-prime-release-date-trailer-cast-martin-compston-iain-glen-emily-hampshire-3971531.

57 Sonia Massai, *Shakespeare's Accents: Voicing Identity in Performance* (Cambridge: Cambridge University Press, 2020), 1.
58 Ibid., 20.
59 Ibid.
60 While not emerging in response to the pandemic. Hampstead Theatre offered an audio-centric production of *Little Scratch* during this period. https://www.hampsteadtheatre.com/whats-on/2021/little-scratch/.
61 Most of the information about KATG derives from their website (https://www.knockatthegate.com/) or from my Zoom interview with its directors, Joe Discher and Sean Hudock on 9 May 2022. I was fortunate to experience both productions and appreciate KATG's willingness to share *Julius Caesar* with me and my students. They also met with my students over Zoom. I was able to link directly into *Macbeth*.
62 Sean Hudock sent me this update in an email exchange in October 2022.
63 Their website also indicates that they have used these productions to raise money for the Actors Fund, which helps artists in need, as many have been during the pandemic. Knock at the Gate, https://www.knockatthegate.com/.
64 Sonya Freeman Loftis, *Shakespeare & Disability Studies* (Oxford: Oxford University Press, 2021), 90. 'Universal design' refers to the concept that many aspects of life can be structured to meet diverse needs: pavement adjustments created for wheelchairs, for instance, can also help those with luggage. There are a number of books describing universal design in education and in architecture. See, for example, Edward Steinfeld and Jordana Maisel, *Universal Design: Creating Inclusive Environments* (Hoboken, NJ: Wiley, 2012).
65 Personal correspondence, 13 January 2023.
66 Discher worked with the Shakespeare Theatre of New Jersey for several years, leaving in 2012.
67 As an undergraduate, Discher did extensive research in the UK on British radio drama, but KATG aims for a more broadly experiential design. For more detail about Shakespeare on the radio, *see* Michael P. Jensen, *The Battle of the Bard: Shakespeare on U.S. Radio in 1937* (Leeds: ARC University Press, 2018), (published in conjunction with Amsterdam University Press); and Jensen, '"Prithee, Listen Well," The Case for Audio Shakespeare', in *The Shakespearean World*, ed. Jill L. Levinson and Robert Ormsby (London: Routledge, 2017), 407–17.

68 The KATG team points out that the connection of this *Julius Caesar* to a NASA project seems appropriate since the Romans were the first to adopt a lunar calendar.

69 NASA, 'The Sonification Project', InsightIAS, 20 September 2020, https://www.insightsonindia.com/2020/09/26/nasas-sonification-project/#:~:text=The%20sonification%20project%20is%20led%20by%20the%20Chandra,visually-impaired%20communities%20%E2%80%94%20to%20experience%20space%20through%20data.

70 Knock at the Gate, https://www.knockatthegate.com/.

71 Zoom interview with Joe Discher and Sean Hudock on 9 May 2022.

72 KATG produced *Macbeth* twice. In the first iteration, they combined the characters of Ross and Lennox; the second production was created in concert with Emory University, so they kept these figures separate in order to provide involvement for as many students as possible.

73 This text has been edited from the Zoom transcript for clarity.

74 *1 Henry IV* 3.1.229.

75 *1 Henry IV* 3.1.230.

76 Jensen, *Battle of the Bard*, 82.

Chapter 3

1 This chapter addresses a diffuse set of programmes, including at least one that simultaneously provokes acclaim and controversy. Given the sensitivity often associated with these communities, it is particularly difficult to designate appropriate terms for them. Some of them are presented as working with those associated with 'learning disabilities', 'learning differences', or 'neurodiversity'; others are presented for persons linked with what used to be termed as the autism spectrum, but who are now more commonly called 'autistic' people or 'autistics'. Still others identify their aim as 'inclusivity', although an increasing number of people are balking at the term 'inclusive'. Throughout this chapter, I work to align my phrasing with respect for how the programmes present themselves, but I remain aware that these may not correlate with the perspectives of others invested in these issues. I endeavour to be respectful of all involved, but 'one size fits all' does not appear to exist in this environment. Petronilla Whitfield discusses some of the controversies, including nomenclature issues, in Petronilla Whitfield, *Teaching Strategies for Neurodiversity and Dyslexia*

in Actor Training: Sensing Shakespeare (Abingdon, Oxfordshire: Routledge, 2020) 4–5. Whitfield's study predominantly addresses the challenges and possibilities associated with dyslexic acting students, but many of her insights offer broader perspectives.

2 The story of this facility can be found in Andy Merriman's 2007 account, *Tales of Normansfield: The Langdon Down Legacy* (London: Down Syndrome Association); Nicholas Chinardet, 'Londonist Discovers Normansfield Hospital Entertainment Hall', *Londonist*, 26 October 2009.

3 John Earl notes that Down was first known as John Langdon Haydon Down, but later became Langdon-Down. Both versions appear in references to him. John Earl, 'Dr Langdon-Down and the Normansfield Theatre', Borough of Twickenham Local History Society, *Occasional Paper* 6 (1997): 6.

4 Merriman, *Tales of Normansfield*, 27.

5 For example, see Dennis B. Downey and James W. Conroy, *Pennhurst and the Struggle for Disability Rights* (University Park: Penn State University Press; Keystone Books, 2020). Such institutions vary widely, and no blanket assumptions are implied here. From a modern perspective, Langdon-Down's contributions to the assessment and care of this population can be seen as progressive, but also as racist and demeaning to the population he worked with. I have found nothing to suggest that Normansfield mistreated its inhabitants, but Langdon-Down's problematic ethnic and socio-economic categorizations of this genetic condition need to be acknowledged. For more information, see O. Conor Ward, 'John Langdon Down: The Man and the Message', *Down Syndrome Research and Practice* 6, no. 1 (1999): 19–24, John Langdon-Down, *On the Education and Training of the Feeble in Mind* (London: H.K. Lewis, 1876), https://ia801302.us.archive.org/29/items/b22305397/b22305397.pdf and Langdon-Down, 'Lettsomian Lectures on Some of the Mental Affections of Childhood and Youth', *The British Medical Journal* 1, no. 36 (1887, January 22): 149–51, https://www.jstore.org/stable/2021034. Earl references archival sources indicating that staff were required to treat children well and that more than one infraction against this dictum would result in termination. John Earl, *Dr Langdon-Down and the Normansfield Theatre* (London: Borough of Twickenham Local History Society, 1997), 16. It must be noted, however, that this treatment may well be linked to the likely affluence of the parents drawn to this facility for the care of their offspring.

6 For a description of Shakespeare for those with learning disabilities at a beloved residential facility now facing potential closure, see Stephen Unwin, 2019. I am grateful to Steve for reading draft chapters and

for providing a good ear and charming company as I was writing this volume.
7 In *Dr. Langdon-Down*, however, Earl observes that some of the Theatre's scenery was appropriate for *A Midsummer Night's Dream* (25) and that *Merchant of Venice* was performed there in 1904 after Langdon-Down's death (33).
8 Merriman, *Tales of Normansfield*, 95.
9 Ibid., 87.
10 Ibid., 90.
11 Cited in Ibid., 89.
12 John Langdon Down, *On Some of the Mental Affects of Childhood and Youth* (London: J & A Churchill, 1887), 140.
13 Merriman, *Tales of Normansfield*, 97–8.
14 'Past Events', Instant Opera, https://www.instantopera.co.uk/past. For information about English classifications of listed buildings, *see* Historic England's guide on designated listed buildings, https://historicengland.org.uk/listing/what-is-designation/listed-buildings/.
15 Merriman, *Tales of Normansfield*, 89.
16 It bears repeating that learning differences vary widely. This term encompasses a wide range of cognitive abilities, and it does not serve anyone well to conflate people under narrow labels that imply congruities that do not exist.
17 Merriman, *Tales of Normansfield*, 97–8.
18 Ibid., 99.
19 Ramps on the Moon, https://www.rampsonthemoon.co.uk/.
20 Information about this production can be found at 'Leeds Playhouse and Ramps On the Moon Co-Production of "Oliver Twist" As Part Of NT At Home', Ramps on the Moon, 8 February 2022, https://www.rampsonthemoon.co.uk/ramps-on-the-moon/leeds-playhouse-and-ramps-on-the-moon-co-production-of-oliver-twist-as-part-of-nt-at-home/.
21 The Apothetae, http://www.theapothetae.org/.
22 Information contained here is drawn from the company website, an in-person interview with Creative Director Amy Cunningham and other members of the staff, as well as from productions co-presented by Ramps on the Moon.
23 Theatrical friends in London indicate that many arts practitioners are hesitant about these strategies, but I have no independent verification of this.

24 For information about Laban, *see* Barbara Adrian, *Actor Training the Laban Way: An Integrated Approach to Voice, Speech, and Movement* (New York: Allworth Press, 2008).
25 Demonstrations of their work can be found on their YouTube channel: https://www.youtube.com/c/DarkHorseTheatreUK.
26 Vanessa Brooks, 'The Silent Approach', blog post, https://vanessabrooks2020.com/the-silent-approach/.
27 Thanks to Amy Cunningham for supplying this information from the Dark Horse Theatre archives. There is a short Vimeo clip available online at https://vimeo.com/308700416.
28 Not all Ramps on the Moon affiliated productions follow this standard. In the Leeds Playhouse 2022 *Macbeth*, for instance, blind actor Karina Jones was regularly assisted, albeit subtly, as she entered and exited the stage.
29 The programme suggests that no Dark Horse Theatre members were in the cast. Karina Jones, however, the blind actor mentioned earlier, plays Hero's mother in this production. Sheffield Theatres and Ramps on the Moon, *Much Ado About Nothing* programme, November 2022.
30 Mackenzie also discusses Blue Apple. *See* Mackenzie, *Creating Space*, 63–5, 180–1, 189–92, 192–4.
31 Blue Apple staff, board members and performers have been very welcoming every time I have visited them in Winchester or elsewhere. It has been a great pleasure to spend time with them. I am grateful for their hospitality.
32 'Our Mission', Blue Apple Theatre, https://blueappletheatre.com/our-mission-1.
33 Jessup's brother created a documentary detailing the progression of the Blue Apple production of *Hamlet*, in which Tommy Jessup played the title role. 'Growing up Downs', directed by William Jessup (London: BBC3, 2015), https://growingupdowns.co.uk/, Jessup's IMDB profile can be found at https://www.imdb.com/name/nm2573241/.
34 British Academy of Film and Television Arts; bafta.org.
35 'Macbeth', Blue Apple Theatre, https://blueappletheatre.com/macbeth#macbeth-performances.
36 Ibid.
37 In conversation with some of the Blue Apple ensemble members in November 2022, they quickly agreed with my assessment that the volume of their activities is 'dizzying'. Be In! (clusive) Festival

and Symposium, Winchester, UK (2 November). 'About Project', Be In!(clusive), https://beintheatres.com/en/about-project/.
38 Ibid.
39 One of the companies partnering with Blue Apple, Warsaw's Teatr-21, which primarily includes autistic actors and those with Down syndrome, devised a play (*Revolution 21*), which has now been made into a documentary of the same name. For over a month in 2018, groups of disabled people, their carers and their families occupied part of the Polish Parliament in pursuit of better conditions and appropriate financial support for those with disabilities and their families, whose caregiving responsibilities often preclude paid employment. In a conversation with the audience after a 2022 sneak preview showing of the film in Winchester, cast members made it clear that the political aspect of this documentary takes precedence over its artistic aims. As this volume demonstrates, such multiple goals are common within these diverse communities currently offering arts programmes. *Revolution 21*, written and directed by Martyna Peszko, https://www.crew-united.com/de/Revolution-21__288337.html.
40 The day I attended rehearsals, the team included Vickers, Alice Rayman, Lewis Penfold, Melissa Toye and John Handscombe, who each demonstrated considerable skill in supporting and encouraging these actors.
41 Brian Edmiston and Iona Towler-Evans, *Humanizing Education with Dramatic Inquiry: In Dialogue with Dorothy Heathcote's Transformative Pedagogy* (New York: Routledge, 2022), 2. Heathcote's works remain available. Edmiston and Towler-Evans volume is one of several recent studies emphasizing her influence.
42 'Meet the Team', Bamboozle Theatre, https://bamboozletheatre.co.uk/meet-the-team/.
43 Christopher Davies, *The Bamboozle Book of Dramatic Starts: 17 ways to Start a Drama Lesson with Special Needs Pupils* (Leicester: Anchorprint, [2006] 2014) and *Creating Multi-Sensory Environments: Practical Ideas for Teaching and Learning* (London: Routledge, [2012] 2020).
44 I appreciate the willingness of Christopher Davies, Bamboozle's artistic director, to offer me a Vimeo version of this production. I also thank him for sharing the company's history, processes and experiences with me via Zoom and in person. YouTube includes excerpts from the English version *The Storm*: 'Storm: A Production for Young AS Audiences from Bamboozle', Bamboozle Theatre Company, https://www.youtube.com/watch?v=hRDdPAdTvd8. The

play has also been presented in Chinese, a process described on the Bamboozle website: 'Storm', Bamboozle Theatre Company, https://bamboozletheatre.co.uk/shows/my-show/. I am also appreciative of his invitation for me to see the troupe in action in November 2022.

45 'How to use creative strategies and reduce conflict and anxiety when working with children who are on the Autism Spectrum', Bamboozle Theatre, https://bamboozletheatre.co.uk/events/as-training/.
46 'Creating & Using Multi-Sensory Environments', Bamboozle Theatre, https://bamboozletheatre.co.uk/events/creating-using-multi-sensory-environments/.
47 Davies, *Creating Multi-Sensory Environments*, 25.
48 This information comes from a conversation with Davies at Curve Theatre, Leicester on 28 November 2022.
49 *Rain Rain: A Showcase Performance for Friends of Bamboozle*, Studio, Curve Theatre, Leicester, UK, 28 November 2022.
50 '""Storm": A Companion Pack for Teachers & Support Staff', Bamboozle Theatre, 4, https://bamboozletheatre.co.uk/wp-content/uploads/2020/07/Storm-Teacher-Companion-Pack.pdf.
51 Conversation with Davies at Curve Theatre, Leicester, 28 November 2022.
52 'Companion Pack', 6–7.
53 Ibid., 8.
54 Ibid.
55 Ibid.
56 Mackenzie has significant experience with Flute and discusses their work in her book. See Mackenzie, *Creating Space*, 28–32, 39–43, 82–5.
57 'Who We Are', Flute Theatre, https://flutetheatre.co.uk/who-we-are/. Bamboozle, by the way, has no affiliation with Flute and the companies are not in contact with each other.
58 Hunter emphasizes the centrality of this aspect of the games in *Shakespeare's Heartbeat*, 8.
59 Ohio State University Nisonger Center, https://nisonger.osu.edu.
60 This information comes from an announcement for a discussion between Hunter and Goldsmith lecturer Dr. Jamie A Ward in conjunction with performances of Flute's two different productions of *Pericles* (one for general audiences; the other for autistic audiences and their carers) in October and November 2022. 'Pericles', Riverside Studios, https://riversidestudios.co.uk/see-and-do/pericles-46148/.

61 Hunter, *Shakespeare's Heartbeat*, 4.
62 Ibid., 9.
63 Kelly Hunter and Robert Shaughnessy, 'Flute Theatre, Shakespeare, and Autism', in *Reimaging Shakespeare Education: Teaching and Learning Through Collaboration*, ed. Liam Semler, et al. (Cambridge: Cambridge University Press, 2023), 271–81.
64 Ibid., 275.
65 Hunter's work is cited in two essays written by Shakespeare Institute graduates aimed at preparing autistic students for GCSE essay exams. *See* Susie Flintham, 'Tailoring Shakespeare to Students with Autism', *Teaching Shakespeare* 12 (2017), https://www.britishshakespeare.ws/wp-content/uploads/2021/10/TeachingShakespeare12_AW_Web1.pdf and Charlotte Roberts, 'The Play's the Thing: Choosing the Right Text for ASC Students', *Teaching Shakespeare* 12 (2017), https://www.britishshakespeare.ws/wp-content/uploads/2021/10/TeachingShakespeare12_AW_Web1.pdf.
66 Material on HHM drawn from this scientific research and elsewhere can be found in Tara Baran, Mary-Grace Kelly and Anne Dickerson, 'The Hunter Heartbeat Method: Evaluating the Impact of a Theater-Based Intervention on Children on the Autism Spectrum', *The American Journal of Occupational Therapy* 72, no. 4, Supplement 1 (2018), https://research.aota.org/ajot/article-abstract/72/4_Supplement_1/7211520313p1/8049/The-Hunter-Heartbeat-Method-Evaluating-the-Impact?redirectedFrom=fulltext; Margaret Helen Mehling, 'Differential Impact of Drama-Based versus Traditional Social Skills Intervention' (Dissertation, Ohio State University, 2017); Margaret Helen Mehling, Marc J. Tassé and Robin Root, 'Shakespeare and Autism: An Exploratory Evaluation of the Hunter Heartbeat Method', *Research and Practice in Intellectual and Developmental Disabilities* 4, no. 2 (2016): 107–20, https://www.tandfonline.com/doi/full/10.1080/23297018.2016.1207202; 'Groundbreaking Intervention Technique, The Hunter Heartbeat Method, Comes to TLS', The Learning Spectrum (2022), https://thelearningspectrum.com/groundbreaking-intervention-technique-the-hunter-heartbeat-method-comes-to-tls/; and Mary Jane Williams, 'Autism and Shakespeare: Ohio State Researchers Study the Hunter Heartbeat Method', *Washington Post*, 9 April 2013, https://www.washingtonpost.com/lifestyle/on-parenting/autism-and-shakespeare-ohio-state-researchers-study-hunter-heartbeat-method/2013/04/09/843cc67e-9003-11e2-9abd-e4c5c9dc5e90_story.html.
67 Robert Shaughnessy, 'Give Me Your Hands', in Forum: Specialized Performers and Audiences, *Shakespeare Studies* 74 (2019): 79.

68 Nicola Shaughnessy discusses her own adult autism diagnosis in 'Life Changing: Meal Deal', BBC *Radio 4*, 2 November 2022, https://www.bbc.co.uk/programmes/m001dndw.

69 Robert Shaughnessy mentions Gabriel's autism and participation as a 'Creative Associate' of Flute in a footnote to a recent article written by Kelly Hunter and Robert Shaughnessy, 'Flute Theatre, Shakespeare, and Autism', 271. Nicola Shaughnessy also comments on her son's autism and his high level of caring needs in 'Life Changing: Meal Deal'.

70 Loftis, 'Autistic Culture, Shakespeare Therapy, and the Hunter Heartbeat Method', 260.

71 Ibid., 257.

72 Ibid.

73 Ibid.

74 Hunter indicates that those objecting about HHM to the BSA were not open to discussion. She also points out that many of the children she works with are in 24/7 care situations, which is distinct from the circumstances of those in the academic community who are voicing complaints, predominantly on Twitter. Kelly Hunter, Conversation at Riverside Theatre, London, 25 October 2022.

75 This meeting, which I attended, was held over Zoom. Loftis was not present at this or any of the other HHM discussions referenced in this chapter.

76 This information comes from a BSA Zoom meeting about this topic and from conversations with several people involved with the conference and in the discussions about responding to complaints.

77 'The Shakespeare Beyond Borders Alliance Launch Event', University of Birmingham, https://www.birmingham.ac.uk/schools/edacs/departments/shakespeare/events/2021/shakespeare-beyond-borders-alliance.aspx.

78 I unsuccessfully tried to encourage such a discussion at the 2021 online Folger Shakespeare Institute/Emory University seminar entitled 'New Scholarly Directions in Premodern Disability Studies and Performance' that I co-directed with Allison Hobgood. As noted, the BSA similarly failed in this regard.

79 Stephen Unwin offers an overview of the kinds of issues at stake in this and related controversies about autism and learning differences, including common demands for self-advocacy on behalf of people without the means to communicate their wishes. I appreciate Unwin's willingness to share this manuscript and look forward to seeing

the book in print. Stephen Unwin, *The Golden Smile: Learning Disabilities in Culture and Society* (Manuscript in preparation).
80 These remarks are drawn from an email narrative provided to me by Karen Saillant on 13 September 2018, supplemented by a Zoom conversation on 12 October 2022, in addition to the time I spent in Umbria with the operatic and Terrarte ensembles.
81 This studio, Associazione Laboratorio Terrarte, can be found at https://www.facebook.com/Associazione-Laboratorio-Terrarte-421551861229943/.
82 Saillant, email narrative, 1 November 2018.
83 Ibid.
84 Saillant, Zoom conversation, 12 October 2022.
85 Email exchange with Saillant, 12 October 2022. This material is excerpted from the outline of a piece she was creating in collaboration with Gianlauro Casodi, a researcher in sustainability at the University of Parma.
86 Ibid.
87 Ibid.
88 Ibid.
89 These remarks are drawn from an email narrative provided to me by Karen Saillant on 13 September 2018.
90 Saillant email, 13 September 2018.
91 Ibid.

Chapter 4

1 As with many of the groups discussed in this study, there are various modes of identifying notation currently being practiced with the people included here. Frequently, the term 'deaf' refers to hearing status, while 'Deaf' alludes to the people and communities using sign language and/or it references 'Deaf culture'. 'Hearing impaired' is often avoided. Since there is no universal agreement about terminology, I am defaulting to d/Deaf, unless I am quoting something from print that makes an alternative choice or if someone included expresses a specific preference.
2 Apothetae Theatre, in New York, regularly presents productions cast with actors possessing a diverse range of abilities. In January 2021,

for instance, they offered a virtual reading of Play On Shakespeare's *Titus Andronicus* in a modern verse translation by Amy Freed, that included both d/Deaf and hearing actors, live captioning and ASL translation. http://www.theapothetae.org/body-of-work.html.

3 d/Deaf actor William Grint performed in the 2021 RSC *Comedy of Errors*. (https://www.signedculture.org.uk/william-grint-is-at-the-rsc-royal-shakespeare-company-in-the-comedy-of-errors/) and d/Deaf actor Russell Harvard appeared in Sam Gold's New York production of *King Lear* (Aja Romano, '82-year-old Glenda Jackson is Towering. But She can't Rescue a Bungled Show', *Vox*, 16 April 2019, https://www.vox.com/culture/2019/4/16/18291744/king-lear-review-glenda-jackson-ruth-wilson-trump). Josie Rourke's 2022 London production of *As You Like It* also includes significant signing and captioning, as noted on the @sohoplace website: '@sohoplace are happy to confirm that Rose Ayling-Ellis and other members of the company will be using BSL as part of the performance and we have announced that all performances of the play will run with captions which will be accessible to the entire audience. The captions have been incorporated into the production to create a fully inclusive experience for all. Screens will be set on all four sides of the theatre so wherever you sit, you will be able to see the screens and the action on stage.' They also indicate, however, that only one performance will be presented fully through BSL and only two will be audio-described. These are only three recent examples of this trend. There is increasing scholarly work being done on the expanding artistic job opportunities for d/Deaf actors. Michael Shurgot, for example, writes about the incorporation of d/Deaf actors in Shakespearean performances in 'Breaking the Sound Barrier: Howie Seago and American Sign Language at Oregon Shakespeare', *Shakespeare Bulletin* 30, no. 1 (Spring 2012): 21–36, 10.1353/shb.2012.0019; while Jill Marie Bradbury discusses recent productions in 'Audiences, American Sign Language, and Deafness', *Shakespeare Bulletin* 40, no. 1 (Spring 2022): 45–67, 10.1353/shb.2022.0000.

4 When I began this study, I worried about my lack of fluency in ASL and BSL. As my investigations continued, however, I realized that since d/Deaf performers were frequently being integrated into productions designed for broad audiences, many of the performers I anticipated including here were not as relevant as I predicted. Those fluent in these languages are better suited to consider the wider range of d/Deaf performances than I am. There are also, of course, many analyses of d/Deaf performers in mainstream theatre still awaited eagerly. I have attended many such performances including d/Deaf actors during my preparation for this study. Thanks to Jill

Bradbury who helped guide me through numerous productions in the United States and Canada.

5   Such productions are increasingly available. The 2022 Edinburgh Fringe Festival, for instance, included numerous germane offerings. In addition, its programme provides an index listing audio described, signed, captioned and relaxed performances. Edinburgh Festival Fringe Society (2022), 233–5. Shortly after the Fringe, London's Arcola Theatre presented Kanze Motomasa's *Sumida River in Sign Language*, directed by Verity Lee, based on a Japanese Noh drama and featuring sign language and audio narration. Arcola Theatre, Grimeborn Opera Festival, 26 July–10 September 2022.

6   For information about these productions, *see* 'Love's Labour's Lost', Deafinitely Theatre, https://www.deafinitelytheatre.co.uk/Event/loves-labours-lost and 'A Midsummer Night's Dream', Deafinitely Theatre, https://www.deafinitelytheatre.co.uk/Event/a-midsummer-nights-dream.

7   *The Tempest—Swimming for Beginners* (2021). A collaboration between the British Council, Owlspot Theatre (Japan) and Graeae Theatre, UK. 'Japan-UK-Bangladesh International Collaborative Project "The Tempest – Swimming for Beginners"', https://www.britishcouncil.jp/en/programmes/arts/tempest.

8   This distinction between companies is not always clearcut or absolute with these groups.

9   *See*, for example, Abigail Rokison-Woodall and Tracey Irish, 'Signing Shakespeare', 23 June 2021. Information about this programme can be found at 'About: The University of Birmingham Signing Shakespeare Programme is Designed to Support Deaf Young People in their Study and Enjoyment of Shakespeare', Royal Shakespeare Company, https://www.rsc.org.uk/learn/schools-and-teachers/teacher-resources/signing-shakespeare-for-deaf-students/about#:~:text=Signing%20Shakespeare%20is%20a%20project%20designed%20to%20support,people%20in%20their%20study%20and%20enjoyment%20of%20Shakespeare; and in 'Signing Shakespeare', Mod-Con, https://modconpak.com/Blog/5265; Hay Festival of Literature and the Arts, 'Signing Shakespeare,' Equality Shakespeare Festival, Shakespeare Institute of the University of Birmingham, Stratford-upon-Avon, transcript of Zoom presentation, 8 June 2021.

10 Abigail Rokison-Woodall and Tracey Irish, 'Signing Shakespeare', Equality Shakespeare Festival 2020, Shakespeare Institute of the University of Birmingham, Stratford-upon-Avon. Transcript of Zoom presentation, 8 June 2020. As anyone who has worked with Zoom transcripts knows well, they are notoriously unreliable. I

apologize profusely for any transcription errors included anywhere in this study. I often do not know, for example, if those included prefer 'Deaf' or 'deaf,' but I feel quite certain they would not choose the frequent Zoom spelling that ends this word with a 'd'.

11 Rokison-Woodall and Irish, 'Signing Shakespeare', Zoom transcript.
12 Ibid.
13 Ibid. Rokison-Woodall subsequently distances the project from the term 'visual vernacular', since that phrasing holds specific connotations in d/Deaf communication that are related, but distinctive, from what this project creates.
14 Ibid.
15 Ibid.
16 Embodied cognition also features in the work of many practitioners included in this study, as the previous chapters suggest.
17 Rokison-Woodall and Irish, 'Signing Shakespeare', Zoom transcript.
18 Ibid.
19 Ibid.
20 Ibid.
21 My understanding is that ToM is accepted in some scientific circles, although it is criticized vis-a-vis autism. The potential role of ToM in the practices described here clearly requires further discussion.
22 Rokison-Woodall, Zoom conversation, 22 September 2022.
23 In the brief conversation noted in October, 2022, Hunter indicated that she was not drawing on ToM while developing HHM. Kelly Hunter, Conversation at Riverside Theatre, London, 25 October 2022. In her book, she attributes her inspiration to Louis Zukofsky's 1963 book *Bottom: on Shakespeare*. Hunter, *Shakespeare's Heartbeat*, 2. Nicola Grove and Keith Park, in contrast, emphasize ToM in their book focused on *Macbeth* with people with learning differences of many kinds. See Nicola Grove and Keith Park, *Social Cognition Through Drama And Literature for People with Learning Disabilities: Macbeth in Mind* (London: Jessica Kingsley, 2021).
24 Jacquie O'Hanlon and Angie Wootten, *Using Drama to Teach Personal, Social, and Emotional Skills* (Los Angeles: Sage, 2007), 10.
25 Hunter, *Shakespeare's Heartbeat*, 19.
26 Ibid.
27 Sheila T. Cavanagh and Allison P. Hobgood, co-directors, 'New Scholarly Directions in Premodern Disability Studies and

Performance', Co-sponsored by Emory University and The Folger Institute, with support from Georgia Humanities, 2021.
28 Hunter, *Shakespeare's Heartbeat*, 4–5. Remarks in the book such as these generated heated comments during the 2021 Emory University/Folger Institute symposium on 'New Scholarly Directions in Premodern Disability Studies and Performance' from those who believe that HHM dehumanizes people with autism due to its adherence to what they perceive as outdated and inappropriate perspectives. Many audience members and participants who attend these performances, however, clearly find them compelling, engaging and compassionate. This disparity emphasizes differences between communities who are not engaged in conversation with each other.
29 O'Hanlon and Wootten, *Using Drama*, x.
30 Ibid.
31 Rokison-Woodall and Irish, 'Signing Shakespeare'.
32 I note, however, that I am not aware that SS has received criticism from this perspective.
33 *See* Augusto Boal, Adrian Jackson trans., *Games for Actors and Non-Actors* (New York: Routledge, 1992).
34 Rokison-Woodall and Irish, 'Signing Shakespeare'.
35 *See* Snyder-Young, *The Theatre of Good Intentions* for a detailed discussion of the kinds of assumptions often brought to this kind of work.
36 These biographical details appear on the back cover of O'Hanlon and Wootten, *Using Drama*.
37 Rokison-Woodall and I discussed her family's choices between 'deaf' and 'Deaf'. She indicated that she uses 'deaf' to refer to her son, as a term referring to his level of hearing. She notes that 'Deaf' is often presented as a mode of social identification and that such referencing would be her son's decision as he aged. Zoom interview, 22 September 2022.
38 Rokison-Woodall and Irish, 'Signing Shakespeare', Zoom transcript.
39 Apparently, Wooten was specifically chosen as Rokison-Woodall's son's teacher due to her interest in using drama in the education of d/Deaf children. Ibid.
40 Ibid.
41 O'Hanlon and Wootten, *Using Drama*, back cover.
42 Ibid., xiv.
43 *See*, for example, Ibid., 32.

44 The practitioners from the programmes including the development of empathy discussed in other chapters did not cite theory of mind when they described their practices.
45 Rokison-Woodall and Irish, 'Signing Shakespeare'. They also note that there are no current publications linking theory of mind with d/Deaf drama education.
46 Ibid.
47 Some of the criticisms of HHM at the Emory/Folger symposium specifically referenced serious concerns about theory of mind.
48 Simon Baron-Cohen, *Mindblindness: An Essay on Autism and Theory of Mind* (Ipswitch: Bradford Books, 1997), 71. Baron-Cohen's ToM work has been challenged by those in the field as well as by disabilities scholars and advocates. *See*, for example, Morton Ann Gernsbacher and Melanie Yergeau, 'Empirical Failures of the Claim That Autistic People Lack a Theory of Mind', *Archives of Scientific Psychology* 7, no. 1 (2019): 102–18, https://www.ncbi.nlm.nih.gov/pmc/articles/PMC6959478/#article-1aff-info. Thanks for Madeline Long for providing this reference.
49 Katherine Wareham and Alex Kelly, *Talkabout Theory of Mind: Teaching Theory of Mind to Improve Social Skills and Relationships* (London: Routledge, 2020). Front matter, np.
50 Henry M. Welman, *Making Minds: How Theory of Mind Develops* (Oxford: Oxford University Press, 2014), 2.
51 Rokison-Woodall and Irish, 'Signing Shakespeare'.
52 Ibid.
53 There does not appear to be a website for this company in 2022.
54 The website containing this link is no longer accessible, but more detail about the production can be found in this announcement about the performance: https://dogandponydcwebsite.files.wordpress.com/2017/09/party-on-program1.pdf.
55 According to the transcript accompanying the NEA-sponsored *Romeo and Juliet* documentary discussed in this chapter, 'Gallaudet has a long history of Shakespeare in American Sign Language (ASL). Students and faculty have been performing Shakespeare's plays since 1884.' *See* Bradbury, et al., ProTactile *Romeo and Juliet*, documentary transcript (2021), https://www.youtube.com/watch?v=btB_nePm860. Gallaudet University enrolls d/Deaf and signing undergraduate and post-graduate students and includes numerous DeafBlind enrollees.

56 'Party On: A Sensory Revelry in Romeo and Juliet', DC Theatre Scene.com, https://dctheatrescene.com/show/party-sensory-revelry-romeo-juliet/.

57 Incorporating scent into filmed performance has a checkered history, including the short-lived 'smell-o-vision', https://www.olorama.com/smell-o-vision and Aromarama, https://nationalboardofreview.org/2014/01/innovations-cinema-aromarama/. Just as video games have developed impressively in sensory experimentation, however, there is room for further inventiveness in the realm of theatre and the senses. I am grateful for my son's work at Naughty Dog (https://www.naughtydog.com/) that enabled me to learn far more about the video game industry than I ever would know otherwise.

58 When I attended this show, I was struck by the powerful choice of these competing foodstuffs, but never learned if they intended for either item to represent a particular family.

59 I must note, however, that while writing this chapter, I learned that one of the pioneering female computer programmers in the 1940s loved the proverbial combination of pickles and ice cream while in her early teens. *See* Kathy Kleiman, *Proven Ground: The Untold Story of the Six Women who Programmed the World's First Modern Computer* (New York: Hachette, 2022), 34.

60 The textural contrast between olives and marshmallows further signals the potential interpretive importance of what Mouritsen and Styrbæk refer to as *Mouthfeel* in such endeavours. As PTT and sensory engagement in other theatre modes develops, this appears to be an important topic to investigate further. As many of us who eat know well, mouthfeel evokes a wide range of emotions and responses, in addition to those emanating from smell and taste. Some instances of mouthfeel can also lead to distaste or feelings of disgust.

61 Shakespeare, *The Norton Complete Works*.

62 This quote draws attention to further linguistic challenges inherent in the overall subject of this inquiry. Words that work well for one community do not serve all populations equally appropriately. In this case, for instance, Grossman uses a phrase that is currently quite common, that is, 'triggering'. DE-CRUIT's Stephan Wolfert, however, uses 'activating' rather than 'triggering' since veterans have specific, potentially unsettling, associations with the term 'triggering'. In a series of webinars sponsored by the Trauma Research Foundation, he explains his word choice several times. See Stephan Wolfert and Dawn Stern, 'DE-CRUIT: Using Theatre to Treat the Effects of

Trauma: Integrating Shakespeare and Science in Healing-Centered Practice', (Collection) Trauma Research Foundation, 4 part TRF Tuesday series (2020), https://traumaresearchfoundation.org/__trashed-3/.

63 Rachel Grossman, in Bradbury, Jill Marie, John Lee Clark, Rachel Grossman, Jason Herbers, Victoria Magliocchino, Jasper Norman, Yashaira Romilus, Robert T. Sirvage and Lisa Van Der Mark, 'ProTactile Shakespeare: Inclusive Theater by/for the DeafBlind', in Forum: Specialized Performers and Audiences, *Shakespeare Studies* (2019): 96. Rick Martínez makes a related point in his cookbook/memoir: 'They Are the Recipes that mean the most to me because Every Single One of them is Connected to a Memory', in *Mi Cocina: A Culinary Journey of Self-Discovery* (New York: Clarkson Potter, 2022), 37.

64 Including food in a performance introduces another reminder that different people and members of various communities possess eclectic sensory needs. Nicola Shaughnessy, for instance, suggests that she always attributed her sensory issues surrounding food to her history of anorexia, but that when she was diagnosed with autism as an adult, she realized that this could also contribute to her responses. Neither these communities nor the individuals included within them are identical and sensitivity to these variations remains significant. See Shaughnessy, 'Life Changing: Meal Deal'.

65 Grossman, in Bradbury et al., 'ProTactile Shakespeare', 96. Grossman acknowledges that they were not initially designing productions specifically for the DeafBlind, although they had DeafBlind consultants.

66 Bradbury is now based at the National Technical Institute for the Deaf in Rochester, where she recently announced The Roving Shakespeare Troupe: 'NTID Performing Arts: The Roving Shakespeare Troupe', YouTube, RIT NTID, https://www.youtube.com/watch?app=desktop&v=b9Ha1FqEpDQ&fbclid=IwAR0IjJ0q3ZG8sBLP5F23NnF4GXJIvHXICPUFRy3pqfcHVsM4DkJD1H1WvFQ.

67 Grossman, in Bradbury et al., 'ProTactile Shakespeare', 95.

68 I had hoped to be able to attend some of the sessions, but as a hearing and sighted person without the same connection as Grossman, I was unable to do so. Several of the people involved, including Bradbury, Grossman and some of the PTT team, describe the project in an essay published in 2019's volume of *Shakespeare Studies*, and there is a documentary about the endeavor available on YouTube. The video can be found at https://www.youtube.com/watch?v=btB_nePm860. Jill Bradbury, Jasper Norman and Yashaira Romilus also presented a panel on the project to the 2021 virtual

Emory University/Folger Institute, 'New Scholarly Directions in Premodern Disability Studies and Performance'.
69 This group began in Seattle, but it is now based in Monmouth, Oregon. Information can be found at tactilecommunications.org.
70 The terms tactile ASL and protactile ASL are each used in this context.
71 Tactile Communication website, https://www.tactilecommunications.org/
72 Grossman, in Bradbury et al., 'ProTactile Shakespeare', 85.
73 Protactile Theatre, home page, http://protactiletheatre.org/. Given the conditions current in many parts of the world, it seems appropriate to note that 'spreading like wildfire' may be a term to be used sparingly in our contemporary circumstances.
74 Information drawn from Jill Marie Bradbury, Jasper Norman and Yashaira Romilus, Protactile Theatre Session from 'New Scholarly Directions in Premodern Disability Studies and Performance', Virtual symposium co-sponsored by Emory University and The Folger Institute, with support from Georgia Humanities, 4–6 March 2021. Zoom recording and transcript and 2021 Pro-Tactile *Romeo and Juliet* transcript, https://www.youtube.com/watch?v=btB_nePm860.
75 Emory/Folger, 'New Scholarly Directions in Premodern Disability Studies and Performance'.'
76 Ibid.
77 Ibid.
78 Ibid.
79 Ibid.
80 Ibid.
81 Ibid.
82 Grossman, in Bradbury et al., 'ProTactile Shakespeare', 90. Presumably due to the experimentation that accompanies devised theatre, an alternate report indicates that Juliet was represented by lavender and that the fiery Tybalt was cued by scents of spice. See Bradbury et al, Pro-Tactile *Romeo and Juliet* Documentary Transcript. Also, *see* the YouTube documentary. 'ProTactile Romeo and Juliet: Theatre by/for the DeafBlind', GallaudetU, https://www.youtube.com/watch?v=btB_nePm860.
83 Retail establishments often use scent to influence their patrons as CNN has reported: Nathaniel Meyersohn, 'How Abercrombie,

Victoria's Secret and Vitamin Shoppe use Smell to Get You to Spend', *CNN Business*, 13 August 2022, https://www.cnn.com/2022/08/13/business/why-stores-smell-good-abercrombie-victorias-secret/index.html.

84 Jude Stewart, *Revelations in Air: A Guidebook to Smell* (New York: Penguin, 2021), xiii.
85 A. S. Barwich, *Smellosophy: What the Nose Tells the Mind* (Cambridge, MA: Harvard University Press, 2020), 10.
86 Rachel S. Herz, 'Influences of Odors on Mood and Affective Cognition', in *Olfaction, Taste, and Cognition*, ed. Catherine Rouby, Benoist Schaal, Danièle Dubois, Rémy Gervais and A. Holley (New York: Cambridge University Press, 2002), 170.
87 Robert Muchembled, *Smells: A Cultural History of Odours in Early Modern Times* (Cambridge: Polity Books, 2020), 8.
88 Harold McGee, *Nose Dive: A Field Guide to the World's Smells* (New York: Penguin, 2020), xvi.
89 Smell is being investigated in a number of important contexts, including the invention of a wasabi-based fire alarm that uses scent instead of noise in order to waken people in an emergency. Sophie Hardach, 'Wasabi Fire Alarm a Lifesaver for the Deaf', *Reuters*, 17 March 2008, https://www.reuters.com/article/us-japan-wasabi-idUST29421020080318.
90 Barwich, *Smellosophy*, 6–7.
91 *Much Ado About Nothing*, 3.2.50
92 Bob Holmes, *Flavor: The Science of Our Most Neglected Sense* (New York: W.W. Norton, 2007).
93 Ole G. Mouritsen, and Klavs Styrbæk further differentiate between these terms: Ole G. Mouritsen and Klavs Styrbæk, *Mouthfeel: How Texture Makes Taste* (New York: Columbia University Press, 2017), 1.
94 Holmes, *Flavor*, 9.
95 Ibid.
96 Edmund T. Rolls, 'The Cortical Representation in Taste and Smell', in *Olfaction, Taste, and Cognition*, ed. Rouby et al., 367.
97 Currently, there are many companies under the 'Drunk Shakespeare' umbrella whereby one of the actors consumes significant alcohol before performing in a play with (presumably) sober cast-mates, but there are many other ways to incorporate food and drink into drama. See https://www.drunkshakespeare.com/.

98 Mouritsen and Styrbæk, *Mouthfeel*, ix.
99 Nicola Perullo, *Taste as Experience: The Philosophy and Aesthetics of Food* (New York: Columbia University Press, 2006), 5.
100 Ibid., 2.
101 Holmes, *Flavor*, 10.
102 While the audience was not offered anything to eat, there was considerable cooking and eating onstage in Sam Gold's 2022 *Macbeth* on Broadway, starring Daniel Craig. In 2022, The Lost Estate presented an immersive *A Christmas Carol*, offering the option of an (expensive) feast during the performance, 'The Lost Estate', *Time Out*, https://www.timeout.com/london/theatre/the-lost-estate.
103 Matthew J. Hertenstein and Sandra J. Weiss, eds, *The Handbook of Touch: Neuroscience, Behavioral, and Health Perspectives* (New York: Springer Publishing Co, 2011), xi.
104 Ibid.
105 Ibid.
106 Constance Classen, *The Deepest Sense: A Cultural History of Touch* (Chicago: University of Illinois Press, 2012), xi.
107 As noted in discussions of trauma-based activities, however, touch needs to be avoided for some Shakespeareans, depending on their personal experiences and preferences. Those involved in these activities, therefore, need to remain sensitive to individual differences of many kinds.
108 'Access', Royal Shakespeare Co., https://www.rsc.org.uk/your-visit/access/.
109 Richard Kearney, *Touch: Recovering Our Most Vital Sense* (New York: Columbia University Press, 2021), Title page.
110 Ibid., 3.
111 Ibid., 85–113.
112 Matthew Fulkerson, *The First Sense: A Philosophical Study of Human Touch* (Cambridge, MA: MIT Press, 2014), xi.
113 F. Murray Schafer, 'The Soundscape', in *The Sound Studies Reader*, ed. Jonathan Sterne (New York: Routledge, 2012), 102.
114 Smith, *The Acoustic World of Early Modern England*, 3.
115 Appropriate sensory experiences are seen as key aspects for what Jake Ernst terms 'routes of safety' which are meant to 'assist people in gaining more access to a felt sense of emotional safety'. Bridget McCarthy CTRT shared these principles with the Shakespeare

Theatre Association (STA) and the Shakespeare in Prisons Network (SiPN) in 2022. See Ernst, 'Routes of Safety', Jake Ernst, MSW RSW (2020) www.mswjake.com. Presented by Bridget McCarthy, Certified Trauma and Resilience Practitioner, at Shakespeare Theatre Association annual meeting (2022), Harrisburg, PA.

116 Mike McLindon, Steve McCall and Liz Hodges, *Learning Through Touch: Supporting Learners with Multiple Disabilities and Vision Impairment Through a Bioecological Systems Perspective* (New York: Routledge, 2020), 50.
117 I am given 'haptic' choices on my cellphone, however.
118 Nathan Williams and Jonas Bjerre-Poulson (Kinfolk & Norm Architects), *Touch: Spaces Designed for the Senses* (New York: Gestalten Publishers, 2019), 7.
119 Ibid., 129.
120 *Henry V* 2.3.25–27.
121 *Henry VIII* 2.3.1310.
122 *Hamlet* 3.3.142.

Chapter 5

1 DE-CRUIT also facilitates groups designed for veterans who have experienced incarceration and many of the practitioners included here participate in SiPN events and presentations. 'Please Share These Two DE-CRUIT programs . . .', DE-CRUIT, 16 September 2021, https://www.decruit.org/wp-content/uploads/2021/09/DE-CRUIT-Please-Share-These-Two-DE-CRUIT-programs.pdf.
2 'THE COMBAT VETERAN PLAYERS UK', the Royal Shakespeare Company, https://www.rsc.org.uk/tickets/the-combat-veteran-players-uk. In Australia, Queensland Shakespeare Ensemble, which includes a robust prison programme, has presented an historic play associated with conscription in Australia during the First World War, 'The Australian Conscription Debates, 1916–17', The University of Queensland, https://hpi.uq.edu.au/australian-conscription-debate.
3 Willy Maley, '*Macbeth* and Trauma', in *The Cambridge Companion to Shakespeare and War*, ed. David Loewenstein and Paul Stevens (Cambridge: Cambridge University Press, 2021), 249.
4 Ibid., 248.
5 Ibid.

6 Paul Stevens, '*Henry V* and the Pleasures of War', in *The Cambridge Companion to Shakespeare and War*, ed. David Loewenstein and Paul Stevens (Cambridge: Cambridge University Press, 2021), 221.

7 Ros King and Paul J. C. M. Franssen trace a range of twentieth century responses to this play (8–11).

8 Claire McEachern, 'Foreign War', in *The Cambridge Companion to Shakespeare and War*, ed. David Loewenstein and Paul Stevens (Cambridge: Cambridge University Press, 2021), 55.

9 King and Franssen cite George MacDonald Frasier's conversation in the Second World War where a sergeant noting Frasier's immersion in *Henry V* expressed his conviction that Shakespeare must have served in the army (3).

10 *See* Patrick Gray, *Shakespeare & The Ethics of War* (London: Palgrave, 2021); and Patrick Gray, ed., *Shakespeare and the Ethics of War* (New York: Berghahn Books, 2019); Ros King and Paul J. C. M. Franssen, eds, *Shakespeare and War* (London: Palgrave, 2008).

11 *Macbeth* 3.2.27.

12 Dawn Stern, Talk-Back with Scott Jackson of Shakespeare at Notre Dame, Emory University and Folger Institute, 'New Scholarly Directions in Premodern Disability Studies and Performance', Virtual (2021).

13 Stephan Wolfert, Talk-Back with Scott Jackson of Shakespeare at Notre Dame, Emory University and Folger Institute, 'New Scholarly Directions in Premodern Disability Studies and Performance', Virtual (2021).

14 Ibid.

15 Martin and Packer, *Shakespeare & Company*, 88. This statement cites a conversation between Dennis Krausnick and Bella Martin in 2016.

16 Wolfert, Emory/Folger talk-back.

17 James W. Pennebaker, 'Overcoming Inhibition: Rethinking the Roles of Personality, Cognition and Social Behaviors', in *Emotion, Inhibition, and Health*, ed. Harald C. Traue and James W. Pennebaker (Seattle: Hogrefe and Huber Publishers, 1989), 103.

18 Pennebaker and Traue, 'Inhibition and Psychosomatic Processes', in *Emotion, Inhibition, and Health*, ed. Harald C. Traue and James W. Pennebaker (Seattle: Hogrefe and Huber Publishers, 1989), 157–8.

19 Kristin Linklater, *Freeing the Natural Voice: Imagery and Art in the Practice of Voice and Language* (Hollywood: Drama Publishers/Quite Specific Media), 25.

20 Shakespeare and Co. regularly emerges in conversations with many of the American-based practitioners discussed in this volume. I have discussed this company's actor training and social justice work with Tina Packer and Kevin Coleman and appreciate their willingness to share their theories, practises, and accomplishments.

21 DE-CRUIT, in consultation with van der Kolk, SBB's Curt Tofteland and others, recently received a National Endowment for the Humanities (NEH) grant for a 'Dialogues on the Experiences of War' project, 'Whats New in 2021 You Ask?' DE-CRUIT, https://www.decruit.org/wp-content/uploads/2021/04/DE-CRUIT-Exciting-News-to-Begin-2021.pdf.

22 Notably, even the books produced by professional trauma specialists, such as Stephen Porges, often include disclaimers. Porges's *Pocket Guide to Polyvagal Theory*, for instance, has a 'note to readers' on the copyright page, stating in part 'standards of clinical practice and protocol change over time, and no technique or recommendation is guaranteed to be safe or effective in all circumstances. This volume is intended as a general information resource for professionals practicing in the field of psychotherapy and mental health; it is not a substitute for appropriate training, peer review, and/or clinical supervision'. Porges, *Pocket Guide to Polyvagal Theory* (New York: W. W. Norton & Company, 2007), copyright page.

23 van der Kolk, *The Body Keeps the Score,* 10.

24 Ibid.

25 Ibid., 14.

26 Ibid., 21.

27 A similar perspective on the intertwined physical and emotional effects of war, sometimes resulting with veterans feeling 'dead inside' appears in the 2022 Rambert Dance production *Peaky Blinders: The Redemption of Thomas Shelby*, written by the popular TV drama's creator, Steven Knight. Programme. 2022. n.p.

28 'Actors: Meet the FoC Staff', Feast of Crispian, https://www.feastofcrispian.org/the-actors; Ogden, Minton and Pain note that sensorimotor approaches to psychotherapy draw heavily from the Hakomi method (xxviii).

29 'About the Hakomi Institute', Hakomi Institute, https://hakomiinstitute.com/about/the-hakomi-institute. In the context of this book, it is striking that Kurtz was living in Ashland, Oregon at the time of his death in 2011 and Hakomi trainings continue to be offered there (https://hakomi.me/). Ashland is the home of the prominent theatrical company, The Oregon Shakespeare Festival.

I have not, however, been able to locate any OSF practitioners associated with Hakomi.

30 Ron Kurtz, *The Hakomi Way: Consciousness & Healing: The Legacy of Ron Kurtz*. (Port Perry: Stone's Throw Publications, 2018), 7.

31 Some details about this issue are offered on the Institute's website (https://hakomiinstitute.com/about/the-hakomi-name).

32 Kurtz, cover.

33 Hakomi's theory and practices are synthesized and explained by the Hakomi Institute Southwest. https://hakomiinstitutesouthwest.com/about-us/the-hakomi-method/.

34 Pat Ogden, Kikuni Minton and Clare Pain, *Trauma and the Body: A Sensorimotor Approach to Psychotherapy* (New York: W. W. Norton, 2006), xxvii.

35 In contrast to many of these practitioners, Wolfert links theatre and therapy closely together and does not hesitate to call DE-CRUIT's work therapeutic. In a conversation at the 2023 STA convention, Wolfert discussed some of the theoretical underpinnings of this belief, including the writings of Yvette Nolan and Gabor Maté. He also indicated that part of his determination to receive his MSW is a desire to help train therapists in the healing work associated with drama.

36 'Shakespeare in the Courts', Shakespeare & Company, https://www.shakespeare.org/education/shakespeare-in-the-courts.

37 Pat Ogden and Janina Fisher, *Sensorimotor Psychotherapy: Interventions for Trauma and Attachment* (New York: W.W. Norton, 2015), 83.

38 I participated in a FoC Milwaukee workshop sponsored by SiPN at Notre Dame University in 2016 and another one at Emory University in 2018 that was organized by Emory PhD students Kelly Duquette, John Gulledge and Mary Taylor Mann.

39 In another instance of varying vocabulary choices, Stephan Wolfert, FoC, and others often refer to 'PTSD' as 'PTS' or PTSS: (post-traumatic stress syndrome), presumably to deflect the possible stigmatic or inaccurate connotation of 'disorder'. I am using 'PTS(D)' in acknowledgement of the challenges associated with the terminology associated with this common experience of veterans.

40 Nancy Smith-Watson, 'Shakespeare for Veterans: Feast of Crispian', in Forum: Specialized Performers and Audiences, *Shakespeare Studies* (2019): 44–5.

41 Smith-Watson, interview via Zoom, 15 February 2022.

42 Kurtz, *The Hakomi Way*, 13.

43 Ibid., 8.
44 Ibid., 3.
45 Martin and Packer discuss the line-feeding exercises undertaken by Shakespeare & Co. (*Shakespeare & Company*, 132–44).
46 Smith-Watson, 'Shakespeare for Veterans', 42.
47 Ibid.
48 Ibid., 42–3.
49 van der Kolk, *Body Keeps the Score*, 337.
50 Ibid.
51 I was able to speak with Ron Heneghan and some of the ensemble members at the Shakespeare Theater Association (STA) where they performed *To Be a Soldier* for the 2022 annual conference as part of Dauphin County, Pennsylvania and Gamut Theatre Group's Classics Fest. I am grateful to CSA, Gamut and to STA for this opportunity and for subsequent communications.
52 The partnership was originally forged through The Institute of Integrative Health (TIIH), which is now NOVA Institute of Health for People Places Planets. The Institute is currently working in other areas, but CSA's commitment to this work remains strong and they continue to offer classes for veterans free of charge. Chesapeake Shakespeare Company, 'To Be a Soldier', https://www.chesapeakeshakespeare.com/education-community/for-veterans/.
53 As CSC's website indicates, the programme also receives support from the National Endowment for the Arts (NEA): Creative Forces®: NEA Military Healing Arts Network is an initiative of the National Endowment for the Arts in partnership with the U.S. Departments of Defense and Veterans Affairs and the state and local arts agencies. The initiative seeks to improve the health, wellness and quality of life for military and veteran populations exposed to trauma, as well as their families and caregivers. Administrative support for the initiative is provided by Americans for the Arts and the Henry M. Jackson Foundation for the Advancement of Military Medicine, inc., https://www.chesapeakeshakespeare.com/education-community/for-veterans/.
54 ClassicsFest.org, *To Be A Soldier* program (Harrisburg, 2022). https://www.paonstage.com/shows/2022/harrisburg/classics-fest.
55 'Classics Fest | Harrisburg | 3–8 January 2022,' PA On Stage, https://www.paonstage.com/shows/2022/harrisburg/classics-fest.
56 'Arts and Nature Experiences Can Help Veterans', Nova Institute, https://novainstituteforhealth.org/arts-and-nature-experiences-can-help-veterans/.

57 'Mission', PsychArmor, https://psycharmor.org/mission.
58 University of Florida Center for Arts in Medicine, 'Talking about Arts in Health', white paper (Gainesville: University of Florida Center for Arts in Medicine, 2017), 7.
59 Ibid., 14.
60 Chesapeake Shakespeare Company, https://www.chesapeakeshakespeare.com/.
61 These quotes come from the Chesapeake Shakespeare Company website. 'Student Matinees & Residencies,' Chesapeake Shakespeare Company, www.chesapeakeshakespeare.com/education.
62 Talk-back, ClassicsFest 2022.
63 I have been fortunate to have had several virtual encounters with DE-CRUIT as well as in-person workshops and discussions in Prague, Rome, and at intermittent STA meetings. I was also able to host a film of *Cry Havoc* and a virtual talk-back during a symposium co-sponsored in 2021 by Emory University and the Folger Shakespeare Library. I have seen *Cry Havoc* several times and always find it a compelling narrative performance.
64 'About DE-CRUIT', DE-CRUIT, https://www.decruit.org/about/.
65 The word 'treating' edges closer to therapeutic claims than most of these initiatives choose.
66 Drew Wiggins, 'Veterans Find a Path to Healing Through Shakespeare', *Mad in America*, 13 October 2019, https://www.madinamerica.com/2019/10/veterans-find-path-to-healing-through-shakespeare/.
67 Jo Reed, host, 'Stephan Wolfert', 3 May 2019, in *NEA Art Works*, National Endowment for the Arts, podcast, https://www.arts.gov/stories/podcast/stephan-wolfert.
68 van der Kolk, *Body Keeps the Score*, 17.
69 Stephan Wolfert, Workshop Course Packet, ESRA Shakespeare Conference, Rome.
70 *1 Henry IV* 2.3.42–62
71 Shay, *Achilles in Vietnam*, 165–6.
72 There are some groups presenting related stage or Zoom productions. Theater of War, for example, is an acting ensemble that presents classic texts (and some modern productions) on challenging issues that resonate for contemporary audiences. Some of their performances are geared towards veterans (https://theaterofwar.com/about). van der Kolk speaks about this group in *The Body Keeps the Score*, 333–4.

73 Wolfert, Workshop Course Packet.
74 Stav Dimitropoulos, 'In Shakespeare, Veterans Find a '"Tower of Strength"'', *Inverse Magazine*, 16 May 2021, https://www.inverse.com/mind-body/shakespeare-as-therapy.
75 Wolfert, Emory/Folger talk-back.
76 Dimitropoulos, 'In Shakespeare, Veterans Find a "Tower of Strength"'. Several of the practitioners discussed in this study, including Scott Jackson and Bridget McCarthy, draw extensively from polyvagal theory, which is most closely associated with the work of Stephen W. Porges.
77 Porges, *The Pocket Guide*, xv.
78 Ibid.
79 Deb Dana, *Anchored: How to Befriend Your Nervous System Using Polyvagal Theory* (Boulder: Sounds True Press, 2021), 5–6.
80 Ibid., 7.
81 Ibid., 8–9.
82 Ibid., 9.
83 Ibid., 10.
84 To add my own disclaimer here: I am not a clinician. I am reporting the interest in polyvagal theory shown by many practitioners of Shakespeare with specialized communities, particularly where trauma is involved. Rosenberg includes autism in his title, but I have not encountered polyvagal theory in the work of those engaged with Shakespeare and autism. Porges discusses autism in relation to polyvagal theory, however (*The Pocket Guide*, 74–96).
85 Stanley Rosenberg, *Accessing the Healing Power of the Vagus Nerve: Self-Help Exercises for Anxiety, Depression, Trauma, and Autism* (Berkeley: North Atlantic Books, 2017), 152.
86 Ibid.
87 Ibid.
88 Jonathan Shay, *Achilles in Vietnam: Combat Trauma and the Undoing of Character* (New York: Simon and Schuster, 1995), xx. Shay acknowledges that 'Homer' is *generally* not considered to be a singular author, but he uses this name as shorthand for the creators of these epics.
89 Shay, *Odysseus in America: Combat Trauma and the Undoing of Character* (New York: Scribner, 2003), 21.
90 Ibid.

91 Shay, *Achilles in Vietnam*, xx.
92 Ibid.
93 Ibid.
94 'Shakespeare with Veterans', Kentucky Shakespeare, https://kyshakespeare.com/programs/shakespeare-with-veterans/.
95 Amy Attaway, 'Shakespeare and Veterans' (Kentucky Shakespeare), Interview via Zoom, 17 March 2022.
96 van der Kolk, *Body Keeps the Score*, 333.
97 Barnes argues, in part, that 'the practices documented [within a series of Shakespeare films] serve and reflect larger projects of neoliberalism'. Barnes, *Shakespearean Charity*, 3.
98 *Hamlet* 2.2.603.

Chapter 6

1 I am extremely grateful to the many people who have shared their Shakespeare in Prison experiences with me in person, on Zoom and through correspondence. I have visited prisons and alumni gatherings in the United States, England and India, and have spoken with practitioners in Argentina and Australia. Sammie Byron, an alumnus of Shakespeare Behind Bars (SBB) visits my classroom in Atlanta regularly. Particular thanks to the many prison participants who have welcomed me in person or electronically into their prison communities and to those who have facilitated these conversations, including Curt L. Tofteland, Scott Jackson, Rowan Mackenzie, Frannie Shepherd-Bates, Matthew Van Meter, Tom Magill, Alokonanda Roy, Hulugappa Kattamani, Amitava Roy, Sergio Amigo, Sarah Higinbotham, Bill Taft, Rob Pensalfini, Jonathan Shailor and Katherine Hennessey. I am also indebted to the additional founders, organizers and indefatigable participants of the Shakespeare in Prisons Network, including Peter Holland, Kate Powers, Kate Kenney, Alejandra Luna, Lynn Baker-Nauman, Melinda Cooper, Devon Glover (The Sonnet Man), Jean Trounstine, Alma Robinson, Lesley Currier, Freedome Bradley-Ballentine, Karen Ann Daniels, and the many speakers and members who make this such a vibrant and informative community. I regret that I never had the opportunity to meet the late Agnes Wilcox, who did pioneering work in this realm.

2 Laura Bates, *Shakespeare Saved My Life*, (Naperville: Sourcebooks, 2013), 109.

3 SIP alumna Asia Johnson was a speaker at the 2022 Theatre Communications Group (TCG) conference: '2022 Speakers and Facilitators', TCG National Conference Hybrid 2022, https://circle.tcg.org/2022pittsburgh/agenda/speakers.

4 First names of SIP alumni are used with their permission. Since Asia Johnson is speaking publicly about her SIP work, I include her surname also.

5 Scott Jackson, Mary Irene Ryan Family Executive Director of Shakespeare at Notre Dame and an SiPN founder, for instance, earned an MFA in Actor Training and Coaching focused on prison Shakespeare at the University of London's Royal Central School of Speech and Drama and trained as a 200 hour certified yoga teacher (CYT-200) in Kundalini Yoga as taught by Maya Fiennes; Kate Powers has a Fulbright-sponsored MA from the Shakespeare Institute in Stratford-upon-Avon and recently completed an MFA in directing with a concentration on social justice and culturally responsive pedagogy at the University of Idaho, which included extensive coursework in sociology and criminal justice; Kate Kenney has an MS from the University of Cincinnati in criminal justice focused on corrections and offender rehabilitation; and Bridget McCarthy is a Certified Trauma and Resilience Practitioner. Rowan Mackenzie started Shakespeare UnBard while completing her PhD in applied Shakespeare at the Shakespeare Institute and is about to commence an MSc in Criminology and Criminal Psychology at the University of Essex. Jenna Dreier earned her PhD at the University of Minnesota with a concentration on Shakespeare in prison before becoming Minnesota Prison Education Program Coordinator. Sarah Higinbotham and Bill Taft founded what is now Common Good Atlanta while graduate students at Georgia State University. Stephan Wolfert of DE-CRUIT has recently begun an MSW at Simmons University. Apologies to anyone whose credentials I have omitted or misstated.

6 Niels Herold offer an intriguing hypothesis in response to the Why Shakespeare? question, suggesting that there is 'an uncanny, anachronistic alignment of prison theatre conditions with those of early modern theatrical process and practice' (67). Rob Pensalfini provides a valuable overview of this question in relation to prison programmes. Rob Pensalfini, *Prison Shakespeare: For These Deep Shames and Great Indignities* (New York: Palgrave Macmillan, 2016), 188–227.

7 SBB Master Class with Curt Tofteland and Michelle Bombe, STA Conference 2023, course packet, 40.

8 These quotes come from my in-person and Zoom sessions with SIP in May, 2022.

9 There was a session devoted to this project at the SiPC 4 conference that is available at https://shakespeare.nd.edu/service/shakespeare-in-prisons/sipc4/.
10 SIP, '2022 Proposal for *Richard III* volume'. Thanks to Frannie Shepherd-Bates for sharing this.
11 Zoom interview, 2022.
12 I write at length about Kattimani's programme (and another carceral arts program in Kolkata) in the 2021 volume of *Shakespeare Survey* and hosted two sessions about them for the online SiPC4 conference. The SiPC4 conference sessions are available at https://shakespeare.nd.edu/service/shakespeare-in-prisons/sipc4/. I visited Kattimani and Jackson in their respective venues prior to the pandemic. I appreciate their hospitality and the introduction to their incarcerated actors. I have encountered some of Jackson's Kundalini exercises with groups over Zoom, but Covid-19 has precluded any additional visits to Westville since he began teaching Kundalini there.
13 Bates reports that she 'was a failure' as a yoga teacher in prison, but that in her one attempt, the incarcerated students demonstrated their 'trust' of her by closing their eyes when asked, something that is not generally considered safe in such an environment. Bates, *Shakespeare Saved My Life*, 98.
14 This book was published by a press located in Ashland, Oregon, home of the Oregon Shakespeare Festival. Similar to the Hakomi work also being done in Ashland, however, I can find no specific link between this book and OSF, other than a jacket blurb by Barret O'Brien, a member of the Acting Company.
15 Szabo-Cassella is not a scholar. She approaches Shakespeare from a practitioner's perspective, similar to many of the Shakespeare in prison conveners. In her acknowledgements, however, she thanks Columbia University Shakespeare Professor William B. Worthen and Laura Bates, the Shakespeare professor and prison educator who authored the 2013 volume *Shakespeare Saved My Life*. Some scholars may balk at her regular use of 'the Bard' to identify Shakespeare and similar non-scholarly statements, but she is not predominantly addressing an academic audience.
16 Claire Szabo-Cassella, *Shakespeare's Yoga: How the Bard Can Deepen Your Practice – On and Off the Mat* (Ashland: White Cloud Press, 2016), 2.
17 Ibid., 8.
18 Ibid., 2.

19 Ibid., Table of Contents.
20 Ibid., 3.
21 Curt Tofteland, 'Master Artist Class Hand-Out. Arts in Corrections: Building Bridges to the Future Conference' (Loyola Marymount University, 2017), 5–6. These circles used to be termed 'circles of trust,' but given the challenges associated with concepts of trust in prison, they are now deemed circles of truth.
22 SBB Master class with Tofteland and Bombe. STA 2023, course packet, 4–5.
23 While Jackson is deeply involved with Kundalini practice, he denounces the actions of Yogi Bhajan, a kundalini practitioner implicated in serious offenses. Flynn, 'A New Report Details Decades of Abuse at the Hands of Yogi Bhajan'.
24 See, for example, N. E. Sjoman, *The Yoga Tradition of the Mysore Palace* (New Delhi: Abhinav Publications, 1999). There are a range of yoga practices available to draw from by practitioners interacting with trauma survivors. These programmes incorporate similar aims and procedures but vary in the particulars associated with the chosen yoga methodology.
25 See, for example, 'Where the Mind is Without Fear', trans. Savita Karthik, *Deccan Herald,* 18 November 2018. The Kattamani family have an extensive archive of news articles about this initiative at their home, which they graciously shared with me.
26 Cope is founder of the Kripalu Institute for Extraordinary Living in Massachusetts (in the same region as Shakespeare & Co). I have never met him. As far as I know, he is no longer associated with prominent yoga figure Amrit Dessai, who left many Kripalu yoga organizations due to sexual impropriety (Cushman and Montgomery).
27 As noted, van der Kolk was involved in the founding and administration of this institute until he was removed after charges of bullying. He remains prominent in the realms of trauma studies, however, and his work is used by many of the practitioners included in this study. As with other controversial figures emerging in areas relevant to this work, I acknowledge such problems, while recognizing the on-going influence of the work.
28 David Emerson and Elizabeth Hopper, *Overcoming Trauma through Yoga: Reclaiming Your Body* (Berkeley: North Atlantic Books, 2011), 6.
29 This reluctance towards touch raises some important questions about trauma and DeafBlind individuals. In another chapter, this

community emphasizes that touch is an extremely important facet in their communication and ability to form communities.
30 Emerson and Hopper, *Overcoming Trauma*, 123. SIP practitioners and alumni discussed staging scenes in ways that respected some of their actors' resistance to touch.
31 Ibid., 44–5.
32 Lisa Danylchuk, *Yoga for Trauma Recovery: Theory, Philosophy, and Practice* (New York: Routledge, 2019), 8.
33 Ann Swanson, *Science of Yoga: Understand the Anatomy and Physiology to Perfect Your Practice* (London: DK Publishers, 2019), 7. Thanks for Scott Jackson for recommending of a number of relevant yoga texts, such as Swanson's. I also appreciate his willingness to share his MFA writing with me for inclusion in this volume.
34 Ibid., 192.
35 Ibid.
36 Ibid.
37 Ibid.
38 Ibid., 193.
39 Ibid., 201.
40 Ibid.
41 Another useful resource into related realms could be David Fontana's *The Meditator's Handbook*, which considers a vast range of meditative practices that often correlate with the yogic traditions discussed. Fontana exemplifies one of the challenges occasionally facing those seeking to integrate academic knowledge with practicses such as yoga and meditation, however. The handbook was recommended highly to me by a practitioner working in this field. Fontana, who died in 2010, was a professor in transpersonal psychology at Liverpool John Moores University and a Distinguished Visiting Fellow at the University of Cardiff when *The Meditators' Handbook* appeared in print. He published numerous books that have been widely translated, and his volumes contain substantial information about germane topics. At the same time, he delved deeply into paranormal studies, which situates him outside many conventional academic and scientific parameters. His interest in poltergeists and related phenomena do not figure into our discussion here, but I am placing his work in a footnote due to the skepticism his paranormal research is likely to generate. Those interested in exploring the role of meditation in mindfulness and yoga practices can find much of interest in Fontana's volume, however.

42 Michael A. West, ed., *Psychology of Meditation* (Oxford: Oxford University Press, 2016), 3–4.

43 Antonio Raffone, 'The Cognitive and Affection Neuroscience of Meditation', in *Psychology of Meditation*, ed. West, 221.

44 For more information about their artwork, *see* 'Bringing about a Dramatic Change in Jail Inmates', *Express News Service* (n.d.), n.p. Kattamani archive.

45 Sarah Higinbotham and Bill Taft combine literary and artistic projects in their Common Good Atlanta classes at Phillips State Correctional Facility and elsewhere in Georgia. Many of these artifacts, which are now housed in Emory's Stuart A. Rose Manuscripts, Archives, and Rare Book Library, contain Shakespearean material. Just prior to lock-down, a symposium featuring Common Good alumni took place at Emory to celebrate the magnificent undergraduate exhibit entitled 'Voices from the Other Side: Artist Books from Phillips State Prison'. Chief Curator Kassie Sarkar guided the work of her fellow undergraduates with considerable support from Kathy Dixson, John Klingler, and the rest of the Emory Library Exhibition team. She also ensured that Common Good alumni received stipends for their participation in this striking event, which took place in the nick of time before the pandemic truly hit. https://libraries.emory.edu/events-exhibits/exhibits/voices-other-side.

46 Emergency Shakespeare, performance programme, *Othello*, HMP Stafford, November 2021.

47 Ibid.

48 Ibid.

49 Ibid.

50 Barnes, *Shakespearean Charity*, 2.

51 Courtney Lehmann, 'Double Jeopardy: Shakespeare and Prison Theatre', in *Shakespeare and the Ethics of Appropriation*, ed. Alexa Alice Joubin and Elizabeth Rivlin (New York: Palgrave McMillan, 2014), 92.

52 Barnes, *Shakespearean Charity*, 3. Barnes' book focuses on Shakespearean documentaries, including the Philomath SBB film, but he does not appear to have any direct experience with Shakespeare in prison programs.

53 Pensalfini, *Prison Shakespeare*, 166–71.

54 Ibid., 130–87.

55 'Shakespeare in Prison', Detroit Public Theatre.

56 Ibid.
57 Bates reports that quilting was a popular activity in the prison where she worked and that some of the Shakespeareans were also quilters.
58 Cathy A. Malchiodi, *Trauma and Expressive Arts Therapy: Brain, Body, & Imagination in the Healing Process* (New York: Guilford Press, 2020), xi.
59 Ibid. Trounstine describes the costumes and props crafted by her performers in Massachusetts. 'Revisiting Sacred Spaces', in *Performing New Lives: Prison Theatre*, ed. Jonathan Shailor (Philadelphia: Jessica Kingsley Publishers, 2011), 252.
60 Jamie Marich, *Process not Perfection: Expressive Arts Solutions for Trauma Recovery* (Warren: Creative Mindfulness Media, 2019), 1–2.
61 Lukasz M. Konopka, 'Neuroscience Concepts in Clinical Practice', in *Art Therapy, Trauma, and Neuroscience: Theoretical and Practical Perspectives*, ed. Juliet L. King (New York: Routledge, 2016), 12.
62 Ibid., 13.
63 Vija B. Lusebrink and Lisa D. Hinz, 'The Expressive Therapies Continuum as a Framework in the Treatment of Trauma', in *Art Therapy, Trauma, and Neuroscience: Theoretical and Practical Perspectives*, ed. Juliet L. King (New York: Routledge, 2016), 45–7.
64 Johanne Hamel, ed., *Somatic Art Therapy: Alleviating Pain and Trauma through Art* (New York: Routledge, 2021), 8.
65 As noted elsewhere, DE-CRUIT's Wolfert more readily links this kind of dramatic work with therapy.
66 Email exchange Cavanagh/Tofteland, 2022.
67 In addition to some of the other SBB events and contacts mentioned elsewhere, I spent several days with Tofteland and SBB participants in their Michigan prison programs in 2017. I am very appreciative of that opportunity and am grateful to Tofteland and everyone from SBB for their warm welcome. When that visit concluded, I was able to join Jackson's Shakespearean interactions with prisoners at Westville Correctional Facility. I am also grateful for that significant experience.
68 'The 4th International Shakespeare in Prisons Conference (SiPC4)', University of Notre Dame, n.d., https://shakespeare.nd.edu/service/shakespeare-in-prisons/sipc4/.
69 'The 4th International Shakespeare in Prisons Conference (SiPC4)', University of Notre Dame.
70 'Shakespeare in Prison', Detroit Public Theatre. I have been fortunate to meet with SIP alumni in person and on Zoom. I appreciate

the hospitality, candor, commitment, and enthusiasm of staff and participants in this impressive programme.

71 'Award-Winning Doctoral Researcher Rowan Mackenzie of the Shakespeare Institute Responds to Coronavirus Crisis in Prisons', University of Birmingham, 3 April 2020, https://www.birmingham.ac.uk/news/2020/award-winning-doctoral-researcher-rowan-mackenzie-of-the-shakespeare-institute-responds-to-coronavirus-crisis-in-prisons.

72 'Award-winning doctoral researcher Rowan Mackenzie of the Shakespeare Institute responds to Coronavirus crisis in prisons.' University of Birmingham. As a Liveryman of the Worshipful Company of Educators, I am pleased at the group's ongoing attention to prison education. I am sorry, however, that Covid-19 rescheduling of many events made it impossible for me to attend Mackenzie's award ceremony.

73 It is important to acknowledge that some corrections personnel are very supportive of these kinds of efforts and that others resist them mightily. I have heard numerous accounts of both kinds of responses from practitioners and participants.

74 'Shakespeare in Prison', Detroit Public Theatre.

75 I met with SIP alumni in person and on Zoom on 28–29 May 2022.

76 Tofteland and I spoke about the juvenile programme and Shax BEYOND Bars via Zoom on 1 June 2022. I am deeply grateful for his willingness to share his work and for the breadth and depth of his experience.

77 Zoom conversation Cavanagh/Tofteland, 12 June 2022.

78 Thanks to the generosity of Emory's Stuart A. Rose Rare Books, Manuscripts and Archives Library, the performance and subsequent conversation from April, 2022 are available on YouTube: Atlanta Shakespeare Co., 'How Shakespeare Connects Us: An Afternoon with Sammie Byron & Harry Lennix at The Shakespeare Tavern', YouTube video, posted by Emory University, 17 May 2022, https://youtu.be/Sc1GwPfViOo.

79 I first met Byron at the SiPC gathering at Notre Dame in early 2016. The information contained in this section derives from our numerous in-person, telephone, and Zoom conversations over the past several years.

80 The work of Freire and of Augusto Boal is central in many of these prison programmes.

81 Scott Jackson, 'Finding Light in the Shadow: Illuminating Prison Theatre Practice through the Production of the 4th International

Shakespeare in Prisons Conference', MFA-Sustained Independent Project, Royal Central School of Speech & Drama, University of London, 2021, abstract.

82 Jackson, 'Finding Light in the Shadow', 10. In this section, Jackson cites B. Aronson's 2017 essay 'The white savior industrial complex: a cultural studies analysis of a teacher educator, savior film, and future teachers', from the *Journal of Critical Thought and Praxis* 6, no. 3 (2017): 36–54.

83 Jackson, 'Finding Light in the Shadow', 7.

84 Ibid.

85 Ibid., 24–5.

86 The 2020–2021 SiPN conference won a Shakespeare Publics Award from the Shakespeare Association of America in 2022. Mackenzie won the same award in 2021, https://shakespeareassociation.org/awards-prizes/.

87 Many thanks to Kate Powers for her willingness to share some of the writing she completed at the University of Idaho.

88 Kate Powers, *Exit, Pursued by a Pandemic*, Exit Project (Moscow: University of Idaho Theatre Department, 2021), 16. There are a number of books available about restorative justice, including *Until We Reckon*, written by Emory alumna and former Rhodes Scholar Danielle Sered.

89 Powers, *Exit*, 3.

90 Dameion Brown, who performed in Marin Shakespeare's prison programme, has continued to act professionally since his release, as the company's website notes: Paul Liberatore, 'Ex-Prisoner's Part in Dominican's "Othello" Parallels Tragic Past', *Marin Independent Journal*, July 2016, A1, A6, https://www.marinshakespeare.org/wp-content/uploads/2016/07/Marin-IJ-Paul-Libertore-Dameion-as-Othello-story.pdf. Kattamani has also had prison alumni gain work as actors.

91 Kate Powers, 'Like Bright Metal on a Sullen Ground: The First Six Months of a Prison Shakespeare Program', University of Idaho Theatre Department, 6–7.

92 Ibid., 22.

93 Ibid., 14.

94 Tofteland, 'Master Artist Class Hand-Out', 3.

Chapter 7

1. John Gulledge, Kelly Duquette and Mary Taylor Mann, 'The Puck Project: A Shakespeare Performance and Ethics Program', *Early Modern Culture Online*, 2020, https://doi.org/10.15845/emco.v7i1.
2. One of these Oxford students later helped curate the 'Voices from the Other Side' exhibition, mentioned earlier in this volume: Kassie Sarkar et al., 'Voices from the Other Side: Artists Books from Phillips State Prison', Atlanta: Emory University's Woodruff Library, 2020, https://libraries.emory.edu/events-exhibits/exhibits/voices-other-side.
3. They cite the origin of this concept as the work of bioethicists Gretchen Case and Daniel Brauner.
4. Gulledge et al., 'The Puck Project'.
5. MadLibs, https://www.madlibs.com/.
6. In particular, they cite work by Thomas Fuchs and Sabine C. Koch, 'Embodied Affectivity; on Moving and Being Moved', *Frontiers in Psychology* 5 (2014): 1–12.
7. Gulledge et al., 'The Puck Project', 52.
8. Mackenzie talks about Shakespearean productions performed by Cardboard Citizens, an ensemble in England, featuring people who are experiencing homelessness. *Creating Space*, 22–3.
9. This information comes from a Zoom conversation with Laura Cole on 5 October 2022.
10. Unlike these initiatives for children undergoing homelessness, Savvy Theatre offers a drama group for adults who have experience with substance abuse and/or homelessness. In 2022, this ensemble presented *The Taming of the Shrew Drag Show*, which included a wide range of musical numbers. When Bianca is surrounded by suitors, for instance, the cast danced to The Weather Girls' 'It's Raining Men.'
11. Cole indicates that in *The Tempest*, they focus on magic and agency, not on the subjugation presented in the play.
12. Notre Dame is a prominent Roman Catholic university, with substantial financial resources. South Bend more broadly has a lengthy history of economic deprivation, so the town/gown contrast in these local communities is considerable by numerous measures.
13. Title 1 schools receive special funding for offsetting the challenges facing a significant proportion of a school's population.

14 Information about the Robinson Center is drawn from site visits, several conversations with Christy Burgess and some University of Notre Dame promotional materials.
15 Christy Burgess, Zoom interview, 29 July 2022.
16 'Robinson Shakespeare Company invited to perform in England', *Notre Dame News*, 8 March 2017, https://news.nd.edu/news/robinson-shakespeare-company-invited-to-perform-in-england/.
17 Hrach, *Minding Bodies*.
18 Burgess, Zoom interview, 29 July 2022.
19 Their ten-month ensemble programme consists of approximately thirty young people, aged from 16–25 (Intermission Youth Theatre, https://www.intermissionyouththeatre.co.uk/). I am grateful to Colin Nash for introducing me to Intermission and to Darren Raymond several years ago.
20 Information about Intermission comes from site visits, (*Julius Caesar* in 2015, *Juliet and Romeo* in 2021 and *MSND: A Shakespearean Remix* in 2022), their website, a telephone conversation with Darren Raymond in March, 2022, the programme for *Juliet and Romeo* and a brief chat with Intermission Trustee Sir Mark Rylance at one of the performances. Their logo splits 'Inter' and 'Mission' with a Christian cross in the middle, presumably symbolizing their joint commitment to theatrically and religiously-based activities.
21 Intermission Youth Theatre, https://www.intermissionyouththeatre.co.uk/
22 'Pupil Referral Units: Converting to Alternative Provision Academies', UK Department of Education, https://www.gov.uk/guidance/pupil-referral-units-converting-to-alternative-provision-academies.
23 Intermission Youth Theatre, https://www.intermissionyouththeatre.co.uk/.
24 Ibid.
25 Ibid.
26 Programme, *Juliet and Romeo*, Intermission Theatre, The Chelsea Theatre, 2021.
27 'What's On', Intermission Theatre, https://www.intermissionyouththeatre.co.uk/whats-on.
28 *A Midsummer Night's Dream*, 2.1.
29 Sam Cooke, 'Cupid', recorded 14 April 1961, track number D8 on *Forever*, RCA Studio.

30 This material can be found at https://www.intermissionyouththeatre.co.uk/whats-on.
31 These remarks come from a phone interview with Raymond in March, 2022.
32 Intermission Youth Theatre, https://www.intermissionyouththeatre.co.uk.
33 'Juliet & Romeo – The Chelsea Theatre', North West End UK, 22 November 2021, https://northwestend.com/juliet-romeo-the-chelsea-theatre/.
34 Merlin and Packer, *Shakespeare & Company*, 225.
35 Ibid., 224.
36 I spoke with Coleman at the January, 2022 Shakespeare Theatre Association conference.
37 Merlin and Packer, *Shakespeare & Company*, 226.
38 Coleman did not refer to particular studies, but there are many such reports cited throughout this volume. Interview with Coleman, January 2022.
39 Interview with Coleman, January 2022.
40 Merlin and Packer, *Shakespeare & Company*, 229.
41 I am grateful to Sayuri Carbonnier for introducing me to Sergio Amigo, thus facilitating our Zoom conversations.
42 Radha Spratt, 'In Conversation with Inspirational Theatre Director, Sergio Amigo', Eggs, Beans, and Crumpets, 1 May 2013, https://radhaspratt.wordpress.com/2013/05/01/in-coversation-with-theatre-director-sergio-amigo/.
43 Ibid.
44 Zoom conversations, 2021.
45 *Richard II*. 5.5.2. William Shakespeare, *The Norton Shakespeare*, ed. Stephen Greenblatt et al. (New York: W.W. Norton, 2015).
46 Sergio Amigo, Zoom, November 2021.
47 Spratt, 'In Conversation with Inspirational Theatre Director, Sergio Amigo'.
48 This material about SBB/Illinois comes from in person and Zoom conversations with Glover and Tofteland.
49 This focus on rhythm points out one of the many correspondences found between the varied groups in this study. Rebecca Vaudreuil, for instance, recently published an edited collection about the therapeutic

value of music for military and veteran populations. Rebecca Vaudreuil, ed., *Music Therapy with Military and Veteran Populations* (London: Jessica Kingsley, 2020).

50 Glover has presented twice at Emory over Zoom during the pandemic and in-person in 2023.
51 Devon Glover (the Sonnet Man), Zoom interview, 26 July 2022.
52 'Shakespeare in American Communities', National Endowment for the Arts, https://www.arts.gov/initiatives/shakespeare-american-communities.
53 See Ian Levy, *Hip-Hop and Spoken Word Therapy in School Counseling: Developing Culturally Responsive Approaches* (New York: Routledge, 2021); Ian Levy and Edmund Adjapong, eds, *HipHopEd-Compilation 2: Hip-Hop as Praxis and Social Justice* (Frankfurt, Germany: Peter Lang, 2020); Hadley and George Yancy, eds, *Therapeutic Uses of Rap and Hip-Hop* (New York: Routledge, 2012); and Raphael Travis Jr, *The Healing Power of Hip Hop* (Santa Barbara: Praeger, 2016).
54 Levy, *Hip-Hop and Spoken Word Therapy in School Counseling*, 1.
55 Ibid., 4.
56 Hadley and Yancy, *Therapeutic Uses of Rap and Hip-Hop*, xxxi.
57 Travis Jr, *The Healing Power of Hip Hop*, xvii.
58 Akala, 'Hip Hop and Shakespeare', TEDx Talk, 7 December 2011, https://www.youtube.com/watch?v=DSbtkLA3GrY.
59 The original SBB began as a programme at Kentucky Shakespeare but has now become an independent entity.
60 Amy L. Smith writes about Shakespeare collaborations between her undergraduate students and youth offenders. See Amy L. Smith, '"Think of me as I am": Juvenile Offenders Talk back to Shakespeare', *Teaching Shakespeare* 12 (2017), https://www.britishshakespeare.ws/wp-content/uploads/2021/10/TeachingShakespeare12_AW_Web1.pdf.
61 Eric Mills, Delaware Shakespeare Company, Zoom interview, 20 July 2022.
62 'Beyond Shakespeare', Delaware Shakespeare, https://delshakes.org/beyond-shakespeare/.
63 Hrach, *Minding Bodies*, 3.
64 Ibid., 24–5.
65 'CSF in the Schools: Shakespeare & Violence Prevention Tour', CU Presents, https://cupresents.org/performance/10050/shakespeare/csf

-schools/. Information in this section comes from material available on the Colorado Shakespeare website and a Zoom interview with Amanda Giguere on 4 August 2022.
66 Zoom interview with Giguere, 4 August 2022.

BIBLIOGRAPHY

Adrian, Barbara. *Actor Training the Laban Way: An Integrated Approach to Voice, Speech, and Movement.* New York: Allworth Press, 2008.

Aeppli, Willi. *The Care and Development of the Human Senses: Rudolf Steiner's Work on the Significance of the Senses in Education.* London: Floris Books, 2021.

Akala. 'Hip Hop and Shakespeare'. TEDx talk. Posted 17 December 2011. https://www.youtube.com/watch?v=DSbtkLA3GrY.

Alexander, Scott. 'Review of *The Body Keeps the Score*'. Slate Star Codex, 11 November 2019. https://slatestarcodex.com/2019/11/12/book-review-the-body-keeps-the-score/.

American Psychological Association. *Publication Manual of the American Psychological Association: The Official Guide to APA Style.* Washington, DC: American Psychological Society, 2020.

Andersen, Philip A. 'Tactile Traditions: Cultural Differences and Similarities in Haptic Communication'. In *The Handbook of Touch: Neuroscience, Behavioral, and Health Perspectives*, edited by Matthew J. Hertenstein and Sandra J. Weiss, 351–69. New York: Springer Publishing Co, 2011.

Aristotle. *On the Soul.* Translated by Edwin Wallace. Digireads.com, 2020.

Aronson, B. 'The White Savior Industrial Complex: A Cultural Studies Analysis of a Teacher Educator, Savior Film, and Future Teachers'. *Journal of Critical Thought and Praxis* 6, no. 3 (2017): 36–54.

'Ask Smithsonian'. *Smithsonian* 53, no. 4 (2022): 92.

'Audio Description and Shakespeare'. Vocal Eyes, 27 April 2017. https://vocaleyes.co.uk/audio-description-and-shakespeare/.

'The Australian Conscription Debates, 1916–17'. University of Queensland School of Historical and Philosophical Inquiry. https://hpi.uq.edu.au/australian-conscription-debate.

'Award-Winning Doctoral Researcher Rowan Mackenzie of the Shakespeare Institute Responds to Coronavirus Crisis in Prisons'. University of Birmingham News, 3 April 2020. https://www.birmingham.ac.uk/news/2020/award-winning-doctoral-researcher

-rowan-mackenzie-of-the-shakespeare-institute-responds-to
-coronavirus-crisis-in-prisons.
Baim, Clark. *Staging the Personal: A Guide to Safe and Ethical Practice*. Switzerland: Palgrave Macmillan, 2020.
Baran, Tara, Mary-Grace Kelly and Anne Dickerson. 'The Hunter Heartbeat Method: Evaluating the Impact of a Theater-Based Intervention on Children on the Autism Spectrum'. *The American Journal of Occupational Therapy* 72, no. 4, supplement 1 (2018). https://research.aota.org/ajot/article-abstract/72/4_Supplement_1/7211520313p1/8049/The-Hunter-Heartbeat-Method-Evaluating-the-Impact?redirectedFrom=fulltext.
Barnes, Todd Landon. *Shakespearean Charity and the Perils of Redemptive Performance*. Cambridge: Cambridge University Press, 2020.
Baron-Cohen, Simon. *Mindblindness: An Essay on Autism and Theory of Mind*. Ipswitch: Bradford Books, 1997.
Barwich, A. S. *Smellosophy: What the Nose Tells the Mind*. Cambridge, MA: Harvard University Press, 2020.
Bates, Laura. *Shakespeare Saved My Life*. Naperville: Sourcebooks, 2013.
Bates, Laura. 'Teaching Shakespeare in a Maximum Security Prison'. *Tell Me More*, NPR News, 22 April 2013.
Bennett, Susan. *Theory for Theatre Studies: Sound*. London: Methuen Drama, 2019.
Berry, Cicely. *Voice and the Actor*. New York: Wiley, 1973.
Bishop, Tom and Alexa Alice Joubin, eds. *The Shakespeare International Yearbook: Special Section, Shakespeare and Refugees* 19. London: Routledge, 2021.
'A Blind Shakespearean Debut'. *In Touch*, BBC Sounds, 9 July 2019. https://www.bbc.co.uk/sounds/play/m0006m40.
Block, Giles. *Speaking the Speech: An Actor's Guide to Shakespeare*. London: Nick Hern, 2013.
Bloom, Benjamin S. *Taxonomy of Educational Objectives, Handbook 1: Cognitive Domain*, 2nd edn. Boston: Addison-Wesley Longman, 1969.
Blue Apple Theatre. 'Surviving or Thriving?: A Symposium for Sector Professionals. Hosted in conjunction with Teatr-21 from Warsaw, Poland and Divadlo Aldente from Brno, Czech Republic'. University of Winchester, UK, 1 November 2022.
Boal, Augusto. *Games for Actors and Non-Actors*. Translated by Adrian Jackson. New York: Routledge, 1992.
Boal, Augusto. *The Rainbow of Desire: The Boal Method of Theatre and Therapy*. New York: Routledge, 1995.
Boal, Augusto. *Theatre of the Oppressed*. New York: Theatre Communications Group, 1985.

Bogart, Anne and Tina Landau. *The Viewpoints Book: A Practical Guide to Viewpoints and Composition*. New York: Theatre Communications Group, 2005.

Bradbury, Jill Marie. 'Audiences, American Sign Language, and Deafness'. *Shakespeare Bulletin* 40, no. 1 (2022): 45–67. doi: 10.1353/shb.2022.0000.

Bradbury, Jill Marie, John Lee Clark, Rachel Grossman, Jason Herbers, Victoria Magliocchino, Jasper Norman, Yashaira Romilus, Robert T. Sirvage and Lisa Van Der Mark. 'ProTactile Shakespeare: Inclusive Theater by/for the DeafBlind'. In Forum: Specialized Performers and Audiences. *Shakespeare Studies* 47 (2019): 81–99.

Bradbury, Jill Marie, Jasper Norman and Yashaira Romilus. 'Protactile Theatre Session from "New Scholarly Directions in Premodern Disability Studies and Performance"'. Virtual symposium co-sponsored by Emory University and The Folger Institute, with support from Georgia Humanities. Zoom recording and transcript, 2021.

Brooks, Vanessa. *Separate Doors Same Stage*. Vimeo. Posted by Separate Doors, 2017. https://vimeo.com/173256511.

Brooks, Vanessa. *The Silent Approach*, 2022. https://vanessabrooks2020.com/the-silent-approach/.

Brooks, Vanessa. *The Silent Approach*. Vimeo. Posted by Separate Doors, 29 December 2018. https://vimeo.com/308700416.

Brown, David Sterling and Jennifer Lynn Stoerer. 'Blanched with Fear: Reading the Racialized Soundscape in *Macbeth*'. *Shakespeare Studies* 50 (2022): 33–43.

Bryon, Experience, J. Mark Bishop, Deirdre McLaughlin and Jess Kaufman, eds. *Embodied Cognition, Acting, and Performance*. New York: Routledge, 2018.

Buell, Brent. 'Rehabilitation Through the Arts at Sing Sing: Drama in the Big House'. In *Performing New Lives: Prison Theatre*, edited by Jonathan Shailor, 49–65. Philadelphia: Jessica Kingsley Publishers, 2011.

Bull, Michael, ed. *The Routledge Companion to Sound Studies*. New York: Routledge, 2019.

Byron, Sammie. '"Othello's Tribunal" and Conversation with Actor Harry Lennix. Atlanta Shakespeare Tavern Playhouse, 10 April 2022. https://youtu.be/Sc1GwPfViOo.

Cavanagh, Sheila T. '"All Corners of the World": The Possibilities and Challenges of International Electronic Education'. *Journal of Interactive Technology and Pedagogy* 6 (2014). http://jitp.commons.gc.cuny.edu/.

Cavanagh, Sheila T. '"All Great Neptune's Ocean": iShakespeare and Play in a Transatlantic Context'. In *Digital Shakespeare*, edited by Christie

Carson and Peter Kirwan, 87–99. Cambridge: Cambridge University Press, 2014.
Cavanagh, Sheila T. '"Being Here Together": Global Partnerships in Higher Education'. *Contingencies: A Journal of Global Pedagogy* 1, no. 1 (Spring 2021). https://doi.org/10.33682/m6hx-0wnd.
Cavanagh, Sheila T. '"Come, and Learn of Us": Shakespeare in an Age of Global Communication'. *CEA Critic* 78, no. 2 (2016): 242–255.
Cavanagh, Sheila T. 'The Curiosity of Nations: Shakespeare and International Electronic Education'. *Journal for Early Modern Cultural Studies: The Digital Turn* 13, no. 4 (2013): 121–5.
Cavanagh, Sheila T. '"In India": Shakespeare and Prison in Kolkata and Mysore'. *Shakespeare Survey* 74 (2021): 98–110.
Cavanagh, Sheila T. '"Make New Nations": Shakespearean Communities in the Twenty-first Century'. In *Routledge* Handbook of Shakespeare and Global Appropriation, edited by Christy Desmet, Sujata Iyengar and Miriam Jacobsen, 195–226. London: Routledge, 2019.
Cavanagh, Sheila T. '"The World's Common Place": Leveling the Shakespearean Playing Field'. *Borrowers and Lenders: Journal of Shakespearean Appropriation* 8, no. 2 (2014). http://www.borrowers.uga.edu/.
Cavanagh, Sheila T. 'The World Shakespeare Project'. Quarto: Shakespeare Theatre Association, Winter 2012/Spring 2013.
Cavanagh, Sheila T. '"The World Together Joins": Electronic Shakespearean Collaborations'. for special edition 'Digital Shakespeares: Innovations, Interventions, Mediations'. *The Shakespearean International Yearbook* (2014): 117–32.
Cavanagh, Sheila T. and Allison P. Hobgood, co-directors. 'New Scholarly Directions in Premodern Disability Studies and Performance'. Virtual symposium co-sponsored by Emory University and The Folger Shakespeare Institute, with support from Georgia Humanities, 4–6 March 2021.
Cavanagh, Sheila T. and Steve Rowland. 'Shakespeare in and out of Prison: The World Shakespeare Project and Shakespeare Central'. In *Reimaging Shakespeare Education: Teaching and Learning through Collaboration*, edited by Liam Semler, Claire Hansen and Jacqueline Manuel. Cambridge: Cambridge University Press, 2023.
Cavanagh, Sheila T. and Steve Rowland. '"Those Twins of Learning": Cognitive and Affective Learning in an Inclusive Shakespearean Curriculum'. *Critical Survey* 31, no. 4 (2019): 54–64.
Charlton, James I. *Nothing about Us Without Us: Disability Oppression and Empowerment*. Berkeley: University of California Press, 1998.
Chinardet, Nicholas. 'Londonist Discovers Normansfield Hospital Entertainment Hall'. *Londonist*. https://londonist.com/2009/10/londonist_discovers_normansfield_ho (accessed 6 October 2009).

Clare, Ysabel. 'Stanislavski's System as an Enactive Guide to Embodied Cognition?' In *Embodied Cognition, Acting, and Performance*, edited by Experience J. Bryon, Mark Bishop, Deirdre McLaughlin and Jess Kaufman, 43–63. New York: Routledge, 2018.

Classen, Constance. *The Deepest Sense: A Cultural History of Touch*. Chicago: University of Illinois Press, 2012.

CohenMiller, Anna and Nettie Boivin. *Questions in Qualitative Social Justice Research in Multicultural Contexts*. New York: Routledge, 2022.

Colapinto, John. *This is the Voice*. New York: Simon and Schuster, 2021.

Conlon, Richard and the Blue Apple ensemble. *Macbeth*, 2022. Full-text of Blue Apple script, shared through email.

CU Presents. 'Colorado Shakespeare Violence Prevention Program in the Schools', 2022. https://cupresents.org/performance/10050/shakespeare/csf-schools/.

Cushman, Anne and Lizette Montgomery. 'Yogi Desai Resigns from Kripalu'. *Yoga Journal* 120 (February 1995): 40–2.

Dana, Deb. *Anchored: How to Befriend Your Nervous System Using Polyvagal Theory*. Boulder: Sounds True Press, 2021.

Danylchuk, Lisa. *Yoga for Trauma Recovery: Theory, Philosophy, and Practice*. New York: Routledge, 2019.

Darò, Carlotta. *Avant-gardes Sonores en architecture [Avant-garde in sonic architecture]*. Dijon: Les Presses du Réel, 2013.

Davies, Christopher. *The Bamboozle Book of Dramatic Starts: 17 ways to Start a Drama Lesson with Special Needs Pupils*. Leicester: Anchorprint, [2006] 2014.

Davies, Christopher. *Creating Multi-Sensory Environments: Practical Ideas for Teaching and Learning*. London: Routledge, [2012] 2020.

Davis-Flynn, Jennifer. 'A New Report Details Decades of Abuse at the Hands of Yogi Bhajan'. *Yoga Journal*, 15 August 2020. https://www.yogajournal.com/yoga-101/abuse-in-kundalini-yoga/.

DC Theatre Scene. 'Party On: A sensory revelry in Romeo and Juliet', presented by dog & pony dc, 2017. https://dctheatrescene.com/show/party-sensory-revelry-romeo-juliet/.

Deafinitely Theatre. *Love's Labour's Lost*, 2020. https://www.deafinitelytheatre.co.uk/Event/loves-labours-lost.

Deafinitely Theatre. *A Midsummer Night's Dream*, 2022. https://www.deafinitelytheatre.co.uk/Event/a-midsummer-nights-dream.

DeSalle, Rob. *Our Senses: An Immersive Experience*. New Haven: Yale University Press, 2018.

Dimitropoulos, Stav. 'The Biological Reason Shakespeare can Treat PTSD'. *Inverse*, 16 May 2021. https://www.inverse.com/mind-body/shakespeare-as-therapy.

Doherty, Martin J. *Theory of Mind: How Children Understand Others' Thoughts and Feelings*. New York: Psychology Press, 2009.

Downey, Dennis B. and James W. Conroy. *Pennhurst and the Struggle for Disability Rights*. University Park: Penn State University Press (Keystone Books), 2020.

Dreier, Jenna. '"As you from Crimes would Pardoned Be": Prison Shakespeare and the Practices of Empowerment'. PhD diss., University of Minnesota, 2020.

Dreier, Jenna. 'Decolonising Pedagogies in Prison Performance Programmes: Making Shakespeare Secondary'. *Ride: The Journal of Applied Theatre and Performance* 26, no. 3 (2021): 477–93.

Dunn, Rob and Monica Sanchez. *Delicious: The Evolution of Flavor and How It Made Us Human*. Princeton: Princeton University Press, 2021.

Dunning, Brian. 'The Dark Side of Polyvagal Theory'. Skeptoid Podcast #816, 25 January 2022. https://skeptoid.com/episodes/4816#:~:text=The%20dispute%20arose%20in%201994%20when%20Stephen%20Porges,dorsal%20branch%2C%20active%20when%20you%27re%20in%20immobilized%20mode.

Earl, John. *Dr Langdon-Down and the Normansfield Theatre*. London: Borough of Twickenham Local History Society, 1997.

Edmiston, Brian and Iona Towler-Evans. *Humanizing Education with Dramatic Inquiry: In Dialogue with Dorothy Heathcote's Transformative Pedagogy*. New York: Routledge, 2022.

Edwards, Caryn. 'Homeless Actors in Jo-burg Take Shakespeare to the Street'. *The South African*, 6 December 2017. https://www.thesouthafrican.com/lifestyle/homeless-actors-in-joburg-take-shakespeare-to-the-streets/.

Egan, Gabriel. 'Hearing or Seeing a Play: Evidence in Early Modern Theatrical Terminology'. *Ben Jonson Journal* 8 (2001): 327–47.

Elliott, Esther Ruth. 'The Man Who Saw Backwards'. Extant Theatre podcast #7, 8 November 2018. https://extant.org.uk/media/podcasts/.

Elliott, Esther Ruth. 'The Man Who Saw Backwards' (adaptation of *King Lear*). Extant Theatre, 2018. https://extant.org.uk/project/the-man-who-saw-backwards/.

Elliott, Esther Ruth. 'Reflections on "Social Dreaming" with Shakespeare'. In Forum: Specialized Performers and Audiences. *Shakespeare Studies* 47 (2019): 61–70.

Emerson, David and Elizabeth Hopper. *Overcoming Trauma through Yoga: Reclaiming Your Body*. Berkeley: North Atlantic Books, 2011.

Escolme, Bridget. 'Costume'. In *The Cambridge Guide to the Worlds of Shakespeare* 1, *Shakespeare's World*, edited by Bruce Smith, 105–12. Cambridge: Cambridge University Press, 2016.

Field, Tiffany. *Touch Therapy*. New York: Churchill Livingstone, 2000.
Flintham, Susie. 'Tailoring Shakespeare to Students with Autism'. *Teaching Shakespeare* 12 (2017). https://www.britishshakespeare.ws/wp-content/uploads/2021/10/TeachingShakespeare12_AW_Web1.pdf.
Folkerth, Wes. *The Sound of Shakespeare*. New York: Routledge, 2002.
Fowler, Nancy. 'Remembering Prison Performing Arts Founder Agnes Wilcox, Who Died Unexpectedly While Vacationing'. St. Louis Public Radio/BBC World Service, 1 September 2017. https://news.stlpublicradio.org/show/st-louis-on-the-air/2017-09-01/remembering-prison-performing-arts-founder-agnes-wilcox-who-died-unexpectedly-while-vacationing.
Francis, Jodi. 'Foley Sound: What Is Foley Sound In Film & How Can I Make It?' *Music Gateway*, 25 January 2021. https://www.musicgateway.com/blog/how-to/foley-sound.
Freire, Paolo. *Pedagogy of the Oppressed*. London: Bloomsbury Academic, [1970] 2020.
Fryer, Louise and Amelia Cavallo. *Integrating Access in Live Performance*. New York: Routledge, 2022.
Fuchs, Thomas and Sabine C. Koch. 'Embodied Affectivity; on Moving and being Moved'. *Frontiers in Psychology* 5 (2014): 1–12.
Fulkerson, Matthew. *The First Sense: A Philosophical Study of Human Touch*. Cambridge, MA: MIT Press, 2014.
Gernsbacher, Morton Ann and Melanie Yergeau. 'Empirical Failures of the Claim That Autistic People Lack a Theory of Mind'. *Archives of Scientific Psychology* 7, no. 1 (2019): 102–18. https://www.ncbi.nlm.nih.gov/pmc/articles/PMC6959478/#article-1aff-info.
Gonsalves, Aileen and Tracy Irish. *Shakespeare and Meisner: A Practical Guide for Actors, Directors, Students and Teachers*. London: Arden Performance Companions, 2021.
Gray, Patrick, ed. *Shakespeare and the Ethics of War*. New York: Berghahn Books, 2019.
Greenblatt, Stephen, Walter Cohen, Suzanne Gossett, Katharine Eisaman Maus and Gordon McMullan, eds. *The Norton Shakespeare*. New York: W.W. Norton, 2015.
Grimshaw-Aagaard, Mark, 'What is Sound Studies?' In *The Routledge Companion to Sound Studies*, edited by Michael Bull, 16–23. New York: Routledge, 2019.
'Groundbreaking Intervention Technique, The Hunter Heartbeat Method, Comes to TLS'. The Learning Spectrum. https://thelearningspectrum.com/groundbreaking-intervention-technique-the-hunter-heartbeat-method-comes-to-tls/ (accessed 14 February 2023).
Grove, Nicola and Keith Park. *Social Cognition through Drama and Literature for People with Learning Disabilities: Macbeth in Mind*. London: Jessica Kingsley, 2001.

'Guidelines for Engaging Intimacy Directors for Live Performance'. *Intimacy for Stage and Screen*, 2021. https://www.intimacyforstageand screen.com/uploads/1/3/1/5/131581092/guidelines_for_engaging_an _intimacy_director_in_live_performance_v8.pdf.

Gulledge, John, Kelly Duquette and Mary Taylor Mann. 'The Puck Project: A Shakespeare Performance and Ethics Program'. *Early Modern Culture Online*, 2020. https://doi.org/10.15845/emco.v7i1.

Gulledge, John, Kelly Duquette and Mary Taylor Mann. 'The Puck Project: A Shakespeare Performance and Ethics Program'. Powerpoint slides and script for Public Humanities for presentation at Emory University, 2021.

Hadley, Susan and George Yancy, eds. *Therapeutic Uses of Rap and Hip-Hop*. New York: Routledge, 2012.

Hamel, Johanne, ed. *Somatic Art Therapy: Alleviating Pain and Trauma through Art*. New York: Routledge, 2021.

Hardach, Sophie. 'Wasabi Fire Alarm a Lifesaver for the Deaf'. *Reuters*, 17 March 2008. https://www.reuters.com/article/us-japan-wasabi -idUST29421020080318.

Hart, Henry. 'Innovations in Cinema: "AromaRama"'. *National Board of Review*, January 2022. https://nationalboardofreview.org/2014/01/ innovations-cinema-aromarama/.

Heritage, Paul. 'Stealing Kisses'. In *Theatre in Crisis? Performance Manifesto for a New Century*, editsd by Maria M. Delgado and Caridad Svich, 166–79. Manchester: Manchester University Press, 2002.

Herold, Niels. *Prison Shakespeare and the Purpose of Performance: Repentance Rituals and the Early Modern*. New York: Palgrave Macmillan, 2014.

Hertenstein, Matthew J. and Sandra J. Weiss, eds. *The Handbook of Touch: Neuroscience, Behavioral, and Health Perspectives*. New York: Springer Publishing Co, 2011.

Herz, Rachel S. 'Influences of Odors on Mood and Affective Cognition'. In *Olfaction, Taste, and Cognition*, edited by Catherine Rouby, Benoist Schaal, Danièle Dubois, Rémy Gervais and A. Holley, 160–77. New York: Cambridge University Press, 2002.

Higgins, Jackie. *Sentient: What Animals Reveal about our Senses*. London: Picador, 2021.

Holmes, Bob. *Flavor: The Science of Our Most Neglected Sense*. New York: W.W. Norton, 2017.

Hrach, Susan. *Minding Bodies: How Physical Space, Sensation, and Movement Affect Learning*. Morgantown: West Virginia University Press, 2021.

Humphreys, Joe. 'Aristotle Got It Wrong: We Have a Lot More Than Five Senses'. *Irish Times*, 16 May 2002. https://www.irishtimes.com/

culture/aristotle-got-it-wrong-we-have-a-lot-more-than-five-senses-1.3079639.

Hunter, Christopher. *States of Mind*. Extant Theatre, Bloomsbury Festival, 16 October 2021.

Hunter, Kelly. *Shakespeare's Heartbeat: Drama Games for Children with Autism*. New York: Routledge, 2015.

Hunter, Kelly and Robert Shaughnessy. 'Flute Theatre, Shakespeare, and Autism'. In *Reimagining Shakespeare Education: Teaching and Learning through Collaboration*, edited by Liam Semler, Claire Henson and Jacqueline Manuel, 271–81. Cambridge: Cambridge University Press, 2023.

Jackson, Scott. 'Finding Light in the Shadow: Illuminating prison theatre practice through the production of the 4th international Shakespeare in Prisons Conference'. MFA-Sustained Independent Project, Royal Central School of Speech & Drama, University of London, 2021.

Jacobs, Katrina Bartow. '"I Believe in Home Language, but the Tests Don't": Addressing Linguistic Diversity within Assessment Practices across Literacy Teacher Preparation and Classroom Practice'. *Teachers College Record* 121, no. 7 (2019): 1–42. https://journals.sagepub.com/doi/abs/10.1177/016146811912100705.

Jensen, Michael P. *The Battle of the Bard: Shakespeare on U.S. Radio in 1937*. Leeds: ARC University Press, 2018.

Jensen, Michael P. '"Prithee, Listen Well," The Case for Audio Shakespeare'. In *The Shakespearean World*, edited by Jill L. Levinson and Robert Ormsby, 407–17. London: Routledge, 2017.

Jessup, William, dir. 'Growing up Downs'. London: BBC3, 2015. https://growingupdowns.co.uk/.

Karthik, Savitha, trans. 'Where the Mind is Without Fear'. *Deccan Herald*, India, 18 November 2018.

Kearney, Richard. *Touch: Recovering Our Most Vital Sense*. New York: Columbia University Press, 2021.

Kemp, Rick. *Embodied Acting: What Neuroscience Tells Us About Performance*. New York: Routledge, 2012.

Kilgarriff, Michael. 'The Voice of Henry Irving'. The Irving Society. https://www.theirvingsociety.org.uk/the-voice-of-henry-irving/ (accessed 14 February 2023).

King, Juliet L., ed. *Art Therapy, Trauma, and Neuroscience: Theoretical and Practical Perspectives*. New York: Routledge, 2016.

King, Ros and Paul J. C. M. Franssen, eds. *Shakespeare and War*. London: Palgrave, 2008.

Kleiman, Kathy. *Proven Ground: The Untold Story of the Six Women who Programmed the World's First Modern Computer*. New York: Hachette, 2022.

Konopka, Lukasz M. 'Neuroscience Concepts in Clinical Practice'. In *Art Therapy, Trauma, and Neuroscience: Theoretical and Practical Perspectives*, edited by Juliet L. King, 11–41. New York: Routledge, 2016.

Kowalczyk, Liz. 'Allegations of Employee Mistreatment Roil Renowned Brookline Trauma Center'. *Boston Globe*, 7 March 2018. https://www.bostonglobe.com/metro/2018/03/07/allegations-employee-mistreatment-roil-renowned-trauma-center/sWW13agQDY9B9A1rt9eqnK/story.html.

Krathwohl, David R., Benjamin S. Bloom and Bertram B. Massia. *Taxonomy of Educational Objectives, Handbook II: Affective Domain (The Classification of Educational Goals)*. Philadelphia: David McKay Publishers, 1956.

Kurtz, Ron. *Body-Centered Psychotherapy: The Hakomi Method*. Mendocino: LifeRhythm Press, 2015.

Kurtz, Ron. *The Hakomi Way: Consciousness & Healing*. Port Perry: Stone's Throw Publications, 2018.

Laban, Rudolf. *The Mastery of Movement*. Alton: Dance Books Ltd., [1950] 1980.

Lamb, Christina. 'I'm a Psychologist with a Gun. My Job is to Help Troops Swallow Fear'. *Sunday Times*, 15 May 2022. https://www.thetimes.co.uk/article/im-a-psychologist-with-a-gun-my-job-is-to-help-troops-swallow-fear-08dghkllf.

Langdon-Down, J. 'Lettsomian Lectures on Some of the Mental Affections of Childhood and Youth'. *The British Medical Journal* 1, no. 36 (1887, January 22): 149–51. https://www.jstore.org/stable/2021034.

Langdon-Down, J. *On the Education and Training of the Feeble in Mind*. London: H.K. Lewis, 1876. https://ia801302.us.archive.org/29/items/b22305397/b22305397.pdf.

Lehmann, Courtney. 'Double Jeopardy: Shakespeare and Prison Theatre'. In *Shakespeare and the Ethics of Appropriation*, edited by Alexa Alice Joubin and Elizabeth Rivlin, 89–106. New York: Palgrave McMillan, 2014.

Levy, Ian. *Hip-Hop and Spoken Word Therapy in School Counseling: Developing Culturally Responsive Approaches*. New York: Routledge, 2021.

Levy, Ian and Edmund Adjapong, eds. *HipHopEd-Compilation*. Volume 2: *Hip-Hop as Praxis and Social Justice*. Frankfurt: Peter Lang, 2020.

Liberatore, Paul. 'Spotlight on Dark Past'. *Marin Independent Journal*, July 2016, A1, A6. https://www.marinshakespeare.org/wp-content/uploads/2016/07/Marin-IJ-Paul-Libertore-Dameion-as-Othello-story.pdf.

Linklater, Kristin. *Freeing the Natural Voice: Imagery and Art in the Practice of Voice and Language*. Hollywood: Drama Publishers, 2006.

Linklater, Kristin. *Freeing Shakespeare's Voice: The Actors Guide to Talking the Text*. London: Nick Hern, 2009.
'Listed Buildings (U.K)'. Historic England, 2022. https://historicengland.org.uk/listing/what-is-designation/listed-buildings/.
Lloyd, Megan and Elizabeth Brown. 'Staging "Skimble-skamble Stuff": *1 Henry IV* and the Welsh Voice'. In *Shakespeare's Auditory Worlds: Hearing and Staging Practices, Then and Now*, edited by Laury Magnus and Walter W. Cannon, 115–36. Fairleigh Dickinson Press with The Rowman & Littlefield Publishing Group, 2021.
Loewenstein, David and Paul Stevens. *The Cambridge Companion to Shakespeare and War*. Cambridge: Cambridge University Press, 2021.
Loftis, Sonya Freeman. 'Autistic Culture, Shakespeare Therapy, and the Hunter Heartbeat Method'. *Shakespeare Survey* 74 (2019): 256–67.
Loftis, Sonya Freeman. *Shakespeare & Disability Studies*. Oxford: Oxford University Press, 2021.
Lucas, Ashley E. *Prison Theatre and the Global Crisis of Incarceration*. London: Methuen Drama, 2020.
Lucia di Lammermoor. Instant Opera Company. Normansfield Theatre, 2022. https://langdondowncentre.org.uk/product/instant-opera-lucia-di-lammermoor/.
Luckett, Sharrell and Tia M. Shaffer, eds. *Black Acting Methods: Critical Approaches*. London: Routledge, 2016.
Lugering, Michael. *The Expressive Actor: Integrated Voice, Movement, and Acting Training*. New York: Routledge, 2013.
Lusebrink, Vija B. and Lisa D. Hinz. 'The Expressive Therapies Continuum as a Framework in the Treatment of Trauma'. In *Art Therapy, Trauma, and Neuroscience: Theoretical and Practical Perspectives* edited by Juliet L. King, 42–66. New York: Routledge, 2016.
Mackenzie, Rowan. *Creating Space for Shakespeare: Working with Marginalised Communities*. London: Arden Shakespeare, 2023.
Magnat, Virginie. *The Performative Power of Vocality*. London: Routledge, 2020.
Malchiodi, Cathy A. *Trauma and Expressive Arts Therapy: Brain, Body, & Imagination in the Healing Process*. New York: Guilford Press, 2020.
Maley, Willy. '*Macbeth* and Trauma'. In *The Cambridge Companion to Shakespeare and War*, edited by David Loewenstein and Paul Stevens, 239–55. Cambridge: Cambridge University Press, 2021.
Marich, Jamie. *Process not Perfection: Expressive Arts Solutions for Trauma Recovery*. Warren: Creative Mindfulness Media, 2019.
Marowitz, Charles. *The Other Chekhov: A Biography of Michael Chekhov, the Legendary Actor, Director, and Theorist*. New York: Applause Theatre & Cinema Books, 2004.

Martin, Michel. 'Teaching Shakespeare in a Maximum Security Prison'. *Tell Me More*, NPR, 22 April 2013. https://www.npr.org/2013/04/22/178411754/teaching-shakespeare-in-a-maximum-security-prison.

Martínez, Rick. *Mi Cocina: A Culinary Journey of Self-Discovery*. New York: Clarkson Potter, 2022.

Mask, Deirdre. *The Address Book: What Street Addresses Reveal about Identity, Race, Wealth, and Power*. New York: St. Martin's Press, 2020.

Massai, Sonia. *Shakespeare's Accents: Voicing Identity in Performance*. Cambridge: Cambridge University Press, 2020.

Matamala, Anna and Pilar Orero, eds. *Researching Audio Description: New Approaches*. London: Palgrave Macmillan, 2016.

Maté, Gabor. *The Myth of the Normal: Trauma, Illness, and Healing in a Toxic Culture*. New York: Avery Press, 2022.

McAllister-Viel, Tara. '"Embodied Voice" and Inclusivity: Ableism and Theater Voice Training'. In *Inclusivity and Equality in Performance Training: Teaching and Learning for Neuro and Physical Diversity*, edited by Petronilla Whitfield, 188–99. New York: Routledge, 2022.

McAllister-Viel, Tara. *Training Actors' Voices: Towards an Intercultural/Interdisciplinary Approach*. London: Routledge, 2018.

McCaskill, Carolyn, Ceil Lucas, Robert Bayley and Joseph Hill. *Hidden Treasure of Black ASL: Its History and Structure*. Washington, DC: Gallaudet University Press, 2011.

McConnell, Susan. *Somatic Internal Family Systems Therapy: Awareness, Breath, Resonance, Movement, and Touch in Practice*. Berkeley: North Atlantic Books, 2020.

McEachern, Claire. 'Foreign War'. In *The Cambridge Companion to Shakespeare and War*, edited by David Loewenstein and Paul Stevens, 54–74. Cambridge: Cambridge University Press, 2021.

McGee, Harold. *Nose Dive: A Field Guide to the World's Smells*. New York: Penguin, 2020.

McLaughlin, Deirdre. 'Embodiment: A Cross-Disciplinary Provocation'. In *Embodied Cognition, Acting, and Performance*, edited by Experience J. Bryon, Mark Bishop, Deirdre McLaughlin and Jess Kaufman, 36–42. New York: Routledge, 2018.

McLindon, Mike, Steve McCall and Liz Hodges. *Learning Through Touch: Supporting Learners with Multiple Disabilities and Vision Impairment Through a Bioecological Systems Perspective*. New York: Routledge, 2020.

Mehling, Margaret Helen. 'Differential Impact of Drama-Based versus Traditional Social Skills Intervention'. PhD diss., Ohio State University, 2017.

Mehling, Margaret Helen, Marc J. Tassé and Robin Root. 'Shakespeare and Autism: An Exploratory Evaluation of the Hunter Heartbeat Method'. *Research and Practice in Intellectual and Developmental Disabilities* 4, no. 2 (2016): 107–20. https://www.tandfonline.com/doi/full/10.1080/23297018.2016.1207202.

Merlin, Bella. *The Complete Stanislavsky Toolkit*. London: Nick Hern: 2014.

Merlin, Bella and Tina Packer. *Shakespeare & Company: When Action is Eloquence*. London: Routledge, 2020.

Merriman, Andy. *Tales of Normansfield: The Langdon Down Legacy*. London: Down's Syndrome Association, 2007.

Meyersohn, Nathaniel. 'How Abercrombie, Victoria's Secret, and Vitamin Shoppe Use Smell to Get You to Spend More'. *CNN*, 13 August 2022. https://www.cnn.com/2022/08/13/business/why-stores-smell-good-abercrombie-victorias-secret/index.html.

Moreland, Alex. 'The Rig: Amazon Prime Release Date, Trailer, and Cast with Martin Compston, Iain Glen, and Emily Hampshire'. *The Scotsman*, 6 January 2023. https://www.scotsman.com/culture/television/the-rig-amazon-prime-release-date-trailer-cast-martin-compston-iain-glen-emily-hampshire-3971531.

Mouritsen, Ole G. and Klavs Styrbæk. *Mouthfeel: How Texture Makes Taste*. New York: Columbia University Press, 2017.

M.S.N.D.: A Shakespeare Remix. Intermission Youth Theatre at the Chelsea Theatre, London, 26 November 2022. https://www.intermissionyouththeatre.co.uk/whats-on.

Muchembled, Robert. *Smells: A Cultural History of Odours in Early Modern Times*. Cambridge: Polity Books, 2020.

'NASA's Sonification Project'. InsightsIAS, 20 September 2020. https://www.insightsonindia.com/2020/09/26/nasas-sonification-project/#:~:text=The%20sonification%20project%20is%20led%20by%20the%20Chandra,visually-impaired%20communities%20%E2%80%94%20to%20experience%20space%20through%20data.

Nestor, James. *Breath: The New Science of a Lost Art*. New York: Riverhead Books, Penguin, 2020.

Nolan, Yvette. *Medicine Shows: Indigenous Performance Cultures*. Toronto: Playwrights Canada Press, 2015.

Norris, Kyle. 'Shakespeare Helps Prisoners Change'. Michigan Radio, NPR, 28 April 2013. https://www.michiganradio.org/arts-culture/2013-04-28/shakespeare-helps-prisoners-change.

'NTID Performing Arts: The Roving Shakespeare'. YouTube video. Posted by RIT NTID, 20 December 2022. https://www.youtube.com/watch?app=desktop&v=b9Ha1FqEpDQ&fbclid=IwAR0IjJ0q3ZG8sBLP5F23NnF4GXJIvHXICPUFRy3pqfcHVsM4DkJD1H1WvFQ.

Ogden, Pat and Janina Fisher. *Sensorimotor Psychotherapy: Interventions for Trauma and Attachment*. New York: W.W. Norton, 2015.

Ogden, Pat, Kekuni Minton and Clare Pain. *Trauma and the Body: A Sensorimotor Approach to Psychotherapy*. New York: W.W. Norton, 2006.

O'Hanlon, Jacquie and Angie Wootten. *Using Drama to Teach Personal, Social, and Emotional Skills*. Los Angeles: Sage, 2007.

O'Mahony, Holly. 'David Tennant in "Good", Harold Pinter Theatre Review'. *Culture Whisper*, 13 October 2022. https://www.culturewhisper.com/r/theatre/david_tennant_good_play_london/15181#:~:text=One%20of%20them%20is%2C%20of%20course%2C%20TV%20star,make%20Cooke%E2%80%99s%20confusing%2C%20overtly%20intellectual%20production%20wholly%20engaging

Pallant, Cheryl. *Writing and the Body in Motion: Awakening Voice through Somatic Practice*. Jefferson: McFarland, 2018.

Pearlstine, Elise Vernon. *Scent: A Natural History of Fragrance*. New Haven: Yale University Press, 2022.

Pennebaker, J. W. 'Overcoming Inhibition: Rethinking the Roles of Personality, Cognition and Social Behaviors'. In *Emotion, Inhibition, and Health*, edited by Harald C. Traue and James W. Pennebaker, 100–15. Seattle: Hogrefe and Huber Publishers, 1989.

Pennebaker, J. W. and H. C. Traue. 'Inhibition and Psychosomatic Processes'. In *Emotion, Inhibition, and Health*, edited by Harald C. Traue and James W. Pennebaker, 146–63. Seattle: Hogrefe and Huber Publishers, 1989.

Pensalfini, Rob. *Prison Shakespeare: For These Deep Shames and Great Indignities*. New York: Palgrave Macmillan, 2016.

Perullo, Nicola. *Taste as Experience: The Philosophy and Aesthetics of Food*. New York: Columbia University Press, 2016.

Pisk, Litz. *The Actor and His Body*. London: Bloomsbury, [1975] 2018.

Porges, Stephen W. *The Pocket Guide to The Polyvagal Theory: The Transformative Power of Feeling Safe*. New York: W.W. Norton, 2017.

Powers, Kate. *Exit, Pursued by a Pandemic*. Exit Project, University of Idaho Theatre Department, 2021.

Powers, Kate. 'Like Bright Metal on a Sullen Ground: The First Six Months of a Prison Shakespeare Program'. University of Idaho Theatre Department, 2020.

Prentki, Tim and Sheila Preston. *The Applied Theatre Reader*. New York. Routledge, 2009.

'ProTactile Romeo and Juliet: Theatre by/for the DeafBlind'. YouTube video. Posted by Gallaudet University, 2 May 2019. https://youtu.be/btB_nePm860.

'Pupil Referral Units'. UK Department for Education, 26 March 2014. https://www.gov.uk/guidance/pupil-referral-units-converting-to-alternative-provision-academies.

Radcliffe, Allan. 'Edinburgh Theatre Review: Venus and Adonis at C Primo'. *The London Times*, 26 August 2017. https://www.thetimes.co.uk/article/edinburgh-theatre-review-venus-and-adonis-at-c-primo-ldx65ss8p.

Raffone, Antonio. 'The Cognitive and Affection Neuroscience of Meditation'. In *The Psychology of Meditation*, edited by Michael A. West, 221–40. Oxford: Oxford University Press, 2016.

Revolution 21. Written and directed by Martyna Peszko. Teatr-21, Warsaw, Poland, 2022. https://www.crew-united.com/de/Revolution-21__288337.html.

Roberts, Charlotte. 'The Play's the Thing: Choosing the Right Text for ASC Students'. *Teaching Shakespeare* 12 (2017). https://www.britishshakespeare.ws/wp-content/uploads/2021/10/TeachingShakespeare12_AW_Web1.pdf.

Rodenburg, Patsy. *The Actor Speaks: Voice and the Performer*. London: Methuen, 2019.

Rodenburg, Patsy. *Speaking Shakespeare*. New York: St. Martin's, 2004.

Rogerson, Hank, dir. *Shakespeare Behind Bars*. Philomath Films, 2005.

Rogerson, Hank and Jilann Spitzmiller, dirs. *Still Dreaming*. Philomath Films, 2014.

Rolls, Edmund T. 'The Cortical Representation of Taste and Smell'. In *Olfaction, Taste, and Cognition*, edited by Catherine Rouby, Benoist Schaal, Danièle Dubois, Rémy Gervais and A. Holley, 367–87. New York: Cambridge University Press, 2022.

Romano, Aja. '82-Year-Old Glenda Jackson is Towering. But She Can't Rescue a Bungled Show'. *Vox*, 16 April 2019. https://www.vox.com/culture/2019/4/16/18291744/king-lear-review-glenda-jackson-ruth-wilson-trump.

Rosenberg, Sidney. *Accessing the Healing Power of the Vagus Nerve: Self-Help Exercises for Anxiety, Depression, Trauma, and Autism*. Berkeley: North Atlantic Book, 2017.

Rouby, Catherine, Benoist Schaal, Danièle Dubois, Rémy Gervais and A. Holley, eds. *Olfaction, Taste, and Cognition*. New York: Cambridge University Press, 2002.

Ryan, Sue. 'Robinson Shakespeare Company Invited to Perform in England'. *Notre Dame News*, 8 March 2017. https://news.nd.edu/news/robinson-shakespeare-company-invited-to-perform-in-england/.

Sanders, V. 'The Passion of Tina Packer'. *The Boston Globe*, 17 August 1997.

Sarkar, Kassie, Greta Goldbart and Jacob Ruhkamp. 'Voices from the Other Side: Artists Books from Phillips State Prison'. Atlanta:

Woodruff Library, Emory University, 2020. https://libraries.emory.edu/events-exhibits/exhibits/voices-other-side.

Saunders, Emma. 'Arthur Hughes: First Disabled Richard III is "Big Gesture" from RSC'. *BBC News*, 17 June 2022. https://www.bbc.co.uk/news/entertainment-arts-61549419.

Sayet, Madeline. 'Reimagining Shakespeare's Legacy with Madeline Sayet'. Howlaround Theatre History Podcast #46, 14 September 2017. https://howlround.com/theatre-history-podcast-46.

Sayet, Madeline. *Where We Belong*. London: Methuen Drama, 2022.

Schafer, F. Murray. 'The Soundscape'. In *The Sound Studies Reader*, edited by Jonathan Sterne, 95–103. New York: Routledge, 2012.

Schafer, F. Murray. *The Soundscape: Our Sonic Environment and the Tuning of the World*. Rochester: Destiny Books, 1993.

Sered, Danielle. *Until We Reckon: Violence, Mass Incarceration, and a Road to Repair*. New York: The New Press, 2019.

Severson, Kim. 'A Bridge between Western Science and Eastern Faith'. *The New York Times*, 11 October 2013. https://www.nytimes.com/2013/10/12/us/seeking-a-bridge-between-western-science-and-eastern-faith-with-the-Dalai-Lama.html.

Shailor, Jonathan. 'Humanizing Education Behind Bars: The Theatre of Empowerment and the Shakespeare Project'. In *Challenging the Prison Industrial Complex: Activism, Arts, & Educational Alternatives*, edited by S. Harnett, 229–51. Chicago: University of Illinois Press, 2011.

Shailor, Jonathan, ed. *Performing New Lives: Prison Theatre*. Philadelphia: Jessica Kingsley Publishers, 2011.

Shailor, Jonathan. 'A Professor's Perspective: The Shakespeare Prison Project at Racine Correctional Institution'. In *Creating behind the Razor Wire*, edited by K. Brune, 38–41. Lulu.com, 2008.

Shailor, Jonathan. 'When Muddy Flowers Bloom: The Shakespeare Project at Racine Correctional Institution'. *PMLA* 123, no. 3 (May 2008): 632–42.

Shakespeare, William. *The Norton Complete Works*, third edition. Edited by Stephen Greenblatt, Walter Cohen, Jean Howard, Katharine Eisaman Maus, GordonMcMullan and Suzanne Gossett. New York: Norton, 2015.

'Shakespeare in Prison: Detroit Public Theatre's Signature Community Program'. Detroit Public Theatre. https://www.detroitpublictheatre.org/shakespeareinprison (accessed 14 February 2022).

'Shakespeare in Prisons Network'. YouTube channel. Shakespeare at Notre Dame. https://www.youtube.com/playlist?list=PLF2QbT7cszC4rAQl4cSx0lqy3yUdBvAP4.

Shapiro, Lawrence. *Embodied Cognition*. New York: Routledge, 2019.

Sharma, Henna. 'Line of Duty Fans Shocked to Discover Scot Martin Compston's Real Accent after Years of Playing Southerner Steve Arnett'. *The Sun*, 2 May 2021. https://www.thesun.co.uk/uncategorized/14831585/line-of-duty-martin-compston-real-accent/.

Sharp, Martin, dir. *Michael Chekhov: The Dartington Years*, introduced by Simon Callow. Michael Chekhov Centre, UK in association with the Dorothy Whitney Elmhirst Trust and Palomino Films. New York: Insight Media, 2002. DVD.

Shaughnessy, Nicola, ed. *Affective Performance and Cognitive Science*. New York: Bloomsbury Methuen, 2013.

Shaughnessy, Nicola. 'Life Changing: Meal Deal'. *BBC Radio 4*, 2 November 2022. https://www.bbc.co.uk/programmes/m001dndw.

Shaughnessy, Robert. 'Give Me Your Hands'. In Forum: Specialized Performers and Audiences. *Shakespeare Studies* 74 (2019): 71–80.

Shay, Jonathan. *Achilles in* Vietnam: *Combat Trauma and the Undoing of Character*. New York: Simon and Schuster, 1995.

Shay, Jonathan. *Odysseus in America: Combat Trauma and the Trials of Homecoming*. New York: Scribner, 2003.

Shepherd-Bates, Frannie. 'Michael Chekhov Technique as a Trauma-responsive Practice in Shakespeare in Prison'. Unpublished manuscript, 2022.

Shona Louise. 'An Open Letter to the Commercial Theatre Industry about Accessibility and Disability Representation'. Blog post, 19 October 2021. http://www.shonalouise.com/2021/10/an-open-letter-to-commercial-theatre.html#.YZYsdb3P3CU.

Shona Louise. 'Meet the Visually Impaired Performers Reimagining Shakespeare'. Blog post, 11 October 2021. http://www.shonalouise.com/2021/10/meet-visually-impaired-performers.html#.YZYrk73P3CU.

Shurgot, Michael. 'Breaking the Sound Barrier: Howie Seago and American Sign Language at Oregon Shakespeare'. *Shakespeare Bulletin* 30, no. 1 (2012): 21–36. 10.1353/shb.2012.0019.

Simpson, Fay. *The Lucid Body: A Guide for the Physical Actor*. New York: Allworth Press, 2020.

Sjoman, N. E. *The Yoga Tradition of the Mysore Palace*. New Delhi: Abhinav Publications, 1999.

'Smell-o-Vision'. Olorama Tech, 31 August 2022. https://www.olorama.com/smell-o-vision.

Smith, Amy L. '"Think of Me as I am": Juvenile Offenders Talk Back to Shakespeare'. *Teaching Shakespeare* 12 (2017). https://www.britishshakespeare.ws/wp-content/uploads/2021/10/TeachingShakespeare12_AW_Web1.pdf.

Smith, Bruce R. *The Acoustic World of Early Modern England: Attending to the O-Factor*. Chicago: University of Chicago Press, 1999.

Smith, Mark M. *A Sensory History Manifesto*. University Park: Penn State University Press, 2021.

Smith-Waton, Nancy. 'Shakespeare for Veterans: Feast of Crispian'. In Forum: Specialized Performers and Audiences. *Shakespeare Studies* 74 (2019): 38–48.

Snyder-Young, Dani. *Theatre of Good Intentions: Challenges and Hopes for Theatre and Social Change*. New York: Palgrave Macmillan, 2013.

Spratt, Radha. 'In Conversation with Inspirational Theatre Director, Sergio Amigo'. Blog post, 1 May 2013. https://radhaspratt.wordpress.com/2013/05/01/in-coversation-with-theatre-director-sergio-amigo/.

Steinfeld, Edward and Jordana Maisel. *Universal Design: Creating Inclusive Environments*. New York: Wiley, 2012.

Stephen, Michael J. *Breath Taking: The Power, Fragility, and Future of Our Extraordinary Lungs*. New York: First Grove Atlantic, 2021.

Stern, Tiffany. '"Theatre"+ "Play + House": Naming Spaces in the Time of Shakespeare'. In *Playing and Playgoing in Early Modern England: Actor, Audience, and Performance*, edited by Simon Smith and Emma Whipday, 186–204. Cambridge: Cambridge University Press, 2022.

Sterne, Jonathan, ed. *The Sound Studies Reader*. New York: Routledge, 2012.

Stevens, Paul. '*Henry V* and the Pleasures of War'. In *The Cambridge Companion to Shakespeare and War*, edited by David Loewenstein and Paul Stevens, 221–38. Cambridge: Cambridge University Press, 2021.

Stewart, Jude. *Revelations in Air: A Guidebook to Smell*. New York: Penguin, 2021

Swanson, Ann. *Science of Yoga: Understand the Anatomy and Physiology to Perfect Your Practice*. London: DK Publishers, 2019.

Szabo-Cassella, Claire. *Shakespeare's Yoga: How the Bard Can Deepen Your Practice – On and Off the Mat*. Ashland: White Cloud Press, 2016.

'Talking about the Arts in Medicine White Paper'. University of Florida Center for the Arts in Medicine, 2017. https://arts.ufl.edu/academics/center-for-arts-in-medicine/resources/talking-about-arts-in-health/.

Tcherkasski, Sergei. *Stanislavsky and Yoga*. New York: Routledge, 2016.

Thelen, Esther, G. Schöner, C. Scheier and L. Smith. 'The Dynamics of Embodiment: A Field Theory of Infant Perseverative Reaching'. *Behavioral and Brain Sciences* 24 (2001): 1–86.

Thomas, Jennifer and Robert J. Vrtis. *Inclusive Character Analysis: Putting Theory into Practice for the 21st Century Theatre Classroom*. London: Routledge, 2021.

Tishman, Shari. *Slow Looking: The Art and Practice of Learning Through Observation*. New York: Routledge, 2018.

Traue, Harald C. and James W. Pennebaker, eds. *Emotion, Inhibition, and Health*. Seattle: Hogrefe and Huber Publishers, 1989.

Travis, Raphael Jr. *The Healing Power of Hip Hop*. Santa Barbara: Praeger, 2016.

Trounstine, Jean. 'Revisiting Sacred Spaces'. In *Performing New Lives: Prison Theatre*, edited by Jonathan Shailor, 231–46. Philadelphia: Jessica Kingsley Publishers, 2011.

Trounstine, Jean. *Shakespeare Behind Bars: The Power of Drama in a Women's Prison*. New York: St. Martin's Press, 2022.

Twitty, Michael W. *Koshersoul: The Faith and Food Journey of an African American Jew*. New York: Amistad: Harper Collins, 2022.

'The University of Birmingham Signing Shakespeare Programme is Designed to Support Deaf Young People in their Study and Enjoyment of Shakespeare'. Royal Shakespeare Company. https://www.rsc.org.uk/learn/schools-and-teachers/teacher-resources/signing-shakespeare-for-deaf-students/about#:~:text=Signing%20Shakespeare%20is%20a%20project%20designed%20to%20support,people%20in%20their%20study%20and%20enjoyment%20of%20Shakespeare (accessed 14 February 2023).

Unwin, Stephen. *The Golden Smile: Learning Disabilities in Culture and Society*. Unpublished manuscript, 2022.

Unwin, Stephen. 'Joey's Dream'. In Forum: Specialized Performers and Audiences. *Shakespeare Studies* 74 (2019): 31–7.

van der Kolk, Bessel. *The Body Keeps the Score: Brain, Mind and Body in the Healing of Trauma*. New York: Penguin, 2014.

Varela, Francisco J, Evan Thompson and Eleanor Rosch. *The Embodied Mind: Cognitive Science and Human Condition*, revised edition. Cambridge, MA: MIT University Press, [1991] 2016.

Vaudreuil, Rebecca. *Music Therapy with Military and Veteran Populations*. Philadelphia: Jessica Kingsley Publishers, 2022.

Ward, Ashley. *Sensational: A New Story of Our Senses*. London: Profile Books, 2023.

Ward, O Conor. 'John Langdon Down: The Man and the Message'. *Down Syndrome Research and Practice* 6, no. 1 (1999): 19–24.

Wareham, Katherine and Alex Kelly. *Talkabout Theory of Mind: Teaching Theory of Mind to Improve Social Skills and Relationships*. London: Routledge, 2020.

Welman, Henry M. *Making Minds: How Theory of Mind Develops*. Oxford: Oxford University Press, 2014.

West, Catherine M. P. 'Mary Feilding Guild Scandal Highlights Appalling Insecurity for Elderly Care Home Residents'. https://www.catherinewest.org.uk/latest-news/2021/03/23/closure-of-mary-fielding-guild/ (accessed 14 February 2023).

West, Michael A., ed. *The Psychology of Meditation*. Oxford: Oxford University Press, 2016.

Whitfield, Petronilla, ed. *Inclusivity and Equality in Performance Training: Teaching and Learning for Neuro and Physical Diversity*. New York: Routledge, 2022.

Whitfield, Petronilla. *Teaching Strategies for Neurodiversity and Dyslexia in Actor Training: Sensing Shakespeare*. London: Routledge, 2020.

Wiggins, Drew. 'Veterans Find a Path to Healing Through Shakespeare. Mad in America: Science Psychiatry and Social Justice'. *Mad in America*, 13 October 2019. https://www.madinamerica.com/2019/10/veterans-find-path-to-healing-through-shakespeare/.

Wilbourne, Emily and Suzanne G. Cusick, eds. *Acoustemologies in Contact: Sounding Subjects and Modes of Listening in Early Modernity*. Cambridge: Open Book Publishers, 2021.

'William Grint is at the RSC (Royal Shakespeare Company) in The Comedy of Errors'. *Signed Culture*, 4 September 2021. https://www.signedculture.org.uk/william-grint-is-at-the-rsc-royal-shakespeare-company-in-the-comedy-of-errors/.

Williams, Mary Jane. 'Autism and Shakespeare: Ohio State Researchers Study the Hunter Heartbeat Method'. *The Washington Post*, 9 April 2013. https://www.washingtonpost.com/lifestyle/on-parenting/autism-and-shakespeare-ohio-state-researchers-study-hunter-heartbeat-method/2013/04/09/843cc67e-9003-11e2-9abd-e4c5c9dc5e90_story.html.

Williams, Nathan and Jonas Bjerre-Poulson (Kinfolk & Norm Architects). *Touch: Spaces Designed for the Senses*. New York: Gestalten Publishers, 2019.

Wolfert, Stephan. 'Stephan Wolfert: US Army Veteran, Actor, and Founder of DE-CRUIT'. National Endowment for the Arts Podcast, 23 May 2019. https://www.arts.gov/stories/podcast/stephan-wolfert.

Wolfert, Stephan and Dawn Stern. 'DE-CRUIT: Using Theatre to Treat the Effects of Trauma: Integrating Shakespeare and Science in Healing-Centered Practice' (Collection). Trauma Research Foundation, 4 part TRF Tuesday series, 2022. https://traumaresearchfoundation.org/_trashed-3/.

'Wooden O Symposium'. Southern Utah University/Utah Shakespeare Festival, 2022. https://www.bard.org/about/education/wooden-o-symposium/.

Zukovsky, Louis. *Bottom: On Shakespeare*. Austin: University of Texas Press, 1963.

INDEX

Achilles in Vietnam (Shay) 125, 128
acting
  and embodiment 7, 18, 56, 94, 106
  as a healing practice 111–15, 125, 144–5
American Sign Language (ASL) 97–8, *see also* d/Deaf and DeafBlind; protactile communication; Signing Shakespeare
Amigo, Sergio 168–70, *see also* Marcos Paz Penitentiary Centre; youth
anti-racism and social justice 72, 158, 163
  Bamboozle 73
  Redeeming Time Project 165
  Shakespeare & Co. 112, 153
  SiPN 149–53, 173
  Terrarte 81
Aristotle 11, 29
'arts in health' 122, *see also* therapy
  somatic art therapy 146
Atlanta Shakespeare Company
  youth outreach 160–1
autism 7, 9, 24, 74–80, 83, *see also* Bamboozle Theatre; Flute Theatre; Hunter Heartbeat Method
  theory of mind 88–93

Bamboozle Theatre 73–6,
  see also autism; Hunter Heartbeat Method
  'Bamboozle Approach' 76
  Storm 74–6
Barnes, Todd Landon 22, 131, 144
  'the perils of redemptive performance' 22, 131
Barwich, A. S.
  on smell 100–1
Berry, Cicely 31, 40
Block, Giles 40–3
Blue Apple Theatre 69–72
  Be In! (clusive) Festival 72
  list of productions 69–70
Boal, Augusto 20–1
The Body Keeps the Score (book),
  see van der Kolk, Bessel
bodywork 25, 112–16, 140–1
  Hakomi method 114–16, 118
breath
  breathwork 37, 43–5, 126, 131, 136, 175
  in Shakespearean performance 41–2, 73
  therapy 36, 111
  training 39–40, 44–5
British Sign Language (BSL) 86–7, 91, 94, *see also* protactile communication; Signing Shakespeare
Burgess, Christy 161–4, *see also* 'Why Shakespeare?'
Byron, Sammie 43–4, 150–1

Chekhov, Michael   18–19
Chesapeake Shakespeare
   Company   107, 120
   Olive Branch and Laurel
      Crown Ensemble   120
   To Be a Soldier   120
Classics Fest (2022)   121–3
Colapinto, John   29–30, 37
controversy
   autism   88–93
   Hakomi method   115
   Hunter Heartbeat Method
      (*see* Hunter Heartbeat
      Method)
   Porges   24
   theory of mind and d/Deaf
      children   93
   van der Kolk   24, 189 n.99
Cooper, Melinda   153, *see* anti-
   racism and social justice
Covid-19 pandemic   12, 71,
   146–8, 152–3
   adaptations   69–71, 120,
      133
   in prisons   147–52

Dana, Deb   126–7, *see also*
   polyvagal theory
Dark Horse Theatre   68–70
   'silent approach'   68
d/Deaf and DeafBlind, *see also*
   Deafinitely Theatre
   audiences   61, 86–8, 95–6
   children   87–92
   performers   97–8
   use of scent   99–101
   use of sign language   86–99
      (*see also* ProTactile
      Theater; Signing
      Shakespare)
   visual adaptation   47–55, 61
Deafinitely Theatre   86, 91
   list of productions   86

DE-CRUIT   107, 110–12, 123–8
   founders (*see* Stern, Dawn;
      Wolfert, Stephan)
   process and principles
      110–11, 123–8
Department of Veterans Affairs
   (United States)
   partnerships with theatre
      groups   117
   and Shay   128–9 (*see also*
      Shay, Jonathan)
   and van der Kolks (*see* under
      van der Kolk, Bessel)
   Walter Reed National Military
      Medical Center   122
DeSalle, Rob   12–13
dog and pony dc   94–6, 100
   Party On   95–7
   Sense-Able initiative   96
   use of other sensory
      modalities   96, 100–1
Down Syndrome   65–6
drama games   76, 92
Dreier, Jenna   8

Elliott, Esther Ruth   50–5, 57,
   see also Royal
      Shakespeare Company
embodied cognition   16–17, 87,
   94, 174–5
Emergency Shakespeare   143–4
Emory University
   and Feast of Crispian   110,
      158
   and the Folger Institute (*see*
      Folger Shakespeare
      Institute)
   and Puck Project (*see* Puck
      Project)
   and Shakespeare Behind
      Bars   150
expressive therapies continuum
   145–6

INDEX

Extant Theatre 13, 47–54, 60, 100
  The Man Who Saw Backwards 52, 100
  States of Mind 47–51 (*see also* Hunter, Christopher)

Feast of Crispian 53, 110, 114, 158, *see also* veterans
  partnership with the VA 117–18
  strategy of questioning 118–20
  use of Hakomi method 118
Flute Theatre 9, 15, 77–8
  criticism 88–9 (*see also* autism; Hunter Heartbeat Method)
Folger Shakespeare Institute 147
  SiPC 9
  symposium with Emory University 98–9
Freire, Paulo 20, 151

Glover, Devon 170–1
Graeae Theatre 4, 86

Hakomi Institute 115
  development 114–16
  Hakomi method (*see* bodywork)
  and Ron Kurtz 115, 118
Heneghan, Ron 120–2, *see also* VetArts Connect
Hip-Hop and Spoken Word Therapy (HHSWT) 171–3, *see* Glover, Devon Susan Hadley and George Yancy 172
homelessness 35, 150, 160
  Nicholas House 157
Hunter, Christopher 47–51, 58

Hunter, Kelly 7, 76, 80, *see also* Hunter Heartbeat Method
Hunter Heartbeat Method 88–9
  and autism 76–80, 93 (*see also* autism)
  criticism of 7, 79–80
  list of productions 77

iambic pentameter 43–4, 73, 77, 87, 110–11, 126, *see also under* voice
The Institute for Integrative Health, *see* Nova Institute for Health of People Places and Planet
integrative somatics, *see* bodywork
Intermission Youth Theatre, *see also under* youth
  Juliet & Romeo (2021) 165–7
  M.S.N.D: A Shakespeare Remix (2022) 165–6
  objectives 164
  social justice 165–8
Irish, Tracey 86–8, 91–2

Jackson, Scott
  Shakespeare at Notre Dame 147
  SiPN (*see* Shakespeare in Prisons Network)
  yoga 136–8
Justice Resource Institute 138–9

Kemp, Rick 17
Kentucky Shakespeare 107, 130–1, 173
KNOCK AT THE GATE (KATG) 60–3, 99
Konopka, Lukasz M. 145
Kurtz, Ron, *see* Hakomi Institute

Linklater, Kristin   30–3, 38–40, 112
Louise, Shona   48–53

McLaughlin, Deirdre   17–18
Malchiodi, Cathy A.   24, 144
Maley, Willy   108–9
Marcos Paz Penitentiary Center, *see under* youth
Merlin, Bella, *see under* Shakespeare & Co.
music
   in productions   53–4, 71–3, 77–9, 161, 166
   rap   170–4 (*see also* Hip-Hop and Spoken Word Therapy)
   in rehearsal   68–9

National Endowment for the Arts (NEA)   124, 167
   NEA-funded initiatives   170, 173
   NEA Institute   99
neoliberalism   144
Nestor, James   36–8
Normansfield Hospital and Theatre   65–7
Nova Institute for Health of People Places and Planet   120–2
   'Talking about Arts in Health' (white paper)   121–2

Packer, Tina, *see* Shakespeare & Co.
Pallant, Cheryl   17, 25
Parachi, The Honorable Paul E.   167–8
Pennebaker, James W.   111–12
Pensalfini, Rob   144
polyvagal theory   126–8, *see also* Porges, Stephen

Porges, Stephen   24
   influence on other practitioners   112, 130
   neuroception   127
   on polyvagal theory   126
   on trauma   34
post-traumatic stress disorder/post-traumatic stress syndrome, *see also* Porges, Stephen; Shay, Jonathan; van der Kolk, Bessel
   in carceral settings (*see under* prisons)
   and Shakespeare   130
   symptoms   128–9
   in veterans (*see under* veterans)
Powers, Kate, *see* Redeeming Time Project
prisons
   incarcerated veterans (*see* DE-CRUIT)
   in India   20, 27, 138, 142 (*see also* yoga)
   recovery and rehabilitation   134–6, 138–40, 152–5
   theatre initiatives   135–6, 143–4, 147–9
   trauma   134–5
   in the United Kingdom   143
   in the United States   133, 136–9, 147–52
pro-tactile communication   95, 97–8, 103–4
ProTactile Theater   12, 97–100, 103–5
   sensory signaling   95, 100–1
PsychArmor   121
psychotherapy, *see* therapy
Puck Project   157–60

racism   153, 173
Ramps on the Moon UK   68–70

Raymond, Darren   164–6
Redeeming Time Project   152
　Covid-19 pandemic   153–4
　partnerships and
　　collaborations   153
　Rehabilitation Through the
　　Arts   153
Rodenburg, Patsy   30–1, 43
Rokison-Woodall, Abigail   86–92, *see also* Irish, Tracey
Rosenberg, Stanley   127–8, *see also* polyvagal theory
Royal Shakespeare Company (RSC)   30, 49–55, 77, 86, 91–4, 103
　The Combat Veteran Players UK   108
　and Esther Ruth Elliott (*see* Elliott, Esther Ruth)
Rylance, Sir Mark   40, 166

Savvy Theatre   4, 73
　The Taming of the Shrew Drag Show   4
Sayet, Madeline   8
senses
　definition   11, 12 (*see also* Aristotle)
　description by Shakespeare   106
　hearing   60–4 (*see also* d/Deaf and DeafBlind; music; sound)
　other senses   12, 17–18
　sight   13, 49
　smell   99–100
　taste   101–2
　touch   103–6
Shakespeare Behind Bars (SBB)   43–4, 147–51, 170–4
　Core Values/Creed Statement   155

Shakespeare & Co.   37–9, 73, 112–17, 153, 160, 167–8
　Bella Merlin and Tina Packer   38–9, 111, 119, 167–8
　collaborations and partnerships   160
　Kevin Coleman   167–8
Shakespeare in Prison (SIP)   1–5, 29, 133–4, 147–50
　Shepherd-Bates, Frannie   1–3, 147
Shakespeare in Prisons Network (SiPN)   9, 43, 146–53
Shakespeare in Prisons Conference (SiPC)   9–10, 146, 153
Shakespeare's Globe Theatre (London)   162
Shakespeare's plays
　As You Like It   5, 52, 102, 137, 169
　Hamlet   59–60, 65, 70, 106, 137, 154, 169–71
　Henry IV   64, 125
　Henry V   106–10, 114, 125 (*see also* Feast of Crispian)
　Henry VI   68
　Henry VIII   106
　Julius Caesar   42, 60–2, 118, 125, 175
　King Lear   1, 52, 100, 135, 137
　Macbeth   60–1, 70–2, 76, 91–4, 108–10, 125, 137, 165
　Merchant of Venice   175
　A Midsummer Night's Dream   4–6, 68–70, 73, 77, 80–3, 86–9, 122, 159–61, 165

Much Ado About Nothing 6, 69–70, 101, 120, 137
Othello 143, 150–1, 166, 173
Richard II 162, 169
Richard III 124, 136, 173
Romeo and Juliet 21, 93–9, 103, 137, 163–7, 173
Taming of the Shrew 4, 102
The Tempest 60, 63, 68, 70, 74–6
  Storm 77, 86, 160, 175
Titus Andronicus 163
Twelfth Night 4, 137, 175–6
Shakespeare UnBard
  Mackenzie, Rowan 9, 142–8
Shay, Jonathan 128–30, *see also* post-traumatic stress disorder/post-traumatic stress syndrome
  Achilles in Vietnam 125
Signing Shakespeare 86–94
Simpson, Fay 32
Smith-Watson, Nancy 112–20, *see also* Feast of Crispian
somatic bodywork, *see* bodywork
The Sonnet Man, *see* Glover, Devon
sound, *see* music; voice
  noise 36, 45, 47, 56
  Shakespearean soundscapes 55, 57–62
  sound studies 55–8
Stephen, Michael J. 35
Stern, Dawn 9, 110
Szabo-Cassella, Claire 136–7

tactile American Sign Language (TASL), *see* pro-tactile communication
Terrarte 81–4
  with Flute Theatre, the World Shakespeare Project and the International Opera Theater 80

theory of mind (ToM) 88, 92–3, *see also* autism
therapy, *see also* Hip-Hop and Spoken Word Therapy (HHSWT)
  controversy 77–8, 112, 122, 130
  sensorimotor psychotherapy (*see* bodywork)
Tofteland, Curt L. 43, 134, 146–51, 158, 170–1
trauma, *see also* DE-CRUIT homelessness; post-traumatic stress disorder/post-traumatic stress syndrome
  in carceral environments (*see under* prison)
  in the military (*see under* veterans)
  in Shakespeare 108–9
  studies 24, 125, 139–42, 175

universal design 61

vagus nerve, *see* polyvagal theory
van der Kolk, Bessel 24, 112–13
  on therapy 33–6
  on trauma 113–14, 117–20, 125
  on the VA 113–14, 117
VetArts Connect 120–1
veterans
  The Combat Veteran Players UK 108
  list of Shakespeare initiatives 107–8
  Shakespearean therapy 117–20, 124–6 (*see also* DE-CRUIT; Feast of Crispian)
  suicide 125 (*see also* post-traumatic stress disorder/

post-traumatic stress syndrome; war)
trauma   112–14, 117
voice   29–30
  accents   58–9, 201 n.56
  embodied speech   31, 45
  and emotional expression   32–3, 36, 40–1
  poetic rhythm   41, 44, 73, 77, 87, 94, 110, 154, 169–73 (*see also* iambic pentameter)
  in Shakespearean performance   43–5, 56–8
  training   57–8

war
  historical   38, 108, 109, 115
  in Shakespearean drama   108–10, 118–19
  Ukraine War   115
  Vietnam War   113 (*see also* Shay, Jonathan)
  'Why Shakespeare?' (question)   31, 41, 55, 109–11, 134–5, 163
  colonialism   8, 144

Wolfert, Stephan   9, 110–11, 123–4
  Cry Havoc   124

yoga   14, 17, 19–20, 24, 34–7, 136–41
  breathing   33–4, 37, 136–7
  Hulugappa Kattamani   20, 138
  Kundalini   138, 151
  Scott Jackson (*see* Jackson, Scott)
  trauma-sensitive   138–9
  and the voice   32–3, 138–40
youth
  with ASC (*see* Atlanta Shakespeare Company)
  at-risk   35, 107, 151
  autistic (*see* autism)
  dramatic education   158–63
  incarcerated   149–51, 164–8, 170–5
  IYT (*see* Intermission Youth Theatre)
  Marcos Paz Penitentiary Centre   168–9
  Puck Project (*see* Puck Project)
  The Robinson Center   161–2

www.ingramcontent.com/pod-product-compliance
Lightning Source LLC
Chambersburg PA
CBHW071811300426
44116CB00009B/1275